AUGUSTUS CAESAR'S WORLD

AUGUSTUS

AUGUSTUS CÆSAR'S WORLD

A STORY OF IDEAS AND EVENTS FROM
B.C. **44** TO **14** A.D.

ILLUSTRATED BY
THE AUTHOR:

GENEVIEVE FOSTER

28322

CHARLES SCRIBNER'S SONS
NEW YORK

IN MEMORY OF
ORRINGTON

CONTENTS

PART I

PART II

PART III

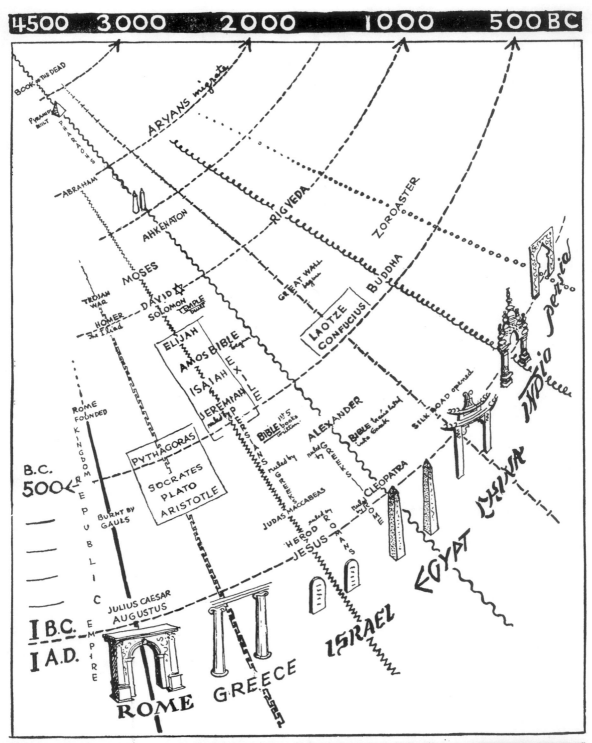

4500   3000   2000   1000   500 BC

LOOKING TO THE PAST

JANUS

INTRODUCTION

OLD JANUS, WHO COULD see two ways at once, both in time and space, was one of the earliest gods of ancient Rome. Guardian spirit of the house door, he also protected the city gate, and was even believed to hold the key to the gates of heaven. A temple to Janus in the market place of Rome always stood open in time of war, but was closed with great ceremony in those rare times when there was peace.

It was for Janus that the first month of our calendar was named.

And since he watched over all openings and beginnings, it seemed right that he should also be here at the opening of this book.

For this is a story of the world, centered in old Rome, during the lifetime of Augustus Caesar, Rome's first emperor, who closed the gates of Janus for the first time in over two hundred years, and established peace and order in the Roman Empire.

That peaceful age had not yet dawned, and Augustus was only Octavius, a boy of eighteen, when our story opens in March, 44 B.C. with the murder of his great-uncle Julius Caesar.

The story tells of the exciting events that followed those fatal Ides of March—of the conspirators, Brutus and Cassius, and what became of them—of Antony and Cleopatra and their famous love affair—of Cicero, the orator, and Virgil, the poet—of Herod, the hated King of Judaea—of Hillel, the wise and patient rabbi—and of Jesus, the boy of Nazareth, who, according to Luke, was born when a decree had gone out "from Caesar Augustus that all the world should be taxed," and was still living in Galilee when the year 14 A.D. brings the life of that first Roman emperor to a close.

We are now almost 2,000 years away from those days when the Roman world was kept in order by Augustus Caesar. What was it like—that ancient world, under the Roman law? How did people live and travel? What did they believe? To what great heroes of the past did they look back? To what Golden Age to come did they look forward? What did they think about the stars and planets? Had they discovered that the earth was round?

And of that far world outside of the Empire on the Mediterranean—What of ancient China, which had recorded 2,000 years of history before Rome was born? And of India? And of those undreamed of continents that would one day be America—were civilized people living there? Or were they like the semi-savages of Britain who painted themselves blue? And what of the rest of Europe—the people in the deep forests of Germany and along the rivers of France—what were their customs and their gods?

And of all the beliefs and customs and superstitions of that ancient world—which ones have we discarded, like that of offering burnt animals to God? Which pleasant ones, like using lights and holly at the Christmas season do we still observe?

And above all, what thoughts and beliefs were there in that old world that will be forever new, and forever will be true, as they have always been true, no matter in what century or in what land or by what race of people they have been spoken?

The answer to some of these questions may be found in this book. For this is not merely a record of events. It tells also what was thought and believed by people everywhere, in that world of Augustus Caesar.

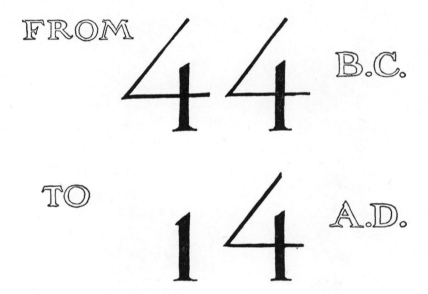

FROM 44 B.C.

TO 14 A.D.

OCTAVIUS

PEOPLE WHO WERE LIVING

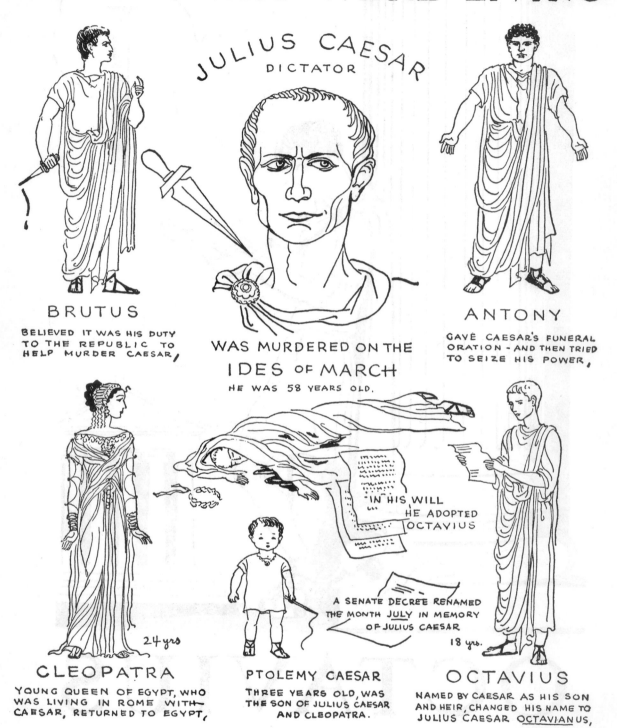

JULIUS CAESAR
DICTATOR

WAS MURDERED ON THE
IDES OF MARCH
HE WAS 58 YEARS OLD.

BRUTUS
BELIEVED IT WAS HIS DUTY
TO THE REPUBLIC TO
HELP MURDER CAESAR,

ANTONY
GAVE CAESAR'S FUNERAL
ORATION - AND THEN TRIED
TO SEIZE HIS POWER,

"IN HIS WILL
HE ADOPTED
OCTAVIUS

A SENATE DECREE RENAMED
THE MONTH JULY IN MEMORY
OF JULIUS CAESAR

24 yrs

18 yrs.

CLEOPATRA
YOUNG QUEEN OF EGYPT, WHO
WAS LIVING IN ROME WITH
CAESAR, RETURNED TO EGYPT,

PTOLEMY CAESAR
THREE YEARS OLD, WAS
THE SON OF JULIUS CAESAR
AND CLEOPATRA.

OCTAVIUS
NAMED BY CAESAR AS HIS SON
AND HEIR, CHANGED HIS NAME TO
JULIUS CAESAR OCTAVIANUS,

AND SOME EVENTS THAT TOOK

WHEN AUGUSTUS WAS OCTAVIUS

WAR

FOLLOWED, BETWEEN CAESAR'S ENEMIES AND FRIENDS,

AGRIPPA

LOYAL FRIEND OF
OCTAVIUS, ALWAYS HIS
MOST TRUSTED ADVISOR

3 MEN FORMED

THE TRIUMVIRATE

OCTAVIAN + ANTONY + LEPIDUS

SEIZED THE POWER AND CLEARED ROME
OF THEIR ENEMIES, BY OFFERING LARGE
REWARD FOR THEIR HEADS,

a wax writing tablet

a box of books

15 yrs

LIVY

FAMOUS HISTORIAN
WAS A YOUNG BOY,
LIVING IN PADUA,

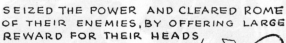

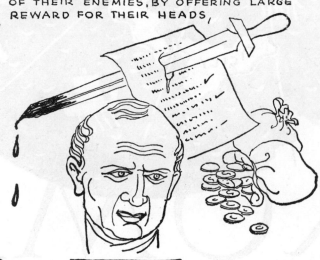

(in Greek dress)

MAECENAS

A FRIEND OF OCTAVIUS,
VERY WEALTHY, AND FOND
OF ALL KINDS OF ART,

CICERO

ROME'S GREAT AND FAMOUS
OLD ORATOR WAS BEHEADED,

OCTAVIA

THE SISTER OF OCTAVIUS,

HER BABY SON, MARCELLUS

PLACE BETWEEN 44 AND 42 B.C.

ROMA

UNDER A LUCKY STAR

OUT OVER THE GRAYING waters of the Adriatic, a single bright star, the planet Venus, shone in a pale pink evening sky. Inside a house, whose windows faced the sea, young Octavius was curiously but cautiously following his friend Agrippa up a flight of dusty, winding stairs that led to the studio of a Greek astrologer.

It was a winter day, one of the first in that year now known to us as 44 B.C. Octavius was eighteen, and, like most of the other young Roman students there in the Greek college town of Apollonia, he had become interested in astrology.

Study of the stars he felt was the most scientific way of foretelling

5

the future and discovering the divine will of the gods. Not even examining the liver of an animal, though it united with the soul of the god to whom it had been sacrificed, could compare with astrology.

Octavius and his best friend Agrippa, eager to know what was written for them in the stars, had thus decided to consult the celebrated astrologer. But now, as Octavius climbed the stairs, he hesitated, somewhat fearful of finding out what the future held for him lest it prove to be dismal and discouraging.

How little he knew then, this slim, pale, eighteen-year-old Octavius, that before he had lived another eighteen years, he would be ruler of the Roman empire, the great Augustus Caesar! How preposterous, at this time, that would have sounded.

In 44 B.C. there was no Roman emperor. Rome was a Republic.

And this boy, this future emperor, was not a Caesar. Although he was the grand-nephew of Julius Caesar, the most powerful Roman of the day, his own family name was not Caesar, but Octavius.

As for Augustus! That was not a name at all. It was an adjective, used to describe the holiness of some sacred shrine, or the majesty of Jupiter himself, but never a human being.

So Octavius, being naturally cautious, and likewise fearful that he had not been born under a lucky star, entered rather doubtfully into the presence of the gray-haired astrologer.

In a high room, where he could see the sky, the old man was found squinting over a table of figures, completely surrounded by maps and charts and diagrams. He looked up as the two young Romans entered, the one, sturdy and brown; the other, slim and pale, with delicate, clear-cut, very regular features. Both were dressed, he noted, in expensive togas of the very finest, pure, white wool.

Though scarcely anyone in Apollonia would have failed to recognize Octavius as the favorite nephew of Rome's foremost citizen, if the astrologer knew him, he shrewdly gave no indication of it. Instead, he followed the boy's sharp, keen eyes to a certain map, which he saw had attracted his attention.

It was a map of the universe, believed to be correct. On it, the earth was pictured as standing motionless in the center, while the sun, moon, and five planets revolved about it, all underneath a dome-like heaven, upon which the more distant stars were fixed.

As the astrologer explained the map, he spoke in Greek, the one language, beside their own, which all educated Romans also spoke. Just where the sun, moon and planets were, he continued, at the very hour when a man was born, determined his character and his future.

And was that not reasonable? he argued. Did not the sun have its effect upon the earth? Did not the seasons change as sun, moon and planets moved about the sky? Why, then, should not people also be affected by the heavenly bodies?

"Indeed," said the astrologer, with professional pride, "for centuries people have been guided by this old Chaldean wisdom."

To speak of astrology as "Chaldean wisdom," Octavius knew, came from the fact that it had originated among the Chaldeans or native priests of ancient Babylon. From them, centuries later, the Greeks had learned it, and had now passed it on to the Romans.

Agrippa, having heard enough about the system, was now impatient to see how it worked, so he boldly gave the year, month, day and hour of his birth, whereupon the astrologer named the sign of the zodiac under which Agrippa had been born. Then he started on another rather lengthy explanation.

The zodiac, he pointed out, was a band or circular pathway of twelve star patterns, marked out around the heavens, in front of which the sun, moon and planets were continually passing, like stations along the way. Since most of the star patterns had been named for animals, they were all referred to, he said, as the zodiac, or "little animal." It took the sun exactly twelve months to make the round trip through all the twelve star signs, he added in conclusion. Then he turned back to his charts and tables, and having busied himself for some time, predicted for the active young Agrippa a brilliantly successful career.

Though pleased at his friend's good fortune, Octavius's heart sank.

Surely, by comparison, his own future would seem dull indeed. Reluctantly, he gave the necessary dates.

Suddenly, to his amazement, the astrologer looked up with an exclamation of awe and surprise. Then, dropping to his knees, without a word, he threw himself at the feet of Octavius, as before a mighty ruler of the east.

The boy was speechless with astonishment, and, although he did not show it, was still trembling with excitement as he and Agrippa

made their way down the winding stairs again, and out under a sky now bright with stars.

What could be the glorious destiny, thought Octavius, that was written for him in those stars? What had the gods in store for him? What did the future hold?

Of one thing only he felt certain: whatever he might become depended upon the tremendous and far-reaching plans of his great-uncle, Julius Caesar.

THE IDES OF MARCH

THE IDES OF MARCH HAD COME! Spring was almost here! Octavius was looking for a letter. Each day he was expecting to hear from Julius Caesar that he had left Rome and was on his way to Apollonia. The soldiers, too, waiting on the outskirts of the city, were growing bored with idleness. As soon as the great general arrived, they were ready to break camp, leave Greece behind, and be off to the east on a fierce campaign against Parthia, Rome's last unconquered enemy.

All winter, Octavius had been counting the days ahead. This was to be his first real experience in a foreign war. Now, as the time approached, he was almost as excited as on that proud day in Rome, two years ago, when he, out of all his young kinsmen, had been chosen by Caesar to ride beside him in his African Triumph.

From that glorious day on, Octavius had looked upon Julius Caesar as his guardian and protector, and had dared to hope that, someday, Caesar might make him his adopted son.

Of his own father, Octavius had but the haziest memory. His step-father, though a Senator, was not an outstanding man.

But this great-uncle Julius! Never could he remember when his grandmother's bold, brilliant, fascinating brother had not been his hero! As a small boy, long before he had ever seen him, he knew how Caesar had conquered Gaul, invaded Britain, built the big bridges over the Rhine, and fought back the wild Germans. How later he had dared to cross the Rubicon River with an army, though as Governor of Gaul he was forbidden to do so. How he had then marched against his enemies, defeated them all, and become the most powerful man in Rome.

Then, before Octavius had seen him, Caesar was gone again, this time to spend the winter with the Queen of Egypt. But the next year, when he was fourteen, the boy had finally met his hero.

Caesar had come dashing back to Rome from a brief campaign in Asia Minor. With three short words he had summed up his lightning victory "Veni, vidi, vici." "I came, I saw, I conquered," he had told them in his tense, exciting voice.

Two months later, he was off for Africa and another victory. Octavius was ill, and to his great disgust had to be left behind. But after the African Triumph Octavius had followed Caesar into Spain. And now, in this spring of 44 B.C., he was waiting here in Greece, to go east on what he was sure would be his great-uncle's most magnificent and spectacular campaign.

Then, on a day before the end of March, came the shocking news: There would be no campaign.

JULIUS CAESAR WAS DEAD!

A message from his mother brought Octavius word of the tragedy. Her letter had been written on the Ides of March, the very day that

Julius Caesar had been killed. "Killed by his enemies" were her words.

But how, thought Octavius, could such words possibly be true? Yet there they were in his mother's familiar writing.

And there, too, before him in the open courtyard was the dust-covered messenger who had made the trip from Rome in record time. A freedman, he was, a former slave in their family. At first sight of his familiar face, Octavius had felt that he brought dreadful news. But this was dreadful beyond belief, beyond imagination.

JULIUS CAESAR could not be DEAD!

The boy's throat grew tight. Shivering, as a damp breeze whipped the folds of his toga against his thin bare legs, he beckoned to Agrippa. Unable to say a word, he held out the letter and watched his friend scan the message rapidly, angry color mounting on his neck.

"You should go to Rome at once," Agrippa said. His quick mind mapped out a positive course of action. "Take command of these legions that are here, march on Rome and wipe out those enemies of Caesar, all of them, whoever and wherever they may be."

Many of the officers gave the same advice. The loyal soldiers also stood for revenge. As soon as the news spread, as it did, like fire, through the town and camp, they were ready to hunt down and kill with their own hands those cowards who had murdered their great commander.

Octavius kept a cool head. Cautious and not given to rash moves, he was inclined to agree with those who advised him to go slowly, spy out his enemies first, find out who and where they were, and then have them tried for murder according to the law.

Night found the group of young Romans still discussing various suggestions. One of them, as he spoke or listened, kept watching the light from the boat-shaped lamp about which they were gathered play through the huge emerald in his ring.

That was Maecenas, the young art collector. Like Agrippa, he was an especial friend of Octavius, and about the same age, though possibly he had been wearing the toga of manhood a few years longer.

"It is highly probable," said Maecenas in his smooth, tactful manner, "that in his will Julius Caesar has named you his heir. If so, you'll want to return quickly to claim your inheritance. However, if you go about it too quickly, you may lose both your inheritance and your head. Who knows what further plan the enemies may have? All relatives of Caesar may well be in danger."

Octavius nodded. He was determined to avenge his great-uncle's death; he intended to claim his inheritance. But at the same time he also wanted to remain alive.

And how should he go about it? That was the bewildering question which he faced.

Toward morning, still awake and tossing on his couch, Octavius thought again of the great destiny that the gods were supposed to have in store for him. Unbelievable as it seemed now, he yet had faith that somehow or other the Divine plan would be carried out and he would be protected.

That faith gave him the courage that he needed.

Early in April he set the day for his departure. First, however, he took great pains to make sure that it was not a date considered dis-astrous (contrary to the stars) to embark upon a journey.

Then, finding the auspices favorable, and bearing the good wishes of his friends, Octavius boarded a ship and set out alone for Italy.

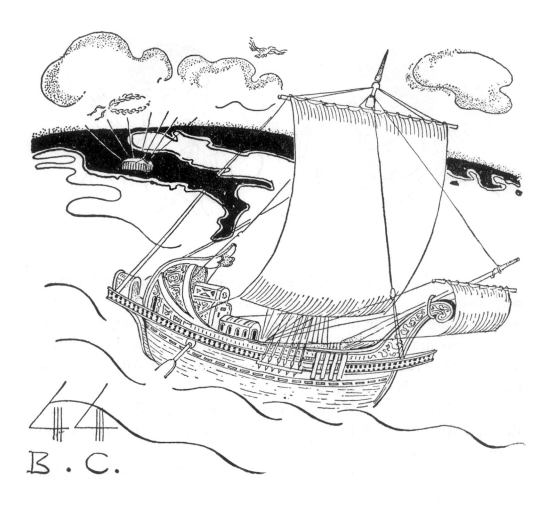

B.C.

CLEOPATRA AND HER SON

ON ONE OF THOSE same early April days, as Octavius was nearing Italy, a royal Egyptian galley was leaving the harbor of Rome. On board ship, with a retinue of slaves, guards and attendants, was a beautiful young queen. "The siren of the Nile" people often called her, for she was the enchanting, glamorous, young queen of Egypt, CLEOPATRA.

As her ship pulled out into the bay, one might have seen her standing in the stern, with a tiny boy beside her, taking a last look at Italy.

14

(CLEOPATRA)

ISIS

For a year and a half, Cleopatra had been living there, making her home in Julius Caesar's lovely villa and gardens overlooking the Tiber River. With Caesar dead, and no reason to stay longer, she had now left Rome, and was taking her small son back to Egypt where he had been born. A half sigh escaped her lips as she watched the receding shoreline, and she clasped tighter the small warm hand in hers. Overhead, the sky was bright and high; blue water sparkled in the sun, but for Cleopatra it was no shining day.

15

Julius Caesar was dead. And with him had died all their dreams—all their plans for a great world empire, to be shared by them together, and inherited by their son. Julius Caesar was dead; he had not lived to found an empire.

"Little Caesar," his son and hers, would never become king of all the earth, though he was now too little to know or care.

Cleopatra smiled down at him. How much he looked like Caesar. Strange that a child of barely three could so resemble a man of fifty-eight! Yet even his walk, as he trudged off with his nurse across the sunny deck, was like his father's. There seemed to be no Ptolemy in him —none of her family in his make-up. He was all Julius Caesar's son. Seated now among the cushions of a golden couch, she watched him play, reliving in memory the summer he was born.

How delighted Julius Caesar had been to have a son! How he had paced about the palace halls in Alexandria, unwilling to leave for Rome until the baby was born—doubting, yet daring to hope that it would be a boy. Four times he had been married before, and his only child had been a daughter. Now, at last, there in Egypt, in that summer of 47, he had had a son. And what a son! Cleopatra smiled to think of Caesar's pride in him, that son who was both royal and divine.

No one of Caesar's Roman wives, she thought, though they might call themselves patricians, could have given Caesar a son of royal blood, for there was no royalty in Rome. Those four wives, the two divorced, the one dead, and the one still married to him, were common mortals, all of them, while she, Cleopatra, had been born into the world's most royal family, the Greek Ptolemies of Egypt.

Her son would rule Egypt as his Greek ancestors had ruled over the native Egyptians, for more than three hundred years. For it was from Alexander the Great, who had conquered Egypt and founded Alexandria, that the first Ptolemy had inherited the throne.

And he would also be hailed, that son of hers, as a Pharaoh, and wear the ten times more ancient crown of the native Pharaohs whose ruined Capitol and gigantic pyramid tombs had been standing years before Alexander and his general, the first Ptolemy, had come to Egypt.

The gentle motion of the ship, gliding through the blue water, reminded Cleopatra of the houseboat on which she and Caesar had once journeyed leisurely southward up the Nile, to see the remains of that marvelous old civilization. There, falling on their faces before her, the poor native Egyptian fellahins or farmers had greeted Cleopatra, just as their forefathers had hailed the ancient Pharaohs. She remembered the envy on Caesar's face as he saw such homage paid to her as had never been accorded him, the most brilliant, powerful and foremost citizen of Rome.

Rome was a Republic. Roman citizens hated kings. They had the idea that they ruled themselves and chose their leaders. A most ridiculous idea! How could a mob of ignorant, common people take the place of a king, when kings were gods on earth!

She, Cleopatra, queen of Egypt, had been born a goddess. She was the earthly form of the holy mother Isis. And her son, little Caesar, was actually the son of almighty Amen, the great god of Egypt. So the high priests had announced to the people at his birth. Julius Caesar, they explained, was merely the human form in which the great god had appeared on earth to wed Cleopatra.

As a hardheaded Roman, Julius Caesar could see how much it inspired the people with awe and respect to believe that their rulers were divine and immortal. He adjusted himself quite readily to the new position, and claimed additional proof of his divinity.

"My own Roman clan, the Julian," he had told her, "have a divine ancestor. We are descended from Aeneas of Troy, who was the son of Venus."

Venus, many believed, was but another name for Isis. Later in Rome, Julius Caesar had built a temple to his ancestor Venus, and had placed in it a statue of her, for which she, Cleopatra, had posed. In those last months of his life, she had been happy to see Caesar begin to dress and act the part of a divine king, and prepare to carry out their dream of empire which had now failed so miserably.

17

And why had it failed, that dream of theirs?

Cleopatra sat up suddenly, clenching her small fists as if some quick action might yet save the day.

Why had Caesar died, and their dream died with him? Why?

Because, for once in his life, he had not been bold and quick enough, she said to herself.

If only he had not waited to take the final step of declaring himself king until after the campaign in the east, he might have swept the people with him, before his enemies had found time to organize.

Certainly, if only he had spied out those enemies first, and had them poisoned, as any Ptolemy would have done, he would still be alive. But he had been too generous with his enemies, too ambitious to cover himself with glory in one last victorious campaign, and so now he was dead.

Julius Caesar was dead. And she was on her way back to Egypt with their small son, Caesarion, who had not even been mentioned in his father's will. That Cleopatra understood. Having no empire, Caesar had had nothing to leave his son but money, which, as son also of the richest queen on earth, he did not need.

Caesar had therefore left most of his fortune to his favorite nephew, Octavius. How fond Caesar had been of that boy Octavius! Cleopatra remembered seeing him for the first time, soon after she had come to Rome, riding beside his uncle in the African Triumph. He was a pale-faced young fellow, about six years younger than she was herself. Probably agreeable enough, but he had a nasty complexion and such little mousy teeth! She wondered how he would make out in claiming his inheritance. It would be a dangerous attempt.

To her it looked as if Rome might be in for another civil war. And on this April day, as she sailed for Egypt, it also appeared to Cleopatra that the man most likely to come out on top in the coming struggle was Mark Antony.

It would be wise to keep watch of Antony—he might be of use to her and to Egypt.

CAESAR'S ADOPTED SON

OCTAVIA WAS MOST unhappy about her brother Octavius. Seated with the family in the garden pergola, where the dappled shade of a rose trellis fell on her brown hair, she was trying to sew. She had hoped that morning to hem the crimson border on a toga she was making for her husband, Marcellus. But she could hardly thread a needle, she was so worried about her brother. He was determined to face the danger.

Nothing they could say seemed to have any effect upon him.

The family had been at Puteoli, their summer villa on the bay of Naples ever since they had hurried out of Rome after the fearful Ides of March. It was now about the twentieth of April.

Octavius had just arrived a day or so before, and had shocked them all with the announcement that he intended to go right on to Rome and carry out the terms of Julius Caesar's will. Though their mother and stepfather kept telling him how dangerous and foolhardy it would be, Octavius remained firm in his purpose. He was determined to claim his inheritance, and to register himself under the new name of Caesar— Julius Caesar Octavian.

The soldiers, he said, were already calling him "Caesar." At the port of Brundisium, the legions waiting to be shipped east on the great campaign had given him a wonderful welcome, and hailed him as their new commander-in-chief, their "imperator."

"Commander-in-chief of Caesar's legions!" exclaimed his mother. "You are too young! You have had almost no military experience."

"Nor any experience in politics," added the stepfather. "You have never held office, and have no power among the people."

"Money buys power," said Octavius. "With my inheritance, I could celebrate Victory Games, in Caesar's honor, and pay the 300 sesterces ($15.00) which he so generously left in his will to every citizen of Rome. That would certainly give me a following."

At these words spoken so surprisingly like a man, Octavia sent her young brother a swift smile of pride. But her stepfather shook his head in grave misgiving. He said that it would be impossible for Octavius to obtain the money from Mark Antony.

"In his will, Caesar made you his heir and his adopted son, that's true," he said. "But Antony, who was his friend and consul with him this past year, took over Caesar's money the day that he was killed —also all of his papers and records, and since then has been running affairs in Rome with a high hand."

Octavius was listening without a word, so his stepfather went on. "As for the soldiers, Antony is a popular general, the best in Rome, now that Caesar is dead. Those legions at Brundisium may go over to him, when they find him in Caesar's place."

To this Octavius replied that the legions were loyal to Caesar. They wanted revenge on the men who had murdered him. They would never follow Antony when they found out that he had come to temporary terms with the conspirators and allowed even the ringleaders, Cassius and Brutus, to leave Rome.

"Brutus! That Brutus!" Octavia repeated the name with sadness in her gentle voice. "To think that Brutus, who always seemed so noble and good, should have taken part in that dreadful plot. And Caesar was so fond of him. No wonder he was shocked when Brutus stabbed him. 'Et tu, Brute' was what he said. 'And you, too, Brutus'!"

Octavia sighed, and a tear dropped on the crimson border as she turned back to her sewing. The four fell into silence. Octavius stood beside a marble bench, looking out toward the blue water, in the direction of Pompeii, another Roman summer resort, which a little over a hundred years later the old Volcano Vesuvius was both to ruin and preserve.

"You are determined, then, to go to Rome," said his mother finally, seeing her son's small mouth set in a firm line.

Octavius nodded.

"Then," said his stepfather, "there is nothing further to be said except that it might be well before you leave to see our old friend Cicero. The old gentleman is here now, in Puteoli, at his villa, writing, and giving the two consuls elected for next year lessons in public speaking. It is true that Cicero considered your uncle Julius Caesar a tyrant, and believed that by killing him, Brutus and those others rendered a service to the state. Yet, on the other hand, he loathes and despises Antony. So if he thought it would lessen Antony's power, Cicero might be persuaded to help you."

So, either that day, or the next, Octavius went to call on Cicero, the old Roman orator, who, as it happened, had made his most famous oration the year Octavius was born.

CICERO

CICERO HAD NO APPETITE. It was the day after Octavian's visit, and he was a perplexed and baffled man. He took one disinterested peck at the luncheon before him, then nervously took up his pen and scratched off the first words of a letter.

"Oh, my dear Atticus," he wrote, "I fear that the Ides of March have brought me no gain."

He put down the pen again. Resting his forehead in his left hand, he leaned heavily on his elbow, as if his thin neck could no longer support that large cranium of his, now so weighted down with anxiety for the future of Rome.

On the Ides of March, when Caesar had been assassinated, Cicero had believed that the worst was over, that the Roman Republic had been saved, authority would be restored to the Senate, and be back again in the hands of good old conservative republicans.

Alas! Such had not been the case. It seemed that they had rid themselves of one tyrant, only to have another take his place. Every day came fresh word of the outrageous use Mark Antony was making of Caesar's money, and of records forged to further his own ends.

"Wouldn't you think he would have been warned by the fate of Caesar?" Cicero spoke aloud to his accountant reclining on the couch across the table. At the man's worthless reply, mumbled through a mouthful of asparagus, Cicero, in exasperation, picked up his pen again. Better to talk by letter to his good friend Atticus, he thought.

Atticus, besides being his best friend, was also Cicero's publisher. At his thriving establishment in Rome, he kept a large staff of handwriting experts constantly busy turning out copies of Cicero's latest books, for which there was always a great demand. Every few days letters passed between them. After the first paragraph of this letter, which was fairly long, Cicero continued:

"Octavius is here; he is treating me in a very honorable and friendly manner; his followers are saluting him as Caesar; but his stepfather and I refuse to do so. What do you think of that boy going into Rome, where our liberators cannot safely be?"

With a few more sentences, Cicero finished the letter, rolled the sheet of papyrus, tied and sealed it and slipped it into a small tubular case, in which the runner would carry it to Rome.

That done, the old gentleman, laying a napkin over his eyes, settled himself back on his dining couch for a few winks of sleep. But sleep did not come. Anxiety over Rome's uncertain future led to speculation about Octavius, and that brought him back to the subject of a book on which he was at work, *The Nature of the Gods*.

Young Octavius seemed convinced that the gods had written his future in the stars. Well, that was not surprising; it was a common enough belief, or mistake.

No one, thought Cicero, who looked up into the starry heavens, and observed the orderly movements of the planets, could fail to believe that the universe was ruled by a Divine Mind, and that human life in general was part of the one great plan.

But that did not mean that the fate of any one person could be determined from the position of the stars at the time that he was born. If so, why were not all the soldiers who died in a certain battle born under the same unlucky star?

No, astrology, though it might seem so, was hardly less inaccurate than those other popular forms of foretelling the future, and the will of the gods, all of which he had described in an earlier book.

Yet Octavius seemed to draw courage from the thought that he had been born under what he considered the lucky sign of Capricorn. Nineteen years old, did he say, he was to be in September?

"According to that," thought Cicero, "he must have been born the year that I was Consul—on the very day, perhaps, that I made my great oration against Cataline, and exposed his vile plot to overthrow the Republic. Ah! What a speech that was! How my ringing words drove the traitor fleeing in disgrace from the Senate Chamber!"

For a few happy moments, the old gentleman basked in the memory of his most celebrated day, that day on which the Senate had hailed him "Saviour of the State" and "Father of his Country." But such escape from the unhappy present could not last.

"Ah, my poor country," he was soon thinking, "now again in an hour of peril! And what can I do to save her? I dare not even return to Rome. . . ."

Four days later, he was writing Atticus of his dilemma:

"If civil war breaks out, I am not clear as to what I ought to do . . . I shall not be allowed to remain neutral. Anyone whom Caesar's friends believe to have rejoiced at the death of Caesar they will count as an enemy. The only thing that I can do, then, is to betake myself to the camp of . . . BRUTUS. If I set out for Greece . . . I am sure to be criticized for having failed the state in its hour of peril. If I stay in Italy, I do so at some risk; but I suspect I can be of some service to my country . . . Therefore, do think this matter over, as is your wont, in whatever concerns me . . ."

That was written April twenty-sixth.

May first, he was writing from Cumae. Tired of Puteoli, Cicero had moved to another one of his seven country villas. He was in better spirits, having heard that a certain "marvelous fellow" in Rome "had hurled some of Caesar's partisans from the Tarpeian rock, crucified others, pulled down the column erected in Caesar's honor, and let a contract to pave the site!"

"In short," wrote Cicero, "he acted like a hero of old . . . Now I agree with you. Things are beginning to go better. I'll not go to Greece. I will not desert my Brutus."

Brutus, too, Cicero felt, had acted like a hero of old in striking down the tyrant.

Indeed, since the Ides of March, he had felt that the one hope of the Republic lay in Brutus. And since that day he had been waiting for Brutus to take charge.

A month and a half he had been waiting. And what had Brutus done? Nothing. Nor Cassius, either. They had fled Rome, as had all the other "liberators," and since then had been letting things take their course. And what a course—steered by Mark Antony!

Opposed by no one, Antony had gone on his way unhindered. As Consul, he had now called a meeting of the Senate for June first. Cicero had considered going, but upon advice had decided not to, so June first, the day of the meeting, found him at another one of his seven villas, writing another letter to Atticus.

The place was Arpinum, a quiet little town near his own farm birthplace in the mountains; "charming," he said, "and retired, and free from interruption, if one wishes to write. But I should soon tire of the

25

scenery here; it is so tame. I fear rainy weather, too, for I hear the frogs declaiming."

He must have missed the rain, for very shortly Cicero had received a message which made him leave Arpinum at once. About June fifth, he was seated in his travelling litter and was being carried by his slaves down the dusty hillside road, then out along the fine Appian Way, paved with its smooth square blocks of stone and over to the sea coast.

Riding along, he felt more optimistic and hopeful than for many a day. This time he was not going to another villa, to fret about the future. He was on his way to Antium, to meet Brutus.

Brutus and Cassius. They had sent for him! They wanted his advice —those younger men! They must have a plan of action that included him! And why not? He was not too old to be of service. The citizens of Rome might yet hail him for a second time as "Saviour of the Country." Who could tell?

Who could tell what that meeting at Antium might lead to? thought Cicero, as he settled back comfortably in his litter, and pulled aside the curtains to look out upon the passing scenes.

Some great plan must be waiting his approval!

CONSPIRATORS WITHOUT A PLAN

FIVE VERY NERVOUS PEOPLE were waiting for Cicero at Antium. There he found them: five people with NO plan. "No plan—no order—no reason among them," he thought with disgust, and no idea at all of how to keep the ship of state from going to pieces.

First of all, there was BRUTUS, a very serious man in his late thirties, who seemed to guard his honor and virtue with a rigid dignity. It was plain to see that he carefully weighed his every act, and hoped never to be found guilty of evil.

The second was PORTIA, the good wife of Brutus.

The third was Brutus's mother, SERVILIA, a spirited, tangy woman, obviously popular with men. In her younger days, it was said, she had been so friendly with Caesar that he practically looked upon Brutus as his son. According to gossip, that was the reason for his keen grief and shock when Brutus stabbed him.

The fourth was TERTIA, a half-sister to Brutus, who was now married to Cassius.

CASSIUS, himself, made the fifth, a lean hungry man, with a sharp nose and a sharp tongue. Having formed the original plot against Caesar, and enlisted Brutus in it, he was now annoyed at Brutus for not letting them kill Mark Antony, too, while their daggers were out. Brutus tried to conceal his righteous indignation. He had behaved only as he believed his great ancestor would have behaved—that noble Brutus of old, whose statue stood on the Capitoline. Cassius had no ancestor to worry him, thank Jupiter, and he didn't spare his critical remarks about lost opportunities.

Cicero answered that they should all let bygones be bygones, then, in the next breath, offered his own ideas of mistakes that had been made.

"After Caesar was killed," he said, "you two, Brutus and Cassius, should have taken charge."

"Nonsense," exclaimed Servilia, cutting him short.

Brutus said flatly that they had had no wish to become dictators. If they had seized control, they would have been guilty of just what they had killed Caesar for. Their part was over when they got rid of the tyrant, and returned the Republic to the people of Rome. Now it was up to the Senate to take charge again. Not that he wished to shirk his duty, he hastened to add. He would gladly go back to Rome, if Cicero thought best.

Cicero did not think best—not at all. It would not be safe. True, he had persuaded the Senate to pass an "Act of Oblivion" the day after

Caesar's death. In other words, for the sake of peace, they had agreed to forget what the conspirators had done. But, now, who could tell when Antony would choose to ignore that decree or have it set aside?

Portia trembled at the thought, and spoke of how near the mob had come to burning down their house after Caesar's funeral. Servilia thought Brutus and Cassius ought to go abroad as grain commissioners. She had taken pains to have Antony (who was still her friend) get those jobs assigned to them. They should be glad of a real excuse to leave Italy . . . and avoid civil war, if they could. Brutus admitted he would be willing to go anywhere to avoid war, though he would hardly choose to be a grain commissioner.

Choose it! sneered Cassius. It was an insult. Judges deserved a better assignment than that! He and Brutus had been praetors (judges) for the year. Would they now take a job rustling grain to feed that common mob of Rome, whom Caesar had toadied to? Not by Jove's thunderbolt, he wouldn't!

"What, then, will you do?" inquired Cicero.

"Go to Greece, perhaps." Somewhere—anywhere—Cassius was thinking, that he could get hold of troops and money, in case the friends of Caesar should organize for war.

Brutus was inclined to go to Asia when the gathering broke up. As for Cicero, he returned home, disgusted with his journey, in despair over the poor old rickety ship of state, and pleased with nothing at all, as he wrote Atticus, except the fact that he had not let his dear Brutus leave Italy without seeing him again.

It was not long before Brutus and Cassius both set forth from Italy, but, as it turned out, they switched their destinations. Cassius headed for Asia, and Palestine. Brutus went to Greece.

From the port, he sent a parting letter to Antony, who probably laughed aloud when he read it.

"Do not flatter yourself that you have frightened us," wrote Brutus. "Fear is beneath our character. We hate war. Nothing can drag us into it."

MARK ANTONY

THIS IS ANTONY. Big, handsome, full-blooded fellow he was, with warm color under his olive skin, and a strong, hard, muscular body that made him look like the statues of Hercules. He had the same short curly hair, thick neck and bold

29

expression. He had, too, a flamboyant, colorful way of doing spectacular deeds on the spur of the moment. One might easily imagine him starting out to capture the man-eating horses, fight the bull, bring back the golden apples of Hesperides, or attempt any one of those other twelve fabulous labors of that old mythical Greek hero and half god.

Antony was proud of his likeness to Hercules. Appearing in public, he often dressed the part, wearing a short tunic, low belted about his hips, a coarse cloak flung over his shoulders, and a broad sword at his side. Thus he would go striding along the Forum, feeling, no doubt, as if the very blood of Hercules were pumping through his heart. And he believed it did—a few drops of it!

According to family tradition, Antony's immediate ancestors were descended from Anton who was a son of Hercules. And since Hercules was a son of almighty Zeus, that gave a divine ancestor to Mark Antony. It put him almost in the class with Julius Caesar, if not quite equal to that most delightful goddess-woman, Cleopatra, to whom, by the way, he wished he could have given even more help than he had, before she left Rome to return to Egypt.

Antony's wife was a shrew, Fulvia, by name. A driving, scheming, ambitious woman who was annoyed at her husband most of the time for acting so like a big, overgrown, carefree boy. Though his friends had laughed and cheered and applauded, it hadn't amused his wife one bit to see him go leaping about the Forum, on the day of the Lupercalia, stark naked, except for a loincloth of goatskin. She could never forget it—neither would anyone else who had been there.

That was by far the most famous Lupercalia in all the hundreds of years that the festival to the old wolf-god had been celebrated. It was the day on which Antony, prancing up to the rostrum, and holding aloft a crown, had offered it to Julius Caesar, either in jest or in earnest, and Caesar, sensing the temper of the crowd, had refused it.

That was just a month to the day before Caesar died. So it was February, the month which took its name from the "februa" or thongs of skin used in the celebration. The old idea had been that if women were flicked by the februa, they would be sure to have children. That was what Antony had been doing, striking right and left with his flying whip, as he went leaping through the crowd, a cross of blood on his forehead from the dog and goat slain in the opening sacrifice. He was master of ceremonies, heading the crowd of leaping, naked boys.

Also he was the chief priest of the newly formed order of priests, devoted to the new god, Julius Caesar. For Julius Caesar, seated that day in his gold chair on the rostrum, had been recently raised by a decree of the Senate to the status of a god, or national saint.

A month later, Caesar was dead. There, on that same rostrum where he had so lately been holding up a crown, Mark Antony was holding up a blood-stained toga. Launching into a funeral oration, he had moved the crowd to such tears and fury that they had set fire to their hero's pyre and burned it there upon the Forum.

Two months later, Antony seemed to have slipped in, and to be comfortably established in the dead man's place, when suddenly, on a May morning, Fate jogged his elbow. Or, to be more exact, Fate, in the strange disguise of a pale young man, with a cold in the nose, was waiting in his vestibule.

Mark Antony, Consul of Rome, and successor to Caesar, kept the pale-faced young heir to Caesar's fortune waiting a long time before he saw fit to talk to him. First Octavian had waited in the small courtyard, or vestibulum, leading to the house. Then he had waited in the atrium.

Octavian had turned in at the vestibule, shortly after sunrise, when the day's business always began at Rome. He had waited there until Antony's clients, hanging about as usual, had either given up in disgust or hastened off, one by one, to present themselves to some other wealthy patron who did not sleep so late.

Finally, passing the ever-present "janitor" guarding the front door with his dog, Octavian was admitted to the atrium. Seating himself on a bench in the large reception hall, he waited another hour or two. He amused himself by counting the tiles on the floor. He studied the pattern painted on the ceiling, watched the clouds float by the opening in the center of it, and even bet with himself which of the final drops from last night's rain would drip first into the pool below.

Meanwhile he went over carefully, word by word, exactly what he planned to say to Mark Antony.

At last he heard voices behind the curtains of the tablinum, Antony's familiar deep tone, a flatter one, which he recognized as that of the man who formerly had been Caesar's secretary, and also the voice of a child.

When the curtains were finally parted to admit him, he found Antony alone. Seated carelessly, his legs wide apart, one arm flung over the low back of his chair, he was looking out through the large doorway into the peristylum. Out there, a nurse could be seen crossing the open flowery courtyard, with a small boy in her arms, who waved to his father as they disappeared into one of the surrounding rooms.

Antony then turned toward Octavian, who, with his eye for order and detail, had already noted among the jumble of papers on the table between them two elaborate inkwells, both carelessly left open for the ink to dry, and a water clock which seemed to be running.

In reply to Antony's first question, Octavian stated simply that he had come to see about the money left to him by Caesar, as he wished to carry out the terms of Caesar's will.

Antony laughed aloud. Was he crazy? How could a boy of his age expect to act as an executor? He, himself, an experienced man, had had a tough time, in the face of Caesar's enemies, to do as much as he had.

Just what had he done, so far, asked Octavian, calmly. To be exact, what had he done with the private funds which he had received on March sixteenth from Caesar's wife, Calpurnia?

What! Antony scowled incredulously. Was this young upstart asking him for an accounting! It seemed he was, for now he was inquiring about the 7,000,000 sesterces which had been stored in the Temple of Ops. What had become of that?

32

R●MAN HOUSE

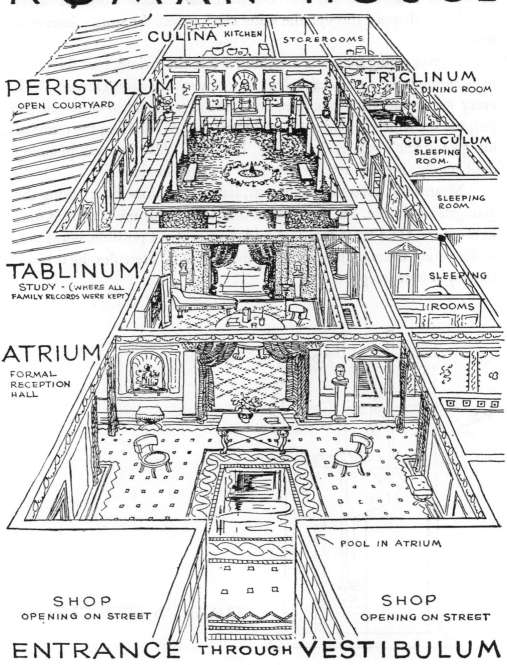

CULINA KITCHEN   STOREROOMS

PERISTYLUM
OPEN COURTYARD

TRICLINUM
DINING ROOM

CUBICULUM
SLEEPING ROOM.

SLEEPING ROOM

TABLINUM
STUDY - (WHERE ALL
FAMILY RECORDS WERE KEPT)

SLEEPING

ROOMS

ATRIUM
FORMAL
RECEPTION
HALL

POOL IN ATRIUM

SHOP
OPENING ON STREET

SHOP
OPENING ON STREET

ENTRANCE THROUGH VESTIBULUM

33

For answer, Antony blew up with rage and exploded in a torrent of words. The result was that less than ten minutes worth of water could have dripped through the water clock before the stormy interview was over.

A grim young man was marching across the atrium, past the doorman, through the vestibule, and out onto the street again, growing, with every step, more grim, more set, and more determined to carry out the purpose for which he had come to Rome—that of fulfilling the terms of his great-uncle's will and avenging his death. Also, he was planning deliberately, step by step, exactly how it might be done.

Meanwhile, Antony, cooling off, laughed at himself for taking the youngster seriously. Yet there was a cold look in his eye, and firm tone in his voice. He'd try to turn him aside peaceably, if possible, but if not, if the young upstart didn't stop his meddling, by Hercules, he'd block the boy at every step!

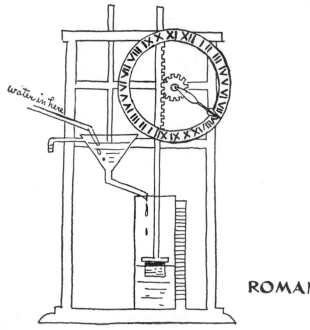

ROMAN WATER CLOCK

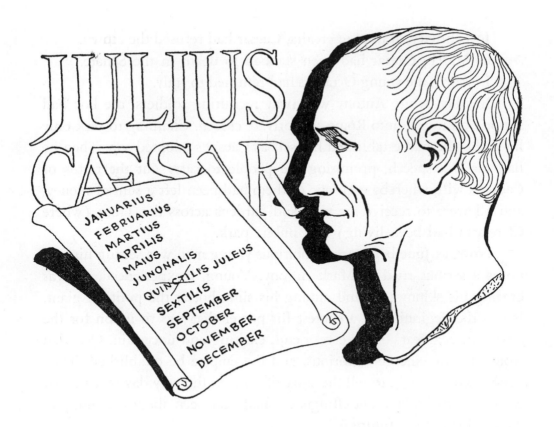

JULIUS CAESAR

JANUARIUS
FEBRUARIUS
MARTIUS
APRILIS
MAIUS
JUNONALIS
QUINCTILIS JULEUS
SEXTILIS
SEPTEMBER
OCTOBER
NOVEMBER
DECEMBER

WHY IS JULY?

MARCH, APRIL, MAY—those months of 44 B.C. had now sped by, filled with danger, change, uncertainty for everyone. Liberals and conservatives, democrats and aristocrats, friends of Caesar and Caesar's enemies, had all been shaken by the upheaval. All had had their lives greatly changed by Caesar's sudden and violent death.

In January, on the Kalends, or first day of the month, when the fatal year began, Antony had taken office as second highest in the Roman state, co-consul with Caesar. To him, Octavius was then merely a young nephew of Caesar's who had grown up down in the country somewhere, and was in school in Apollonia.

35

In February, at the Lupercalia, Caesar had refused the crown.

In March, Caesar had been stabbed to death in the Senate.

In April, the young Octavius had returned to Italy.

In May, while Antony was away recruiting soldiers, the boy had slipped cautiously into Rome as a private citizen. Claiming to seek only his rights, he had established himself as Caesar's adopted son. Then he had made a speech, promising the people to carry out the terms of Caesar's will, whereby each one of them had been left a sum of money, and all were to receive his villa and gardens across the Tiber (where Cleopatra had been living) as a public park.

Now, as June began, the ambitious young man was setting himself up as a serious rival to Mark Antony. Young, inexperienced, he was bracing his skinny legs and aiming his slingshot at the political giant. It was the beginning of a contest for power that was to go on for the next fourteen years—to the very end, exciting and uncertain. Octavian would finally emerge victorious, and the empire be established. Then people would begin to tell the story of how on the very day that he first entered Rome, a "radiant effulgence" had been seen about the sun, predicting his radiant future.

Octavian could see nothing very radiant as he left the house of Antony that May day after the stormy interview. But the month of June was well spent.

First he appealed to Caesar's old friends for help, telling them how Antony had mistreated him.

Then he undertook to raise all the money that he could, gathering together his own resources and borrowing more. His stepfather, mother and two cousins loaned him all they had. He put the money to use at once and with it, in the next month, QUINCTILIS, he achieved a minor victory, and won loud cheers from the mob.

A motley lot they were, those common people of Rome, more foreigners than natives, speaking a medley of tongues. Gauls, Spaniards, Germans, Africans, Syrians, Greeks, Jews, they had come from all parts of the Roman world. From the backwoods of Europe and the crowded old cities of the East, they had been drawn, or brought to this commercial, thriving, and most western metropolis. They were not, most of them, citizens interested in good laws, but a fickle, hungry lot, ready to cheer and cast whatever votes they had for anyone who would feed them well and pay for Games to entertain them.

In the month of Quinctilis, it was up to Brutus and Cassius to furnish Games in honor of Apollo. Having been praetors or judges, they dared not fail to do so yet they dared not return to Rome. So they put up the cost, had someone else round up the gladiators and wild beasts, and the Games went on. It was the 13th day of Quinctilis, as the excited crowds went surging through the narrow, dirty streets that led to the Circus. Hot, sweaty, under the blistering sun, breathing garlic, they jostled one another, laughing, shouting and cheering in a frenzy of joy, but not for the Games. Not for Brutus and Cassius were they cheering, but for Octavian.

Planning to make the Games a flop, Octavian had shrewdly chosen that day to distribute the $15.00 each, that Caesar had left the people in his will. Each citizen, therefore, in that crowd—butcher, fuller, baker, peddler, or whatever—had in his hot, sticky fist more money than he could earn in a month, or perhaps in two months. No wonder that they were shouting loud cheers for the dead Caesar, who had not forgotten his people, loud cheers for the young Caesar, who had kept his promise.

That was the first thing that Octavian did with his money, but not all. Later in the month, he, too, furnished Games, in honor of Caesar and his latest victory. For, in celebration of all victories, the people expected Games to be given them by the successful general. Caesar had died too soon. So Octavian put them on.

Once more, in that hot, midsummer month of Quinctilis, the streets were full of an uproarious, holiday crowd, streaming out to take their seats on the long wooden grandstands of the Circus Maximus. There they would bet on their favorite gladiators, as they strode in, flexing their strong, naked muscles, glistening with olive oil. Or they would argue and wager about the comparative strength of the lions, pitted against each other, whose deep roars, as they caught the human scent, could be heard through the uproar of the crowd and the shrill blare of the trumpets.

Wild beasts, tearing each other to pieces, and young men hacking each other to death. That made a wonderful spectacle for the Roman crowd, a thrilling and successful day!

One thing only marred it for Octavian. He had hoped to display the glittering crown of golden laurel leaves that Caesar had been allowed to wear, and also his golden chair, but that had been forbidden. Something far more thrilling, however, than the sight of those tokens of earthly power and glory took place that very night.

As it grew dark, a comet of unusual brilliance flashed its wide arc across the sky. Looking up, the people could see, as they were told, that it might be the soul of their great leader. Julius Caesar, whose genius had been so much greater than that of average men, as to seem to be that of a god on earth, had now gone to take his place among the stars of heaven, the everlasting gods.

On the strength of this heavenly sign, Octavian had a new statue of the god Julius (Divus Julius) made with a gold star on his forehead, and placed in the Temple of his ancestor Venus.

Also influenced, possibly, by that omen from on high, the Senate issued a decree that the month in which the great event had taken place should no longer be known as the fifth month, Quinctilis.

Henceforth, it should bear Caesar's clan name, Juleus or July.

All our months still carry their old Roman names. Our entire calendar, not just the one month of July, is a memorial to Julius Caesar. Though it was made more accurate by Pope Gregory, in 1582, the calendar we use today is still practically the same one that was made for the Romans by Julius Caesar, the year before he died.

For nearly twenty years, Caesar had been Pontifex Maximus, the chief Roman priest, in charge of announcing each month and its events. But the Roman calendar was such a mess that half the time he hardly knew, himself, when a month began or what it was.

The idea of making a new calendar had occurred to him in Egypt. During the winter spent with Cleopatra, Caesar had seen the Egyptians using a far better calendar. It had then been in use more than 4,000 years. having been made by one of those ancient Pharaohs whose pyramids he had visited with Cleopatra on their journey up the Nile.

On his return home, Caesar had sent for an Egyptian astronomer, by the name of Sosigenes, to come to Rome and work out a calendar for him, one that would keep the names of the old Roman months but leave out their connection with the moon.

It was figuring by the moon, Caesar saw plainly, that caused the Romans all their trouble. The Egyptian calendar paid no attention to the moon. Each year had 12 equal months of 30 days, with 5 extra feast days added at the end, which made 365.

The Romans used a moon, or lunar calendar, which had been handed down to them by way of Greeks from the ancient Babylonians.

It also had 12 months, but each one was truly $\frac{1}{\text{"moonth"}}$ as well as $\frac{1}{12}$ of the year. That is, each new moon started a new month. But when several nights were cloudy, and the man on watch for it failed to catch sight of the new moon, who could tell when the month began? Also, 12 of those moon months made only 354 instead of 365 days, so the year was always too short; the months kept coming around too soon, and getting out of season. Spring months turned up before the winter was over, summer months came in early spring, and so on.

Sosigenes found, when he reached Rome, that the year 46 B.C. had come out about 90 days too short. So, the first thing he and Caesar did was to tack on three extra months. Then they figured out new months, discarding the moon entirely. The Roman priests, some of them, were horrified; they said it was sacrilegious to give up the old way. But

Caesar wanted a calendar that would keep itself in order, not one that only the High Priest could manipulate.

This calendar of his would have 365 days, he had thought, just like the one in Egypt, but Sosigenes had said that he could make one still more accurate; 365 days were not exactly the correct number in a year.

"We now know," he said, "that it takes the sun about ¼ of a day more than that to travel around the earth, or 365¼ days."

Caesar was determined to have the best and most scientific calendar that could be made, including that quarter of a day. Thus it was set up, that calendar, which we have inherited and which was made originally in ancient Egypt, at that very earliest date recorded in history, the year 4241 B.C.

45 B.C. was the first year that this new "Julian Calendar" was put into use. To the Romans, who counted time from the founding of their city, that year was 709. 709 years it was said to be since Rome had been founded by Romulus, one of those famous twins, who had been brought up by a wolf.

Mars, the god of war, was supposed by the early Romans to have been the father of those twins, and it was for him that they had named what was then the first month in their year, Martius or March.

January, which later took first place in the calendar, was named for Janus, another early god, who had two faces, showing that he could look both to the past and to the future. He was the gatekeeper of Heaven, and from early times a Temple to Janus, in the shape of a great gate, had stood near the Forum. In time of war the gate stood open, but it was to be closed in those rare times when Rome was at peace. Only twice so far had that gate been closed.

Never during Julius Caesar's lifetime. Now, at his death, Rome was to be plunged into fourteen more years of civil war. Possibly old Janus, looking to the future, could see the end of it, but no one else. Caesar's enemies and friends were marshalling their forces.

Mars, bloodthirsty god of war, was sharpening his sword.

GAULS, GEESE AND BLACK VULTURES

L IVY, THE GREAT Roman historian, was only fifteen, four years younger
than Octavian, when this civil war broke out that was to destroy
forever the Roman Republic. The first battle took place in Cisalpine Gaul, the Roman province in which he lived.

41

That was really northern Italy and was much more civilized than the larger, wilder Gaul across the Alps, which is now France. On this side of the Alps, the Gauls had adopted Roman customs. They wore the toga, instead of their queer breeches, cut short their yellow hair, instead of letting it grow long, and many had given themselves Roman names.

Young Livy, however, was not a Gaul, but an Italian.

For the past two hundred years Italian settlers from southern Italy had been sent up here to Cisalpine Gaul, to form a strong pioneer colony between Rome and the barbarians. Chopping down the tall trees for their fields and vineyards, these pioneers had cut great squares of sunshine into the deep wooded valley of the Po.

But young Livy was not of that pioneer or farmer stock. The boy was city bred; he had been born in a fine house in Padua, where his family had lived for many generations. They prided themselves that their city was as old as Rome. Padua, like Rome, they said, had also been settled by Greek refugees from burning Troy.

As a small boy, Livy had loved to listen to the story of the Trojan War, and to hear how the hero Aeneas had escaped with his band of followers and finally landed on the Tiber. That was long before Rome existed, except as a little camp or village, because Aeneas was the early ancestor of Romulus, by whom Rome was founded.

The story of Romulus and Remus! That, too, was a wonderful story for a small boy to hear, though, at times, he might wonder if it could all be true. The cruel uncle who had thrown the twin babies into the Tiber seemed real enough, but if the god Mars had truly been their father, why hadn't he protected them? And why didn't the good shepherd who had rescued them have his wife care for the poor little fellows, instead of leaving them to a wolf? Yet, people from Padua who had been to Rome said they had seen the actual cave of the wolf, with an iron statue in it, showing the wolf mother nursing the twin babies! It was on the side of the Palatine Hill. Livy always planned some day to go to see it. Then he could also go to the top of the hill! That was where the twelve black vultures had come swooping down from heaven, and

THE 7 VII HILLS OF ROME

Temple of Jupiter · Temple of Juno

CAMPUS MARTIUS OR FIELD OF MARS

QUIRINAL · VIMINAL · ESQUILINE

CAPITOLINE · FORUM · SACRED WAY

TIBER

PALATINE · CAELIAN

CIRCUS MAXIMUS

AVENTINE · APPIAN WAY

circled over the head of Romulus, to show him that it was he, and not Remus, who was to found the city of Rome. Twelve black vultures that had never been seen again!

And the Capitoline! That was another hill to visit, with another exciting story. This one was about the Gauls, and how three hundred and sixty years or so after Rome was founded, a terrible horde of those big, blue-eyed barbarians had come pouring over the Alps, and sweeping down into Italy, so fast that they had taken Rome by surprise.

Without even stopping to shut the city gates, the Romans had fled with their wives and children to the fortress on the Capitoline. Through the wide open gates, then, the Gauls had come pouring in, plundered, sacked and burned the city, and very nearly captured the Capitol. In that extremely steep hill, they had discovered a gulley or tunnel, through which, one starlit night, they managed to creep up, so silently as to wake neither the watchmen nor the dogs. But they could not get by the geese! Those sacred geese of Juno, in her nearby temple, woke with such a gabbling and clapping of their wings that the sleeping Romans were on their feet at once. Jumping into action, they "assailed the invaders with javelins and stones, and soon the whole company lost footing, and were flung headlong to destruction."

Since then, no army of Gauls had ever reached Rome again. Instead, Roman legions had gone over the Alps into the Gauls' own country to overwhelm and conquer them.

One of Livy's earliest memories was of hearing about Julius Caesar, who then, summer after summer, was leading his soldiers against those wild tribes of Gaul across the Alps. Finally the year had come when the last and greatest leader of the Gauls, brave young Vercingetorix, had been led back to Rome in chains, to walk in Caesar's triumph, and all Gaul was under Roman rule.

One winter soon after he had learned to read, Livy had unrolled a brand new book that Caesar had just written about his war in Gaul. It began with the words, "Gallia est omnis divisa in partes tres . . ." Spellbound, he had read through to the very end.

Caesar had then seemed to the boy Livy, not unlike those brave, bold, early Roman heroes who had built up the city and helped make Rome mistress of the world.

But later when Caesar had so boldly crossed the Rubicon River, when he had marched on Rome, and overthrown the government, he seemed no longer a great man, but a traitor to the Republic. Then, for the first time, the boy had realized how good and bad can be blended together in a single man, and in the story of a nation. That thought

44

Livy was to put down in the introduction of his great history of the Roman people, which he was to write in future days.

"That is what makes the study of history so valuable," he was to say—"the fact that you can behold, displayed as on a monument, every kind of conduct; thence you may select for yourself and for your country that which you may imitate; thence note what is shameful in the undertaking and shameful in the result, which you may avoid. . . ."

Much that was utterly shameful young Livy was to see in this civil war that now, in his sixteenth year, was just beginning. . . .

OCTAVIAN PLAYS THE GAME

WAR WAS NOT declared until more than six months later, but this final struggle for control of the Roman State actually began in that newly named month of July, 44 B.C., when Octavian had celebrated the games in Julius Caesar's honor, and Antony was Consul. It was amazing what changes were to take place in a single year.

Just one year and a month later, Octavian would have forced the Senate to give him, a mere boy of nineteen years, the position of Consul, that highest place in the Roman State.

Years later he had forgotten, or chose to overlook the fact that he had seized the consulship by force, but the fact remains. These are the events that led up to it. They are so many, and took place so rapidly, that we have to follow them like moves in a close game of wits. That is what it really was, a cruel hard game of politics and war—a three-cornered game, to begin with, between Octavian, Antony and Cicero (who stood for the Republic).

Month by month, move by move, this is what happened in that bitter struggle that followed the death of Julius Caesar.

JULY, 44 B.C. Antony, looking ahead six months to the end of his term as Consul, got the Senate to decree that, for the following year, he should be governor of Cisalpine Gaul. That arranged, he set the next Senate meeting for September first.

SEXTILIS. Senators were gathering for the meeting.

SEPTEMBER. Cicero arrived in Rome. But when he found to his disgust that, on the first day, the Senate were to discuss divine rites for Julius Caesar, he sent word that he was "too ill" from his journey to attend. That infuriated Antony. Somebody ought to go, he said, break open his house and drag the old man out! That, in turn, made Cicero furious. Next day, dressed in his best toga, he came to the Senate chamber, and launched at once upon the first of what were to be fourteen increasingly bitter orations against Antony. In reply, Antony publicly renounced his friendship with Cicero, and all the other "traitors and assassins."

OCTOBER. Antony was almost assassinated by Octavian. So he himself declared. Men paid by Octavian to do it, he said, had been caught lurking in his vestibule, and he had barely escaped with his life. With that as an excuse for needing soldiers to protect him, Antony set out to take command of those legions of Caesar's which were still stationed at Brundisium. Octavian, hearing of this, set out for the country south of Rome, there to gather into an army for himself all of Caesar's retired soldiers who might now have grown bored with farming.

NOVEMBER. Octavian was back in Rome, with 10,000 men. Marching to the Forum, he declared that he and his soldiers were there to defend the people, and the Republic, against Antony, who had proved to be a traitor.

When Antony returned to Rome with his soldiers the Senators, in utter distress, ran back and forth between the two men, urging them to come to terms, and not start another war.

By this time, poor old Cicero, back home in the country, was also in a dilemma. "Every day," he wrote Atticus, "I have a letter from Octavian, asking me to take up his cause, and to be a second time the Saviour of the Republic, and to come to Rome at once. I am afraid to accept and ashamed to refuse." The boy was certainly acting with vigor, yet how could anyone be trusted who bore the name of that tyrant Julius Caesar? What to do? What a mixup! What a dilemma to be in!

DECEMBER. Antony had now only one month left of his term as Consul; he decided not to wait, but set out at once with his cavalry for Cisalpine Gaul. To the old governor of the province he sent word to clear out, that he, the new governor, was coming. But Decimus, the governor, who was one of the conspirators, fortified himself in the town of Mutina and refused to move. Thereupon Antony laid siege to the town, in order to starve him out. By this time Cicero had arrived in Rome, and sent word to Decimus to hold fast. Then, sweeping together his worst adjectives, he denounced Antony as a "monster, a drunken swine and a brute beast, devoid of all sense and feeling."

JANUARY. The two new consuls took office. Cicero, on his feet again, urged them and the Senate to declare war on Antony—and to put their trust in Octavian. Cicero was now convinced that in this crisis the best thing for the Senate to do was to let Octavian help them defeat Antony, and then settle with him later. "I pledge my word to you, O Senate," cried Cicero, "that Octavian will always be as loyal to the Republic as he is today. To you, to the Roman people —to the State, I pledge my word."

The Senate was impressed, enough so to vote Octavian a seat in the Senate, but not enough so to declare war on Antony—not yet —not until they had first sent a delegation to confer with him. At the same time, however, they sent Octavian and one of the consuls north with armies, to scare Antony into reason.

The delegation soon returned with the report that Antony was willing to trade his one year in Cisalpine Gaul for five years as Governor of Gaul across the Alps.

47

Cicero was alarmed. "Beware," cried he, "lest you let this foul and deadly beast escape!" And finally he convinced the Senate that Antony was a dangerous man.

FEBRUARY. On the second day, therefore, the Roman Senate formally declared war on Mark Antony!

MARCH. The second Consul was sent north with soldiers to join the other consul and Octavian. Moving quickly, Antony tried to prevent their meeting, but ten days later, the three armies of the Senate had joined. Storming Antony's camp, they gained a partial victory, but paid dearly for it with the lives of the two consuls, for both of them died that day.

Antony, not knowing of course that they were dead, and Octavian left alone in command, expected that the next day would bring another attack. So that night he broke camp and made a hasty escape. Thus the siege was raised, and Decimus and his soldiers, after four hungry months, regained their freedom.

APRIL. The glad news reached Rome. Wild with joy, the citizens cheered and applauded Cicero. They carried him in triumph to the Capitol and acclaimed him for a second time, as Saviour of the State! It was Cicero's great day, the day he had long hoped for. No special credit or thanks was given to Octavian, by either the Senate or Cicero, for the part that he had played. And there they made a fatal mistake.

MAY. Octavian was still in command of the army in Cisalpine Gaul when he received word that he had been voted the barest possible thanks for his part in the victory. Now that he had served his purpose he saw that he was to be brushed aside by Cicero and the Senate.

Very well, he thought, the time had then come for him to make a move and he thought up a shrewd one.

The two Consuls were now both dead, and there were still seven months left to finish out the year. He, Octavian, would demand to be made Consul for those remaining months. He was nineteen only, much too young. The Senators would certainly refuse, but if so, he would use that as an excuse to break off all connection with them. If they appointed him, what could be better? Either way, he was bound to win!

JUNE. A delegation of his soldiers went down to Rome to ask the Senate to appoint Octavian Consul. The Senators refused.

JULY. The officers went down to Rome again. This time, Octavian went with them. Also a hundred men. Again the officer in charge demanded the appointment for Octavian and again the Senators refused. The officer then pointed to his sword.

"This," said he, "will make him Consul, if you don't."

That was a threat the Senate dared not disregard. Cicero was broken hearted—"utterly overcome with grief" that this boy, whose loyalty to the Republic he had so confidently pledged, had after all followed in his great-uncle's footsteps. He had marched on Rome, and with force of arms defied the Roman Senate. "Utterly overcome with grief," the old man, so recently flushed with victory, acknowledged his defeat, and gave up the struggle.

SEXTILIS. On the nineteenth day of this month, later to be known as August, Octavian was made Consul of the Roman State.

Nervous inside, but outwardly calm, he stepped forward for the first time to offer the customary sacrifices to Jupiter with which the Senate meeting opened. In a circle about him, stood the disgruntled Senators, each one watching with a cold, critical eye for him to fumble. To their keen disappointment, he went through the service perfectly. It was likewise to their loss, it seems, that they watched him so intently. For, according to the story, told years later, when myths had become mixed with history, if they had looked up that day, they would have seen twelve black vultures come swooping down from heaven, those twelve black vultures of Romulus that had returned again,—this time to circle above the head of the young man who was to become Rome's first emperor, the future Augustus Caesar.

BLOODY FINGERPRINTS

ROME WAS IN TERROR by December, 43 B.C., the last month of
Octavian's consulship. Roman citizens were fleeing for their
lives. Soldiers, with drawn sword in one hand, a list of names
in the other, were searching streets and houses. The Senate
was powerless to stop them, for now, three dictators, working together,
had seized control of the government.

Those three dictators, known as the Triumvirate, had signed a
proclamation, calling for this wholesale murder of their enemies. One
of the three was young Octavian.

It would be a happier thing, if we could skip this black page in
the story of that young emperor to be, and recall only his later years
known as the great Augustan Age. But that would be to write propa-
ganda and not history. For the sake of truth, the whole story of his rise

to power must be told. Signing his name to this proclamation is part of that story.

Another signature was that of Antony. The Senators had celebrated their victory over him too soon, and as Cicero feared, they had let "the foul and deadly beast" escape. That, like brushing off Octavian, was a mistake for which they were to suffer. It gave reason for those two former enemies to unite against their common enemy, the Senate. They were brought together by an older general named Lepidus, the third man in the Triumvirate.

Old "Papa Lepidus," as Antony called him, had been a cavalry commander under Julius Caesar. He was a man of sixty years or more. It was to him, at his camp at Forum Julii, that Antony had fled when he had made his escape, the night following the battle. Lepidus, after receiving Antony, had written to Octavian, suggesting that he join forces with them. The letter had reached Octavian just at the right moment, just when he had made up his mind to break connection with the Senate. To join Antony and Lepidus had then appeared the best thing for him to do.

The idea of forming a Triumvirate also appealed to him. In that, too, he was following in his great-uncle's footsteps, for Julius Caesar himself had once been part of a similar three-man dictatorship. That was the first, and this one, formed by Antony, Octavian and Lepidus, was the second Triumvirate.

The first meeting of the big three took place in October, in Cisalpine Gaul, on a very small island in the middle of a river. In preparation for the great event a tent had been erected on the little island, and two narrow bridges built, one leading from each bank. It was to be a very secret meeting. Each man was to go to the island alone and unguarded. All their troops were to remain on shore.

Accordingly, at the appointed hour, out from one bank could be seen the spindly legs of Octavian moving forward deliberately across one of the narrow bridges. At the same time, striding forth from the opposite bank came a big muscular fellow in a scarlet general's cape

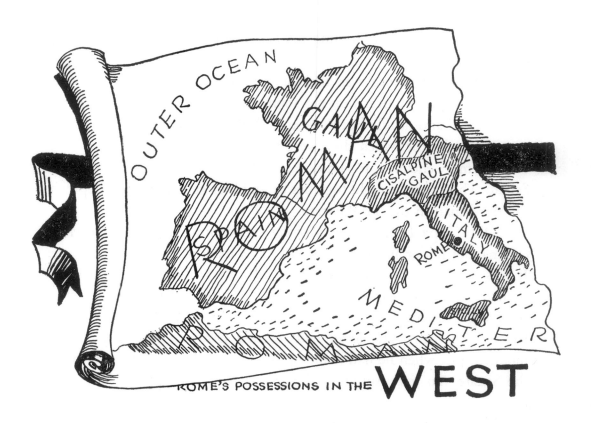

ROME'S POSSESSIONS IN THE **WEST**

which was caught and flung wide by a sudden breeze. Following him, knees and shoulders slightly bent, came an older man with gray bushy hair. Thus, the three men, young, middle-aged and old, approached the island. Each, as he stepped on to it, was alone and unarmed—that is, supposedly unarmed. Octavian and Antony, however, more suspicious than trustful, both took precaution to feel for hidden weapons before embracing too cordially. Convinced of their so-called friendship, the three then entered the tent, seated themselves about the table and got down to business.

First, they drew up an agreement that for five years to come, they would rule Rome and Italy together. Then they divided up Rome's provinces in the west.

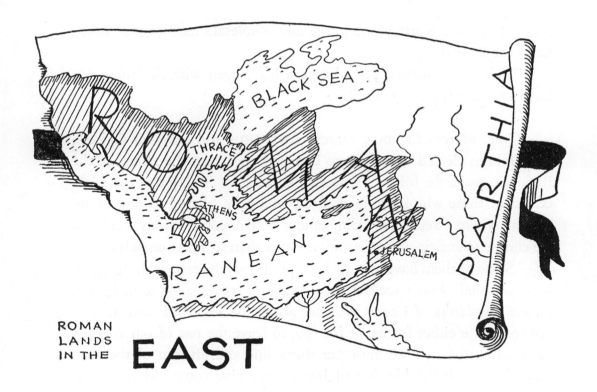

ROMAN
LANDS
IN THE
EAST

Of those in the east, Brutus and Cassius still had control. Not until they had been defeated would Rome's eastern possessions also be in the hands of the Triumvirate.

It was decided, therefore, that while "Papa" Lepidus remained in Rome, Antony, assisted by Octavian, should set out for Greece, or Asia, if need be, to defeat Brutus and Cassius and those armies which they had now raised and equipped.

At this point two tormenting questions arose to perplex these three ambitious gentlemen.

Where would they get money enough to pay for the campaign?

What about the enemies they would leave behind in Rome?

On the third day, they worked out the answer to those questions. On that day the three men drew up a list of their enemies (which included many wealthy men, whose property could be confiscated), and they plotted the worst blood purge and wholesale murder that Rome had ever known.

Their proclamation, preceding the list, began with the following false and self-righteous words:

"We, Marcus LEPIDUS, Marcus ANTONIUS and Octavius CAESAR, having been elected to bring into harmony and order the affairs of the Republic, make the following proclamation. . . . Seeing that the wickedness of those who have insulted us, who have plotted to destroy us, and by whom Caesar was slain, cannot be overcome by any kindness, we choose to anticipate our enemies, rather than to suffer ourselves.

"Some of them have already been punished; the rest, with the gods' help, you shall shortly see chastised. One task yet remains: to make war on the murderers of Caesar who are across the sea. And since it does not seem safe either for us, or for you, to leave the rest of our enemies here behind us . . . we must put them, one and all, out of the way. Therefore, with the blessing of heaven, we give command that none shall harbor any of those whose names are written here below. . . . Whosoever shall bring the head of anyone of them to us, if he be a free man, shall receive $500, but if he be a slave, he shall receive $200, his freedom, and all the civic privileges of his master.

"The same reward shall be given anyone who shall furnish information of their place of hiding."

Then followed a list of names, including approximately 2,000 Knights and 300 Senators.

With the publication of the list, the awful man hunt began, and terror struck the city. Those named on the list, as well as many who were not named, but hunted out for private spite, were tracked down, slain in their beds or murdered on their doorsteps. Every day, soldiers came marching back to the Forum, carrying sacks full of heads, to count and claim their coveted reward.

One day, early in December, the right hand as well as the head ot a man was brought to Mark Antony. On the large head, the grey hair lay thin and rumpled. The middle finger of the hand was slightly stained with ink—the hand that had written many consoling thoughts on the nature of the universe, on Friendship, Old Age and Immortality, that would be read and enjoyed for centuries to come. It was the hand of Cicero. But that severed hand had also written the fourteen orations against Antony, which he never would forget.

"Now," he cried, with satisfaction, "our list is complete."

He ordered the head and hand of the dead orator hung up on the rostrum, that all might see, he said, the penalty for double dealing.

That was December 7, 43 B.C., the day of Cicero's death.

After he had lost hope of saving his beloved Republic, Cicero had returned to the country and his writing. On the day of his death, he had been riding in his litter, trying to escape, when he heard the soldiers coming. Terrified till then, he suddenly became composed. He told the frightened, loyal slaves to set the litter down. A moment later, the soldiers, rushing up with drawn swords, found the old man sitting quietly, one elbow on his knee, his head resting heavily on his hand, as if utterly weary. Without a word, he bent his neck to receive the blow, and knew no more.

"When the time comes," he had once said, "I shall withdraw from life, not as one leaves home, but as from a temporary lodging place. On that brightest of all days, when I depart from the confusion of this world, I shall set out, I believe, for a far-off divine gathering of spirits. . . .

"But, if I am mistaken, in that I believe men's souls to be immortal, I am glad to be mistaken . . .

"And all my life I shall continue to believe it. . . ."

CANDLES AND HOLLY BERRIES

A ND NOW TO ROME, as always in December, came the Saturnalia.
"Io! SATURNALIA!" That was the call that ushered in the mer-
riest holiday of the Roman year—that hilarious, glorious, mid-
December festival, the Saturnalia.

"Io! SATURNALIA! Io! Io! Io!" That was the greeting that echoed
through the holiday season. For it was in honor of Saturn—this gay
carnival of thanksgiving—good, old, generous Saturn, kindest and most
provident of gods.

God of the rich harvest, born of Earth and Sky he was, who,
"once-upon-a-time," so it was said, had lived and reigned on earth.
During that time, the world had known only prosperity and peace.
Crops grew without cultivation; bins and storehouses were always full!
There had been neither want, nor weariness, nor war, in his Golden
Age. So, once every year in memory of that happy time of old, came
these glorious carefree days of the Saturnalia.

56

During those mid-December days (first three, and later seven) no war was ever declared, nor battles fought, no criminals tried or punished. Courts were closed; schools dismissed; even the slave markets were shut down. During those days, all slaves were free as in those golden days of old, all people had been equal. Everyone, rich, poor, young and old joined in a glorious holiday.

The day began with a sacrifice of thanksgiving in the early morning, followed by a public feast at midday, which turned into a wild, hilarious carnival before evening. In red pointed caps and colored costumes, merrymakers went singing and laughing through the streets, showering wheat and barley like confetti, and granting every wish, no matter how wild, ridiculous, or disgusting, made by the lucky one who had been chosen "King of the Saturnalia."

The weeks ahead were always filled with preparation. Candle-makers and makers of dolls were busy pouring out wax, turning out little earthenware images, and setting up booths for the doll fair. Every child would want a doll, and every household would need many candles for the Saturnalia.

Holly branches, with their bright berries, had to be cut and carted into the city, and houses trimmed with evergreen. Gifts for the family and friends must be selected and wrapped. For on the second day, after a family dinner of roast young pig, with all the trimmings, came an exchange of presents!

How Octavia loved that part of it!

As children, she and Octavius had always had such fun wrapping up their gifts together. They had always spent Saturnalia in the country. One year, she remembered, they had hung more than a hundred tiny masks of Bacchus on the small fruit and olive trees. As the wind whirled them round and round, it was fun to think that each time the little laughing face of the wine god turned and touched the tree, another olive or cherry would grow on it!

The next year she got the little doll with the sweet face that she loved so much and planned to keep always until she had a real baby of her own. She still had the little doll.

And now, on this Saturnalia, Octavia also had a darling baby boy. Little rosy cheeked Marcellus, in the cradle beside her, was almost a year old. This would be his first Saturnalia. He was too little to enjoy it, but it might be fun to make him a wee red pointed cap out of a scrap of wool or silk.

Some day, when he was old enough, she would take him to the Forum to see the Temple of Saturn and the statue of the good old god who was, she believed, the most ancient god in Rome. The statue was hollow, and filled with olive oil, because olives had been so plentiful in Saturn's day. And there were ribbons of wool about his feet. Was that because the sheep gave wool in such rich abundance when he reigned on earth? she thought.

Or was it, perhaps, to try and draw him back into this unhappy world which, since he had left it, was so full of hate and poverty and war.

Would he ever come back? she wondered. Would people of the world ever again live in peace and happiness together?

Would there ever be another Golden Age?

IMPERATOR

PEOPLE WHO WERE LIVING

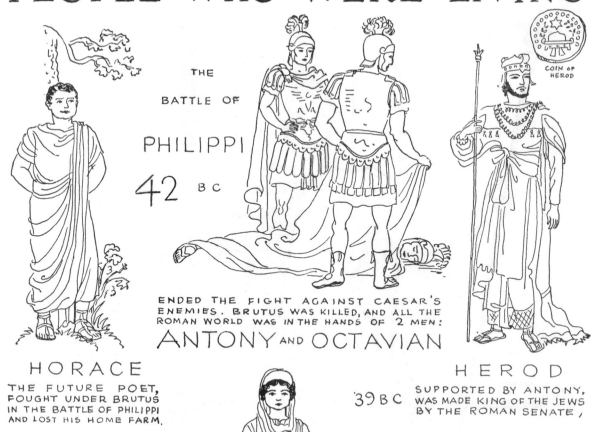

THE

BATTLE OF

PHILIPPI

42 BC

COIN OF HEROD

ENDED THE FIGHT AGAINST CAESAR'S ENEMIES. BRUTUS WAS KILLED, AND ALL THE ROMAN WORLD WAS IN THE HANDS OF 2 MEN:

ANTONY AND OCTAVIAN

HORACE

THE FUTURE POET, FOUGHT UNDER BRUTUS IN THE BATTLE OF PHILIPPI AND LOST HIS HOME FARM.

HEROD

39 BC

SUPPORTED BY ANTONY, WAS MADE KING OF THE JEWS BY THE ROMAN SENATE,

a Trojan horse filled with toy soldiers

HER SON

HER SON

JULIA

DAUGHTER OF OCTAVIAN BY HIS FIRST WIFE, WAS BORN 40 BC

DRUSUS

WAS FOUR YEARS YOUNGER THAN HIS BROTHER TIBERIUS,

LIVIA

WIFE OF OCTAVIAN

TIBERIUS

WAS FOUR WHEN HIS MOTHER MARRIED OCTAVIAN IN 38 B.C.

MARCELLUS

OCTAVIA'S SON, WAS ABOUT TWO YEARS OLDER THAN TIBERIUS

THESE CHILDREN GREW UP TOGETHER ON THE PALATINE)

AND SOME EVENTS THAT TOOK

WHEN OCTAVIAN WAS A GENERAL

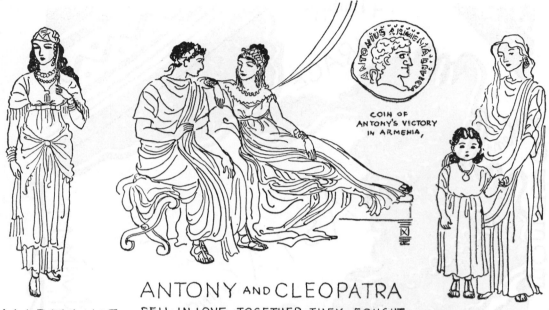

MARIAMNE
GRANDDAUGHTER · OF
THE HIGH PRIEST OF THE
JEWS, MARRIED HEROD,

ANTONY AND CLEOPATRA
FELL IN LOVE. TOGETHER THEY FOUGHT
OCTAVIAN FOR CONTROL OF THE ROMAN
WORLD, BUT WERE DEFEATED IN THE BATTLE OF

ACTIUM

COIN OF
ANTONY'S VICTORY
IN ARMENIA,

OCTAVIA
MARRIED ANTONY, HOPING
TO KEEP PEACE BETWEEN
HIM AND HER BROTHER,
LITTLE ANTONIA WAS BORN 40 B.C.

31 B.C.

dressed for
a Triumph

COIN TO CELEBRATE
PEACE

OCTAVIAN
WAS VICTORIOUS, AND ONE
MAN ALONE, CONTROLLED
THE ROMAN WORLD,

PEACE
CAME AT LAST, AND
THE TEMPLE OF JANUS
WAS CLOSED!

VIRGIL
THE POET, WELCOMED
THE END OF WAR AS THE
DAWN OF A NEW GOLDEN AGE.

PLACE BETWEEN 42 AND 29 B.C.

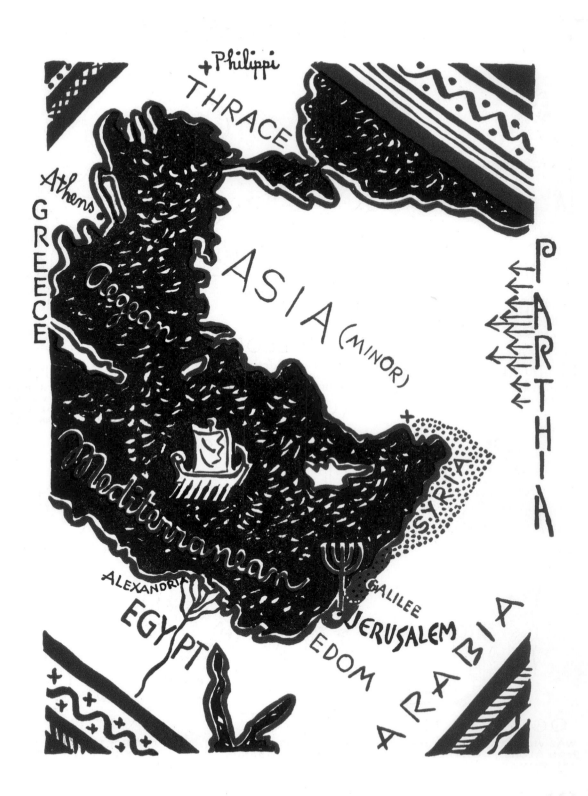

THE FESTIVAL OF LIGHTS

OVER THE TEMPLE and housetops of Jerusalem, over its smoking altar, and its Mount of Zion, a red winter sun was slowly sinking. Much too slowly, it seemed to the two children who were watching it that December afternoon from the palace of their grandfather, the High Priest, Hyrcanus.

Mariamne, a very beautiful little girl of eleven or twelve, stood quietly leaning against the window frame, her long lashes and heavy dark curls turned to red bronze in the sunlight.

Aristobulus, who was nine and more impatient than his sister, kept turning in his hands a small unlighted torch, and wondering aloud if tomorrow was never going to come!

Half an hour or more the two royal children had been watching and waiting for the sun to disappear behind the dark edge of the city wall and let the new day begin. For each new day began, not at midnight, but at sundown in Jerusalem.

And tomorrow was a Festival!—the beginning of Hannukah! Always in December, while the Romans were celebrating the Saturnalia, the Hannukah, or Festival of Lights, was being celebrated by the Jews.

At sundown, as soon as it was dusk, the first one of the eight lamps would be lighted in the Hannukah lampstand. That was what Aristobulus was waiting for. The next evening, they would light two lamps instead of one. The next, three, and so on, until on the last day, all of the eight branches of the Hannukah lampstand would be ablaze with light. Lights would be shining out from all the houses in Jerusalem.

The sacred gold lampstand in the Temple had only seven branches, like the seven days of the week, or the seven planets in the sky. But the Hannukah lampstand had eight lights, in memory of the miracle.

According to a legend, which Mariamne and Aristobulus never tired of hearing repeated, a miracle had taken place in the Temple in the days of one of their early ancestors, Judas Maccabeus. It had been on a December day about one hundred years ago, when the Greeks instead of the Romans had ruled over Palestine.

The Temple, after being long misused by the Greeks for the worship of one of their many gods, had just been won back again by the Jews and was about to be rededicated to Javeh, the one and only God of Israel. Everything was ready. The altar had been cleansed and purified. New golden basins had been provided to catch the blood of the lambs, waiting to be sacrificed. The twelve loaves of unleavened bread had been laid on the table in the Holy Place. And there, too, once more, standing like the tree of life, was the great sacred lamp, or candlestick, with its seven branches. It had only to be filled and lighted.

64

Then, to the dismay of the priests, no pure lamp oil could be found! A frantic search unearthed but one small dusty jar, containing only enough sacred oil to last a single day, but with it the seven cups were filled and lighted. The next day, to the amazement of the priests, it was still burning, and the next. For eight days, it was said, the oil continued to burn. In joy, then, and thanksgiving, Judas Maccabeus had decreed, that every year for eight days the miracle should be commemorated with a solemn festival of joy and thanksgiving.

For eight days, therefore, this year, as every year, while the Hannukah lights were burning, the Temple walls would resound with singing of psalms, and their chorus of Hallel-u-Jah, or "Praise-to-Javeh," God of Israel.

Judas Maccabeus was the great hero who had defeated the Greeks and won back the Temple. He was an ancestor in whom the two royal children felt great pride, though just how they were related to him Aristobulus never could remember.

He knew only that they, too, were Maccabeans, and that since the days of Judas Maccabeus, all the High Priests had belonged to the Maccabean family.

"Judas Maccabeus," Mariamne explained to him again, "had four brothers. One of them was the great-great-grandfather of our grandfather Hyrcanus."

And all those grandfathers have been High Priests," said Aristobulus. "Some day, do you think there may be another High Priest strong enough to fight and drive the Romans out, the same way Judas Maccabeus drove away the Greeks? Judas Maccabeus . . ." he said thoughtfully. "I can spell that name."

Diverted for a moment from his vigil, the boy laid down the small torch, and slowly traced the name of his brave ancestor in Hebrew characters on the dusty window sill.

Then he looked up, and saw that suddenly, while he wasn't watching, the sun had dropped below the western horizon, and it was tomorrow! It was Hannukah. The first day of the Festival of Lights.

HEROD, FUTURE KING OF THE JEWS

IT WAS IN THIS same December of 43 B.C., about the time of the Festival of Lights, that Cassius, the lean and hungry one, was leaving Palestine, taking with him many chests of gold. By taxing the Jews and demanding gold from the Temple treasury, he had been gathering funds for the war against Antony and Octavian.

"You have served us well, thus far," said Cassius, bidding farewell to the young governor of Galilee whom he had found most obliging. And no wonder. This young governor was HEROD (the same Herod who, years hence, it is said, was to be visited by three wise men from the East following a star).

66

PHARISEE PHARISEE

THE LAW

A SHEKEL

Naturally keen and crafty as a fox, young Herod had also been well trained by his father to help the most powerful Roman of the day, no matter who he was, when he arrived in Palestine. And why not? All the power Herod's father held in this kingdom of the Jews depended upon the Romans who controlled the country.

For Herod's father was not a native of Palestine. He had come up to Jerusalem from Edom, the country to the south. So the pious Jews looked upon him as a foreigner, hated him as they did all foreigners, and resented the fact that he held power in their country that should have belonged to their own High Priest.

Among the Jews, who had no other law but the law of their religion, the office of High Priest was similar to that of a king.

But Hyrcanus, who was now the High Priest, had no power left to him at all, outside of the Temple. The actual rule of the country had been taken away from him by the Romans, when they conquered the country, and given to Herod's father. That had been his reward for being shrewd and quick to furnish the Roman general with gold as soon as he arrived, help him bombard and conquer Jerusalem, enter the city, and establish their authority.

67

That had been twenty years ago, and during that stormy time, Herod, who was then eleven, had been left with his grandfather in Arabia. For while his father came from Edom, Herod's mother was an Arabian princess. There, where sandy waste and fertile pasture meet, the boy had learned to hunt and fight and ride high-spirited steeds like any son of the desert. He had come to Jerusalem, a strong boy, with a sinewy body, as quick and agile as his mind. A prophet, seeing how keen and daring he was, is said to have predicted that Herod would one day be King of the Jews.

"You do not believe," said the old man, who had observed the boy's shrewd black eyes narrowing in doubt. "You have been told that no one who is not descended from King David will ever be called 'King' by the Jews. But mark well my words, for I, old seer of the Essenes, can foresee your destiny."

When he was twenty-five, Herod's father had given him the northern province of Galilee to govern. There Herod had found his first opportunity to gain the friendship of the Romans, on his own account. But in doing so, Herod had also earned the everlasting hatred of the Jews.

Galilee was a rich, fertile province, but a troublesome one in which rebellion against Rome was always breaking out. There, in Galilee, were to be found many hot-headed young patriots, so full of zeal to make their country independent that they were always ready to snatch up their daggers and follow almost any new leader in an uprising against the Romans. At that particular time, one of those outlaw patriots, a sort of Robin Hood, was captain of a band of rebels who had become the terror of the countryside.

Roman travellers and merchants carrying their goods along the ancient highway running north from Egypt, were in constant fear of being held up and robbed when they went through Galilee. Roman legions never knew when the robbers might rush from their hiding places down upon their camps, to raid and plunder them.

Herod had gone after these outlaws of Galilee, hunted them down in the hills, tracked them to their caves among the rocks and then killed their leader. By doing that Herod had defied the Law and the whole Jewish nation was aroused.

Only the SANHEDRIN, only that body of seventy-one men, the supreme court of the nation, had the right to condemn any man to death. An angry mob stormed the palace of Hyrcanus, and demanded that Herod himself, that tool of the Romans, who had taken the Law into his own hands be summoned before the Sanhedrin to be tried for murder, and condemned.

Hyrcanus, who, as High Priest, was president of this supreme court of justice, had hesitated. By nature mild and uncertain, he also did not wish to offend the Romans and endanger his comfortable position. Trembling, therefore, between the wrath of the Romans and the fury of the Jews, it was with great hesitation that he finally sent the summons to young Herod.

Herod, high in favor with the Romans, had answered the summons boldly, bringing a company of Roman soldiers with him to Jerusalem. Into the Hall of Hewn Stones he had marched, with clanking sword and polished armor, and flaunting a purple cape.

Before those seventy old men, a man on trial was expected to appear with disheveled hair, and clad in the black robe of a penitent. Herod's arrogance shocked and reduced them to silence. Only one among them had been brave enough to speak.

He was a PHARISEE.

Most of the seventy others who made up the Sanhedrin at this time were SADDUCEES, wealthy, worldly, hard-eyed princes of the land who were more interested in protecting their riches and their high position than in defending the rights of those low born noisy rebels of Galilee whose leader had been killed.

But this old man who rose to speak was a PHARISEE and so he was devoted to the Law. For the PHARISEES were students and puritans. They were continually studying the Law of Moses and searching it diligently for righteousness.

"O you, members of this court, who are judges with me," cried the Pharisee, "God is great, and his law is greatly to be feared. If you absolve this guilty man who now stands before us, armed, as if daring us to find him guilty, he will one day return to punish you, all of you, and your High Priest, as well."

Hyrcanus trembled at the words. Looking about the circle of elders he had seen that they too had been stirred. Not daring to take a vote for fear that this young friend of the Romans might possibly be condemned, he had weakly dismissed the court, and left Herod free to escape.

This affair in Galilee had occurred in the days when Julius Caesar was all-powerful in the Roman world. Soon Herod learned that Caesar had been killed, and his enemy Cassius had arrived in Palestine.

Cassius, scratching and scraping together all the gold within reach of his lean and hungry fingers, had found four cities of Syria unable to meet with his demands, and had therefore sold all the inhabitants as slaves (an unfortunate but not unusual way of raising money in this age of wholesale slavery.)

In Galilee, there had been no need to resort to such means. For here, Cassius had found this most capable and obliging young governor, named Herod, who had rounded up the required taxes in short order and delivered them promptly.

Therefore, on that December day, before leaving Palestine to meet Brutus in Asia Minor, Cassius was assuring Herod that he would be well rewarded for his services.

"Continue to serve us well," he was saying. "And when this war is over, I will make you King of Judaea." Cassius spoke with confidence. But Herod's black eyes looked narrow and suspicious.

When the war was over, would it be Cassius, he was thinking, or some other Roman who held the power in Palestine?

No matter. Whoever the most powerful Roman of that day might be, he, Herod, would be on hand to prove himself a friend.

70

PHILIPPI AND THE GHOST

IT WAS FAR PAST MIDNIGHT. Cassius and Brutus had now met, and with the armies which they had recruited were in camp in Thrace. And Brutus was exhausted. The air in his tent was dead and chill, as the fog crept into it. Words danced and blurred on the page before him, but he read on, driving himself feverishly, as he had been doing day and night for weeks. Suddenly, his lamp flickered; he looked up. Through the haze of light his eyes traveled toward the flap of the tent, and stopped.

"Who are you?" he gasped, in a hoarse whisper. "And what do you want?" He was rigid with horror as the ghost drew nearer.

"I am your evil genius," he heard the spectre say. "You will see me again—at Philippi. At Philippi." he whispered and was gone.

Philippi! Brutus shuddered. Philippi was the town in Macedonia where he and Cassius were to camp and prepare for battle against Antony and Octavian. They were in Thrace on their way to Philippi!

Next morning, Cassius laughed scornfully at the story of the ghost, but Brutus could not shake off the chill of it. It clung to him like cold fingers on his neck.

Philippi proved an easy place to fortify. Brutus and Cassius reached

IMPERATOR
(GENERAL)-SEVERAL LEGIONS

TRIBUNE
(2nd LIEUTENANT) 1000 MEN

CENTURION
(SERGEANT) 100 MEN

there in early autumn (42 B.C.) and were well fortified when Antony and the first troops arrived from Rome. The main road ran through a narrow plain between two long high hills. Cassius had taken the hill near the sea; Brutus, the opposite hill, and across the low plain between them they had built a string of earthworks. Looking the situation over, Antony saw that a steep rock cliff protected the far side of Brutus's camp, and an impassable swamp lay between Cassius and the sea. Octavian, arriving ten days later, found Antony making plans to build a road across the swamp. For ten days after they had landed in Greece, Octavian had been too ill to move, but as soon as possible, he had insisted on being carried to Philippi in his litter. He made his camp opposite to Brutus, as Antony's was opposite to that of Cassius.

For a month, the armies faced each other, all four men growing increasingly nervous as the days went by. Each day, Antony and Octavian were expecting their supply ships from Rome each day they did not come. Day by day, the need for them increased.

72

STANDARD BEARER

ORDINARY SOLDIER OF THE LEGION 6000 SOLDIERS = 1 LEGION

His "evil genius" haunted Brutus. Birds of prey worried Cassius. He could scoff at ghosts, but birds of prey flying above one's camp were another matter. They were an evil omen. Finally, Brutus, unable to stand the suspense any longer, set a day for the battle. Cassius wanted to postpone it. A swarm of bees, he said, had settled on one of his standards. In the face of that, no one ought to undertake a battle. But Brutus insisted. They met in the morning of the appointed day to discuss the final plans.

"If the battle should go against us, what do you propose?" asked Cassius, his thin nose looking very pinched and drawn.

"I once thought," said Brutus, "that killing oneself was a cowardly and irreligious act. But now I am of a different mind. If Providence does not favor us today, I am resolved to die, content with having given my life for my country."

The purification ceremony and sacrifice, customary before any battle, was then performed for the soldiers. Cassius, still uneasy, became more so when the garland which he was supposed to wear was handed to him, upside down! That was bad enough, but when the officer walking in front of him, with the image of Victory, stumbled and dropped it to the ground, Cassius was ready to back out, but then it was too late. Before anyone was quite prepared for it, the battle began, a battle that might be called a "Tragedy of Errors."

The first mistake was made by Brutus's soldiers, who started forward in a rush toward the enemy lines before Cassius's men were ready —even before their own officers had given the signal. Part of them, plunging ahead, divided from the others, passed around the left wing of Octavian's forces, and on into his camp. There, after slaughtering the soldiers left on guard, they came upon Octavian's litter. Piercing it savagely with their pikes and darts, they left him for dead, and set to plundering the camp. Their arms were full when Brutus caught up with them. Their mistake, although profitable to them, was disastrous for the soldiers of Cassius.

Antony was down superintending his road across the swamp when the battle started, but his left wing joined the right wing of Octavian's forces (also without their leader). Together, they rushed against the soldiers of Cassius, sent them scattering in retreat, captured Cassius's camp, and began scooping up the plunder.

Cassius, himself, had escaped. Unable to keep his forces together, he and a small personal guard had fled to the top of a more distant hill that overlooked the plain. Judging by his own defeat, Cassius supposed that Brutus had also been defeated.

Brutus, on the other hand, judging by his own success, believed that Cassius had also been victorious, and so had sent no help to him. In time, being unable, from where he stood, to make out why Cassius's camp looked so peculiar, Brutus sent over a company of horsemen. Cassius, standing on the small hill squinting back across the plain, saw the company of horsemen galloping in the dust and mistook them for the enemy. Not completely sure, he sent one of his officers to investigate. The man soon saw who the soldiers were, and they, in turn, recognizing him, were so glad to see him alive that they completely surrounded him. But to nearsighted Cassius, it looked as though he had been captured by the enemy!

"Great Jupiter," he cried. "How could I now love life so well as to live on! Come," he said grimly to the freedman whom he kept always with him in battle for such an emergency. "Strike," he said, pulling his cloak over his head, and making his neck bare. "Strike," he told him. "The time has come to die!"

The cavalry riding up, and Brutus following later, found the freedman gone and Cassius dead, his head severed from his body. The officer stabbed himself in remorse, and Brutus wept. Then, sending Cassius's body to be buried outside of camp, he rallied all the remaining soldiers and, during the following days, reorganized them. These, together with his own, he promised a large sum of money. Also, if they behaved themselves and were victorious, he told them that instead of merely an army camp, they might have two entire cities in Greece to plunder, rob, and pillage "to their hearts' content." A happy thought!

After dark on the night of the battle, to Antony's surprise Octavian turned up alive. He had been warned by the bad dream of a friend and urged to leave camp in the early morning. So his litter had been empty. He was alive, but shivering, and half ill as usual.

Antony's camp was too near the swamp for comfort. It was cold for October, and the tents were pitched in mud and puddles of half frozen water. They could not stay there long. As soon as the supply ships came they must attack Brutus, Antony said, and defeat him. They waited another twenty days for the supplies to come, and then learned that they would never come. The ships had been destroyed at sea. That night, without further delay, Antony announced to the men that the battle would begin on the following day.

And that night, Brutus saw his "evil genius" again. This time, it did not speak, just floated into his tent and out—like the cold breath of the fog. Brutus would never see it again, nor would he see another night. The next day was to be his last.

His forces met with complete defeat. A few brave soldiers remained to defend their leader, but most of them fled before Antony's opposing legions. It was about three in the afternoon when the attack began. Long after dark, about midnight, a small group of dark figures sat on a rock beside a brook, deep in the woods.

Brutus was bemoaning bitterly those who were not with them—those friends who had been lost in the battle. The man beside him slipped down, dipped his helmet in the brook, and handed him a drink of water. They continued to watch for one who had gone to see what had become of their camp. He was to signal with his torch if he got through. There was no signal.

Far above, the sky was bright with stars; at their feet, the brook gurgled. Occasionally someone spoke, then relapsed into silence. Brutus made a quiet request of one and then another, which each seemed to refuse. He sat silent for a time, leaning on his hand. At length he spoke. He thanked them for their loyalty. He said he was angry at Providence only for his country's sake.

"For my own, I think myself happier than my conquerors. I go, leaving a reputation of virtue. They will be condemned by Posterity for having seized a power to which they had no right."

He rose then, gave his right hand to each in farewell, walked a little way apart from them. He drew his sword, and holding the hilt firmly in both hands, fell upon it, and killed himself.

After daylight had come, they found his dead body—the soldiers, Antony and Octavian. As they stood there, Octavian remarked, with a thin, cold voice, that he wished the head sent to Rome to be placed at the foot of Caesar's statue.

Antony shook his head, as he stood looking down upon the quiet figure, with a sort of puzzled wonder, and a certain respect. Unbuckling the clasp of his scarlet general's cloak, he slipped it off, and with it covered the dead Brutus.

WELL, THAT WAS DONE. The task of avenging the death of Julius Caesar had now been accomplished. Brutus and Cassius were dead, and their army, the only strong republican army left, had been defeated. The Roman Republic was dead. All of Rome's possessions in the East, as well as in the West, were now in the hands of the Triumvirate. Rather, they were in the hands of two of the three men. The two who had shared the victory were now to share the spoils. Lepidus, who had remained in Rome, was to be squeezed out—given just enough to keep him quiet.

Octavian and Antony now divided the world between them.

Antony, who was certainly the hero of the hour, took charge of the dividing. He chose first and unhesitatingly; he chose to take the provinces of the East.

"That leaves you Rome, Italy, Spain, Gaul, Sicily—and all the other islands and provinces in the West," he told Octavian.

At first thought, it might seem that the big man had been overly generous, especially to give up Rome, the capital of the world—but not on second thought!

Rome was going to be a hotbed of troubles for many months to come. It would be a bad job for anyone to try to bring peace and order out of the confusion. Antony had no desire to undertake it. He wanted to relax now—have a good time—enjoy life, with plenty of wine and good food, beautiful women and amusing, boisterous companions to enjoy it with him.

Oh, no, he had no desire to return to Rome, not to Rome. Nor to Fulvia, with her carping criticism and driving ambition that never gave a fellow any peace. No, Rome and its cares were not for him, at the present moment. So, dropping the unwelcome burden on Octavian's narrow shoulders, and wishing him good luck, Antony swung back into his easy stride, and departed for the East.

His trip through Asia Minor was like the royal journey of a potentate, for he was now the most powerful Roman in that part of the Roman world. Everywhere, kings and princes of the subject countries rushed to court his favor. Herod was among them, eager to prove himself as good a friend to Antony as he had been to Cassius. Ambassadors also, for various reasons, came running to him, with huge sum of gold, which he spent at once in a lavish manner.

A whole company of actors traveled with him, singers, pipers, dancers, jugglers and entertainers of all kinds, all those who could add spice to life and joy to living.

Oh, those were gay days for Antony, and merry ones! Bacchus, the god of wine, himself, could scarcely have improved upon them. In fact, at Ephesus, boys and women, falling into the spirit, did actually hail Antony as Bacchus. Dressed as nymphs and devotees of the happy god, they went dancing to meet him at the gates, draped his chariot with flowers, and, dancing and singing, escorted him into the city, winding through the streets in a long, hilarious, jubilant procession. . . .

Octavian, meanwhile, had started on the dismal journey back to Rome. He knew very well what he had to face: first, paying off the soldiers, then driving the pirates out of Sicily. During the sea voyage, although almost too ill to think of anything, he kept turning the two problems over and over in his mind.

The soldiers had enlisted with the promise that they would be given, as their pay, certain cities and estates in Italy, or in Cisalpine Gaul. Now those who had served their term and were to be discharged naturally demanded that Antony and Octavian keep their promise. Not to do it would be fatal, but to do it meant taking the property away from the people who already owned it. Naturally, wealthy owners, robbed of their estates, and farmers, driven from their farms, were going to make trouble. To settle the affair would take most skillful handling, and the best possible advice.

As he was landing at Brundisium, Octavian thought of Maecenas, his old school friend in Apollonia. Maecenas was most diplomatic; his advice should be very valuable. He would get in touch with Maecenas as soon as he reached Rome.

But it was weeks before Octavian could go on to Rome. He fell ill and was unable to leave Brundisium. Week after week, he lay there, tossing in pain and fever, at the point of death. Neither the doctor nor the attendants, looking down upon his small thin body, expected him to live. But he clung to life with grit and determination, pulled through, and was finally able to sit up.

His first thought now was of his other friend Agrippa. During his feverish dreams, and moments of semi-consciousness, it seemed to him that he had been at sea, fighting the pirates for control of Sicily, and Agrippa had been with him.

Sicily was one of the islands which had fallen to Octavian's share when the Triumvirate first divided up the Roman lands, but he had never been able to get control of it. When he left for Philippi, it was still in the hands of a half-pirate by the name of Sextus Pompey. This Sextus was the son of a Roman general who had been an enemy of Julius Caesar. When his father had died, after being defeated by Caesar, Sextus had turned pirate. Seizing Sicily, he had since then used it as headquarters for his pirate fleet. With that as a base, he raided the shores of Italy.

He also caught the ships of wheat coming up from Egypt, and prevented them from getting through to Rome. Without grain from Egypt the people of Rome would starve. There would be a famine if Sextus were not soon defeated and driven out of Sicily.

Soldiers, demanding their pay; angry landowners, robbed of their property; hungry mobs, calling for grain to make into bread, are not pleasant people to deal with.

But those were the people that Octavian knew he had to face. On the day when he was well again, though still weak and wobbly in the knees, he stepped into his litter, and set out for Rome.

No wonder Antony preferred to be far away at the eastern end of the Mediterranean, while such troubles boiled in Rome!

HORACE AND THE COUNTRY MOUSE

SUMMERS WERE HOT IN ROME, and the summer following the battle of Philippi was no exception. Horace, a short, stout young man, who had fought on the losing side of that battle, now sat cooped up in the city quaestor's office, mopping the perspiration from his chubby face.

For two thousand years to come, this short, stout, friendly little Roman, by the name of Horace, was to be known and loved for his poems wherever people could read Latin. But in this year 41 B.C. when he was twenty three, Horace had not yet proved himself a poet; he was only an obscure clerk in the city treasurer's office.

That was neither where nor what he wanted to be, but he had no other way to make his living, and no other place to go. He would have preferred on this hot summer day, or any day, to be in the country, in the shade of a green tree, beside a brook. But he had now lost his old country home forever.

His father's farm, his own birthplace, south of Rome, had been among those taken away from their rightful owners and handed over in payment to the soldiers who had fought for Octavian.

All during the voyage home from Greece, Horace had looked forward to the joy of being home again with his good father on the farm. He pictured the olive orchard, the vineyard on the hillside, the fragrant clover field, the cone-shaped beehives, the sunny garden with its even rows of green—all those dear familiar places.

But when Horace had reached Italy, he had found his father dead. Everything was changed. A soldier's family was living in their old home on the village street. Another soldier had taken possession of the farm. The village of Venusia and all the surrounding countryside had been turned over to those soldiers who had fought on the winning side in the battle of Philippi.

So here he sat in Rome, mopping his hot face, and adding up long columns of figures in the quaestor's office. Probably he ought to be thankful just to be alive, and pardoned, since he had fought with Brutus and all those others who had died at Philippi!

Horace thought back to that first day when Brutus had arrived in Athens and how he and all the other young Roman students there at school had greeted him, and cheered him as the "liberator" of their country. How Brutus had roused their enthusiasm, until they had all enlisted under him to fight for the cause of the Republic.

Brutus had then made him a TRIBUNE! Though he had no ambition for a military career, Brutus, to his surprise, had given him a command which put him in charge of 1,000 men.

Horace thought again of how some of the lesser officers had begrudged him that rank, looked down upon him, and objected to serving under him, because of his lowly birth.

"Why should we," he had overheard them saying, "we, who are sons of Senators and Knights, take orders from one whose father was formerly a slave?"

For the father of Horace had been a freedman, a man who had gained his freedom after having been a slave.

But Horace was not ashamed of it. Slaves in Roman days were often far finer and more cultured people than their masters. And in Horace's grateful heart, there was no one more worthy to be loved and respected than his father.

Years later, when the most important people of Rome were to count him among their friends, Horace was to speak of how much he owed to that father who had worked and saved to give his son as good an education as any Roman boy could have—even sending him to Athens! In a poem, he was to preserve forever the memory of the Roman schoolboy and his devoted father—"who though poor," he says:

Passed by the village school at his own door,
The school where great tall urchins in a row,
Sons of great tall centurions used to go,
With slate and satchels on their backs. . . .
And took his boy to Rome, to learn the arts
Which Knight or Senator to his imparts.
Whoe'er had seen me, neat and more than neat,
With slave behind me in the crowded street,
Had surely thought a fortune fair and large
Two generations old sustained the charge.
Himself the true tried guardian of his son,
Whene'er I went to class, he still made one.
. . . he feared not lest one day,
The world should talk of money thrown away,
If, after all, I plied some trade for hire,
Like him, a tax collector or a crier. . . .
No: while my head's unturned, I ne'er shall need
To blush for that dear father or to plead
As men oft plead, 'tis nature's fault, not mine.
I came not of a better worthier line.

In this next poem, Horace, who loved life in the country, retells one of Æsop's fables which he must have read in Greek as a little boy. It is about the Town Mouse and the Country Mouse.

One day a country mouse, in his poor home
Received an ancient friend, a mouse from Rome
The host, though close and careful, to a guest

Could open still, so now he did his best.
He spared not oats, nor vetches, in his chaps
Raisins he brings and nibbled bacon scraps
Hoping by very dainties to entice
His town-bred guest so delicate and nice,
Who condescended graciously to touch
Thing after thing, but never would take much
While he the owner of the mansion sate
On threshed out straw, and bran and rye grass ate.
At length the townsman cries, "I wonder how
You can live here friend on this hill's rough brow
Take my advice and leave these ups and downs
This hill and dale for human kind and towns.
Come now, go home with me, remember, all
Who live on earth are mortal, great and small
Then take good sir, your pleasure while you may
Were life so short 't were wrong to lose a day."

This reasoning made the rustic's head turn round
Forth from his hole he issues with a bound
And they two make together for their mark
In hopes to reach the city during dark.

The midnight sky was bending overall
When they set foot within a stately hall
Where couches of wrought ivory had been spread
With gorgeous coverlets of Tyrian red
And viands piled up high in baskets lay
The relics of a feast of yesterday,
The townsman does the honors, lays his guest
At ease upon a couch with crimson drest
Then nimbly moves in character of host
And offers in succession boiled and roast
Nay, like a well trained slave each wish presents
And tastes before the tidbits he presents.
The guest, rejoicing in his altered fare
Assumes in turn a genial diner's air.
When hark, a sudden banging of the door
Each from his couch is tumbled on the floor
Half dead they scurry round the room, poor things
While the whole house with barking mastiffs rings
Then says the rustic, "it may do for you
This life, but I don't like, so adieu.
Give me my hole, secure from all alarms
I'll prove that tares and vetches still have charms."

ANTONY AND CLEOPATRA

VENUS!" CRIED THE EXCITED people of Tarsus. "Venus has come!" they cried, as they crowded the waterfront of that city in Asia Minor late one summer afternoon.

"Venus has come to visit Bacchus!" they cried to one another, watching as in a dream, the most beautiful Egyptian galley they

had ever seen, gliding up the river, out onto the lake before them.

They had been expecting Cleopatra. They had known that she was coming to meet Antony, there in the city of Tarsus. They had been prepared to see a gorgeous Egyptian galley, with purple sails, and oars of silver, even a golden stern, but no such ship as this. This was one of such unearthly beauty, as to have come only from that immortal cloudland of the gods.

Music drifted to their ears as it drew nearer, strange enchanting melodies, on harps and flutes and pipes. Exotic, too, was the scent of spices, and the pale blue drifting smoke of incense.

Youths, beautiful as young gods, could be seen standing at the helm and rudder. Girls in draperies thin as evening mist were poised so lightly in the rigging as to seem to be floating in the quiet air. Beings from another world—attendants, courtiers, they might well be, of an immortal queen!

And there, see! There beneath the golden canopy, that reclining figure, was that not a goddess? There, in the shimmering robe and the high shining headdress—that radiant creature, could that be anyone but the immortal Venus, queen of love and beauty?

"Venus!" cried the people, carried along by their imagination, until for them fancy had turned into fact. Venus had come to visit Bacchus! Let someone go to Antony at once. Bid him come quickly to welcome his heavenly visitor!

Antony was easily found, though not attired like Bacchus, that afternoon, but as a Roman magistrate. Seated in the public square of Tarsus, he had been holding court, deciding arguments between petty rulers and ambassadors, (among them, as usual Jews, complaining about Herod). Although the square had been almost emptied of people by the ship's arrival, Antony still sat there, struggling to look dignified and control his curiosity.

He too, had been expecting Cleopatra.

He had sent an ambassador to Egypt, asking the queen to meet him there in Tarsus, and he was very glad that she had come. He had need of her. The cities of Asia had been taxed and retaxed, and squeezed out of almost their last cent, but there was gold in Egypt, if it could be had. And gold was what he needed.

For now, Antony was beginning to think of undertaking the campaign which Julius Caesar had been planning just before he died. Lands yet to be conquered farther east were now tempting him, as they had tempted Caesar—Babylonia, Persia—all that fabulous land east of the Euphrates River which now belonged to Parthia, the only undefeated rival of the Romans.

"Come ashore and have dinner with me," was the message Antony now sent to Cleopatra.

Her reply was an invitation to come aboard ship, instead, and dine with her. It would give her pleasure she assured him.

Antony accepted. Why refuse a lady pleasure? Especially a lovely one! And so with that invitation and acceptance, one of the world's most famous love stories began. Some of Antony's officers and certain dignitaries of the city had also been invited.

Daylight had faded into dark when they reached the harbor. Myriads of tiny lights outlined the ship and were reflected in the water. On board, everywhere, the tiny lights were multiplied a thousand times, in the mirrors, in the wine, in the glistening jeweled gown of Cleopatra, and in the wondrous pear-shaped pearls swinging from her ears. It was a fairyland.

Antony was spellbound at once by the fascinating queen, now, to him, even more glamorous than she had appeared in Rome, when she was there with Caesar. To Cleopatra, the big Roman, too, seemed more attractive, far, than in her memory of him. She admired his hard muscles as he lay stretched upon his dining couch which was placed beside her own.

The feast was lavish; rare, delicious food served on platters of gold. The plates, too, were of gold, and the golden drinking cups were studded with jewels.

"They are yours, all of them," Cleopatra said to Antony, when the feast was over. "They are nothing, truly; just a small remembrance," she added lightly, slowly withdrawing her slim fingers from his large hand which had closed over them too long in parting.

And they were, those plates and cups of gold, a mere fraction of the treasure which Cleopatra had brought with her for a definite purpose. She wanted to dazzle Antony, to convince him of the vast wealth of Egypt that might be his if he would share his power in the Roman world with her. If Antony would lay claim to Rome, in the name of little Ptolemy Caesar, all the riches and power in the world might be theirs together.

Why should Antony support Octavian, Caesar's nephew? Was not Caesar's own son a more rightful heir to his father's power?

Alone, without help, Cleopatra knew that she could do little for the future of that seven-year-old son of hers. She saw clearly that, in days to come, he might not even have the throne of Egypt left to him. With unfriendly rule in Rome, Egypt, instead of being allowed to remain an independent kingdom, might be made just another province in the Roman empire. And the rule of the Ptolemies would end.

But if only she could persuade Antony that his best chance lay with Egypt, then the brightest future possible might be ahead of them. With so much at stake, Cleopatra had now come to Tarsus, prepared to use all her wit and charm upon Antony, to dazzle him with her riches, to hail him as a god, to promise him her love, her self, all that she had to give, in return for his alliance.

Her favorite ladies in waiting, Charmian and Iras, were eagerly watching for her to awake the morning following the banquet. As soon as they saw her eyelids flutter open, they knew that she was in high spirits, and that the first evening had been a great success. There was lilting music in her voice, as she called in Ethiopian to the slave girls who prepared her bath, and spoke to each attendant in her native language, for she spoke them all.

Catching her gaiety, Charmian and Iras planned to outdo themselves, and make their lovely lady even more bewitching for the feast that evening. Which tunic should she wear? Which would display her graceful figure to the best advantage? What jewels? How many necklaces? Which bracelets and earrings? And how should her hair be dressed? Bound in the Greek fashion or coiled back softly, leaving a frame of small tight curls about her face?

These, and a hundred other delightful details, were all to be decided later, when Cleopatra, herself, was seated at the dressing table. It was then a question of which rouge to use, what perfume would be most seductive. Should the clear arch of her eyebrows be made a trifle blacker? And the eye shadow on the lower lid, applied with a swan's feather, should that not be drawn just a little farther toward the corner of her eyes?

"Am I beautiful? Do I please you?" Cleopatra laughed, as they admired their handiwork. "This night as you know, my dears, and each night must excel in every way the one before it."

The banquet of the second night was more splendid than the first. And that of the fourth night was so resplendent that Antony declared that it would be impossible to excel or even equal it in luxury. No one, he wagered, could spend more on a single feast.

"I accept your wager," said Cleopatra, with a tantalizing smile. "I could spend 10,000,000 sesterces on the food alone. I shall prove it— shall we say, tomorrow night?"

At first, the feast of the next night appeared no different from the others, to the disappointment of the guests, but to the satisfaction of Antony, who felt that he had won the wager. But wait! At the end of the last course, Cleopatra was beckoning to a slave. A tiny jewel-encrusted cup of gold was set before her, and filled with vinegar. Raising her hands, she removed from her ear one of the two precious pear-shaped pearls. Watching Antony as she did so, she then dropped it into the little cup, waited a moment for it to dissolve, and then drank its contents.

A gasp of shocked astonishment went up from all who saw the wanton destruction of this rare pearl, worth easily half of the amount wagered. For all believed the pearl had been dissolved—except, perhaps, the very clever little person who had swallowed it.

"Stop!" exclaimed the officer, chosen to decide the wager, as he saw her reaching for the other. "Do not destroy it! You have won!"

Cleopatra had won. She had won the wager, and she had won Antony! His heart went with her when, at the end of a few weeks, she returned to Egypt, where, it had been decided, he was shortly to follow her. All desire for an immediate campaign against Parthia had now faded away before the more glamorous prospect of a winter in Alexandria to be spent with Cleopatra.

Alexandria was the "Paris of the ancient world," its most beautiful and sophisticated city, one in which every kind of pleasure was available, from the highest of the mind and spirit, to the lowest of the senses.

89

In all of them Antony was indulged. It was a winter of extravagant delight, that winter which united the most powerful Roman in the world with the world's most glamorous queen.

Their union, although sanctioned by the Egyptian priests, was outside of the Roman law. But did that matter? Were not queens and rulers above the common law? Could Venus and Bacchus be bound by the ties of this mere mortal world? They could not, and so deeply in love were Antony and Cleopatra that they quite forgot about the Roman world, until early spring, when suddenly bad news broke through their enchantment.

News traveled slowly by land during the winter months when the Mediterranean was rough, but with spring the ships came again. And they brought bad news, in this spring of 40 B.C., both from Rome and from Asia. Antony tried to turn a deaf ear to the loud calls for help, but it was impossible.

At home in Rome, Fulvia, Antony's disagreeable and now jealous wife, had stirred up trouble with Octavian to the point of war.

In Asia, the king of Parthia, not waiting for the Romans to make war on him, had invaded Syria and seized Roman territory!

Bad business both places! Uncertain which place to go to first, Antony set out for Asia Minor. From there he could go either way. Cleopatra watched him leave with a very heavy heart. He kissed her briefly in a hurried parting, assuring her that he would soon return, that they would rule the world together—to be good and not to worry. Then while she watched, his ship disappeared from sight.

And what had she left? Only promises. And could she trust him? Would these vague promises be kept, she wondered, feeling quite alone now, and deserted.

Four years she would have to wait and wonder, for it was to be four years before Cleopatra would see Antony again—or before he would see the twins—his twin baby boy and girl, who were to be born that summer—Alexander the Sun and Cleopatra the Moon.

ANTONY HAD BEEN GONE but a few months when a most excited and distraught young man whirled into Alexandria, intent upon seeing Antony, and most annoyed at finding him no longer there. If not there, where was he? Where had Antony gone? To Rome? He wasn't in Asia. So he must have gone to Rome! Then he, Herod, must follow him there! For this was Herod.

This excited visitor who had paced into Cleopatra's palace on the trail of Antony was Herod. He had now been driven out of Galilee, and out of Jerusalem.

The Parthians were there. The whole country of Palestine from the Sea of Galilee to the Dead Sea was in the hands of the Parthians. They had seized Jerusalem and captured the High Priest. He, Herod, had managed to escape, but not Hyrcanus. Hyrcanus, the High Priest, was a prisoner and would be taken away. And with one ear bitten off.

It was his nephew, his dead brother's son, who had bitten off his uncle's ear. A mutilated man, he could never be High Priest again. The whole business was a revival of an old quarrel between Hyrcanus and his brother. It was this brother's son who had now made himself High Priest, with the help of the Parthians. It was he who had bribed them to invade Jerusalem, and help him get rid of Herod and Hyrcanus. A thousand talents of gold was what he had promised the Parthians for their help. Also five hundred women. Think of it. Five hundred fine Jewish women, all from the best families.

Those women, Herod said, he had been able to rescue. He had carried them off by night, by camel and by horseback, to a fortress in Edom. The rest of his soldiers and many followers he had left behind him, in Arabia. With only a small guard, as they could see, he had come on to Alexandria to find Antony.

Antony was his friend. Not once, but time and again, since the battle of Philippi, when the Jews had sent embassies to Antony at Tarsus, Ephesus, or wherever he was, accusing Herod, and seeking to get rid of him, Antony had upheld his case.

Now he must find Antony again! He must go to Rome—if that was where he was!

Cleopatra could not dissuade him. She offered him a commission as commander of her fleet, but Herod scarcely heard her.

The weather was stormy, the sea was rough. It was suggested to him that he ought at least to wait until the danger of shipwreck was past. Wait! Herod could not wait! He had no time to lose.

Rome was no place to go now, everyone in Alexandria told him. Did he not know that civil war had broken out again in Rome? Antony would have no time to see him: Antony now had war on his hands against Octavian or else a peace to patch up.

According to reports, Fulvia, Antony's wife, was at the bottom of it. Evidently jealous, she had tried to stir up enough trouble in his absence to make her wandering husband forget Cleopatra and come home. Claiming to look out for Antony's interests while he was away, she and Antony's brother had picked a quarrel with Octavian over the way he was managing affairs. Landowners, Senators, soldiers were all dragged into it, on one side or the other, causing an upheaval as bad as that in Jerusalem. Altogether, Rome, they told him, was no place to go.

That argument was of no more avail than the others in diverting Herod from his purpose. Why should he accept an office under Cleopatra? Of what value could that be to him, compared to getting back his power in Jerusalem, which, by the way, he had a strong suspicion the Queen of Egypt might like herself.

As for fear of war and shipwreck—were such fears going to prevent Herod from seeing the one man who could help him? Anyone who might think so knew little about the one-track mind of this intense and violent young man. He would go to any lengths to realize his ambition. That was now taking him to Rome.

VIRGIL AND ISAIAH

WAR AND ITS EVILS had come again to Jerusalem and to Rome. Ambitious leaders, fighting for power, had brought upon their people the horrors and bloodshed of civil war.

Would war never cease? cried the Roman people. Would the Temple of Janus never be closed again? Would there never be another Golden Age? The Jewish people, in the midst of bloodshed, uttered their age-old cry for a Messiah. When, oh when, would that promised king arise to save them from their enemies, and establish the Kingdom of God?

Seven hundred years they had been waiting for him. Seven centuries ago, when Rome had been a young, scrawny village, Jerusalem had been old, and her people disheartened. It was then that the great prophets had first given the Jewish people this hope of a Messiah. In time, they had said, a great saviour king anointed by God would be sent to rescue them from war and destruction and to rule the whole world in righteousness and peace.

The age of the Messiah, as the prophets pictured it, was to be a Golden Age, very like the long lost Age of Saturn, which the Romans held as an ideal, but now despaired of ever seeing repeated.

Four summers had now passed since Caesar's death, which was supposed by those who killed him to restore peace and order to the

93

Roman Republic. Instead, a war of revenge had followed. At the battle of Philippi, Caesar's murderers had been defeated, but still peace and order had not come to Rome. Trouble between the two men who had won the battle had been stirred up by Antony's wife, Fulvia, thus bringing on more bloodshed. Though Fulvia had died before Antony had returned from Egypt, the quarrel she had started with Octavian did not die so easily. Fearful that war between them would continue, friends used every effort and argument and finally brought the two men to a peaceful understanding.

That was a day of jubilation for the Roman people. It was in October, at Brundisium, in front of cheering crowds on shore, before the fleet and the armies, that the two leaders, Antony and Octavian, were seen to clasp hands and exchange the kiss of peace.

To a young poet of Rome, by the name of Virgil, that day seemed to mark the dawn of a new Golden Age. His words used to describe it sound strangely like those spoken by the prophet ISAIAH seven hundred years before to predict the peaceful age of the Messiah.

Virgil may have read Isaiah, for the Jewish Bible had long since been translated into Greek. One cannot be sure where ideas come from, for they know no barriers of time or space.

Once more, Virgil says, the Golden Age is here.

"Once more . . .

> Kind Saturn reigns, and from high heaven descends
> The first born child of promise . . .
> The age of iron in his time shall cease
> And golden generations fill the world.
> For thee, Fair Child, the lavish Earth shall spread
> Thy earliest playthings, trailing ivy wreaths,
> And wild acanthus smiling in the sun . . .
> The goats shall come uncalled weighed down with milk,
> Nor lion's roar affright the laboring kine.
> The treacherous snake and deadly herb shall die
> The field shall thrive unharrowed, vines unpruned.

And stalwart ploughmen set their oxen free.
Wool shall not need the dyers skillful art . . .
But lambs be clothed in scarlet as they feed!
Come then, dear child of gods, Jove's mighty heir
Begin thy high career; the hour is sounding.
See, in the dawning of a new creation
The heart of all things living throbs with joy!"

These words from Virgil's poem may still be read in Latin, as in 40 B.C. they were read for the first time. And here are the far, far older words of Isaiah, which had then been read in Hebrew for centuries in the Jewish synagogues. A child would be born, says Isaiah, to sit upon the throne of Jerusalem, to be called the Prince of Peace, and to so judge among the nations, that . . .

"They shall beat their swords into ploughshares
And their spears into pruning hooks.
Nation shall not lift up sword against nation,
Neither shall they learn war any more.
The wolf also shall lie down with the lamb,
And the leopard shall lie down with the kid;
And the calf and the young lion and the fatling together
And a little child shall lead them.
And the cow and bear shall feed;
Their young ones lie down together;
They shall not hurt nor destroy
In all my holy mountain:
For the earth shall be full of the knowledge of the Lord
As the waters cover the sea."

In those long ago days of Isaiah, when Rome had been but a village, the people of Jerusalem had been under the rule of the Assyrians. So far, they had escaped the dreadful fate of the ten tribes to the north of them, who had been robbed of their homes and driven into exile. But, about one hundred and fifty years later, the people of Jerusalem had also been driven off to Babylon. Their city on the holy mountain had been laid

95

in ruins, their Temple burned and destroyed. Far away then, they had "sat down by the rivers of Babylon and wept." To comfort them, the prophets in exile had revived the old hope of a Messiah. In His own time, they said, God would restore His people to Jerusalem, send them a powerful leader, and glory would be theirs. They had waited fifty years.

Then the Persians, who had conquered Babylonia, allowed the Jewish people to return home to Jerusalem, and they felt that surely the days of the Messiah must be drawing near. In hopeful preparation they had toiled and struggled to rebuild the Temple, and even had a gold crown sent from Babylon to be used in the coronation. But when the Temple was finished, no saviour king had appeared among them to be crowned. Year after year they had waited.

The days of the great prophets had gone. Still the hope in the Messiah would not die. It had been planted too deep in the hearts of the Jewish people. Generation after generation, in some form or another, they had passed it on through seven centuries.

During those centuries, nation after nation had swept over their country and conquered it. After the Assyrians had come the Persians, and then the Greeks—and then the Romans, and now the Parthians were in Jerusalem!

Disappointment, oppression, hatred of their conquerors had made them bitter and eager for revenge, and had changed their idea of a Messiah. Instead of wishing for a Prince of Peace, many, like the rebels of Galilee, were looking for a ruthless conquerer to arise—one who would drive out the Romans, wipe out the Parthians—a powerful king —a warrior—a man of vengeance who would "tread down his enemies, and trample upon them in his fury."

And yet in Jerusalem, in Galilee, and all over Palestine, the people were still hearing read to them Isaiah's great vision of a world at peace —a vision now also caught in words of sunlight by Rome's greatest poet—and the one most pure in heart.

LARES   PENATES

OCTAVIA WEDS ANTONY

A WEDDING, AND A STRANGE ONE, sealed the new peace between Octavian and Antony. Antony, big, sensuous and spectacular, married Octavian's lovely, gentle sister, Octavia.

To marry again, so soon after the death of her husband Marcellus, had not been Octavia's desire, but when her brother had explained how important it was for the peace of Rome, she had willingly consented. So they had been married, Octavia and Antony.

Octavia's sweet face was grave as she entered the dining room of her new home on the Palatine Hill for the first mid-morning breakfast, and there paused before the household shrine. Tenderly she placed a tiny wreath of fresh flowers on each one of the three small, sacred figures, before which a lamp was burning.

They were her LARES and PENATES. Though the small images no longer stood above the hearth, as in early Roman days, wherever they were placed in a home there was its heart, for they held its guardian spirits. The center figure symbolized the Genius or guiding spirit of the family father; the two dancing figures on either side expressed the joy of a well-stocked storeroom and prosperity. In the small flame of the lamp, Octavia could feel the comfort of the glowing hearth, and the clear, steady spirit of the home fire, that was VESTA.

She now sprinkled a bit of salt into the flame, with a quiet prayer

97

that she might make this home a happy one for her new husband.

"Even though I cannot help protect Rome," she thought, "as the Vestal Virgins do, by tending the sacred hearth fire of the city, here in my own home I can do my part." Her face shone with the thought.

Antony, waching her from his couch at the dining table, felt a sudden embarrassment. What had he, with his past, to do with one so delicate and pure? Could he change his life? Forget her, whom he loved in Egypt, and settle down in Rome? Rome was a rough market town compared to Alexandria, but it was home. And this sweet little wife, with her quaint old-fashioned ways, was certainly refreshing.

He drew her to him, as she came near the table, kissed her, and whispered something in her ear that made her blush. At that, he laughed aloud, and patted her hand in his big, easy manner.

Octavia smiled back primly, surprised to find this man of the world so like a boy. How could the ugly things people said about him possibly be true? If he spent his nights drinking and carousing, it was because he never had a real home. If Cleopatra beguiled him, it was because Fulvia had been too busy doing outside things—big, masculine things, for which she, Octavia, had no talent. But now, she would care for Antony, and make him feel comfortable. That was all, she was sure, a man needed to be happy.

As the winter wore on, however, it came as a disappointment to see that Antony was not entirely contented. For instance, he had been most gruff about trying on the new toga she was making for him. And he seemed hardly able to endure the company of her brother, Octavian, without bursting into rage.

At long family dinners, like that of the Saturnalia, it was most difficult to keep the peace. While trying to entertain her sister-in-law (an older woman whom Octavian had now married for political reasons), she had to keep an eye on the gaming table.

That was where the great irritation lay. No matter what game the two men played, Octavian always won. At dice, mora, cock fighting, whatever it was, luck was never with Antony. When he played against

Octavian, it actually seemed as if his Genius, or guiding spirit, grew weak and deserted him.

And there, though Octavia was unaware of it, was the secret thought that was annoying Antony. An Egyptian soothsayer, whom he had consulted in Alexandria, had first put the idea into his mind. Now, at Cleopatra's bidding, the Egyptian had followed Antony to Rome, and was warning him to avoid Octavian.

"When this man is present, I tell you," the Egyptian whispered, "your guiding spirit becomes weak and unmanly. When he is far away, your Genius becomes strong again—and good fortune awaits you. Why, then, do you tarry here in his shadow?"

Why, indeed, thought Antony. Why stay in Rome? What was there to do in this dull western town?

But, though he felt dissatisfied and bored and restless, Antony stayed on in Rome with Octavia through the spring and summer.

And then, one morning, a tiny rosebud of a daughter was laid at his big feet. Following the ancient custom, Antony picked up the little one

to acknowledge her as his child, and laughed aloud to see that wee unfolded face so like his own.

They named her ANTONIA.

At almost the same time, Octavian's JULIA put in her appearance. Octavian divorced her mother, Scribonia, the day that she was born, but from that day on he idolized his little daughter, though in later years she was to cause him nothing but trouble.

In time to come, these two baby girls were to have a great-grandson, by the name of Nero, who, it is said, was playing on his fiddle while Rome burned.

HEROD, KING OF THE JEWS!

AND NOW TO ROME, came Herod, fugitive from Jerusalem. Despite shipwreck and delay, some months after leaving Egypt, Herod arrived in Rome, and turned up one spring morning in Antony's ever popular vestibule. An important visitor, a well tried and useful friend to Rome, he was admitted at once to the tablinum. There, after presenting himself, with proper compliments to this, his most important friend, Herod reviewed the serious situation that existed in Jerusalem.

The treachery! he pointed out. The treachery of that younger Maccabean! The Maccabean prince who had now seized the office of High Priest—that nephew of Hyrcanus. He had called on Parthia for help. Parthia, the worst enemy of Rome, had been urged to enter Jerusalem; together, they had taken over the city and driven out all good friends of Rome.

Was not he, Herod, governor of Galilee, a good friend of Rome? Had not his dead father also been a loyal friend? Wasn't old Hyrcanus himself always agreeable and grateful for protection? What was to be done? Was Rome to stand by, and let Parthia remain in Jerusalem?

Antony was already concerned over Parthia, and he needed no further proof of Herod's loyalty. Appearing before the Senate, he recommended his friend from Palestine as the best man to look after Rome's interests in that rebellious country. A few days later, Herod heard the Roman Senate pass the decree which made him King.

Walking then, between Antony and Octavian, who, he saw, eyed him with a shrewd curiosity, Herod left the Senate Chamber and between the two Romans climbed the long white marble steps of the Capitoline. There, at the Temple of Jupiter, the customary sacrifice was offered to the Roman god, the decree was placed for safekeeping in the Capitol, and the ceremony was complete.

Herod was King of Judea. He was King of the Jews. In name only, however, for his was still an empty title.

He had to return now, this new King Herod, to capture his capital, kill off or win over his enemies, and force himself upon the Jewish people who hated him, and did not want him for their King—this foreigner from Edom, half-Jew, half-Arab, as he was, forced upon them by the Romans.

And no king did they want, those people of Jerusalem, except a descendant of King David, their old warrior king and hero of a thousand years ago!

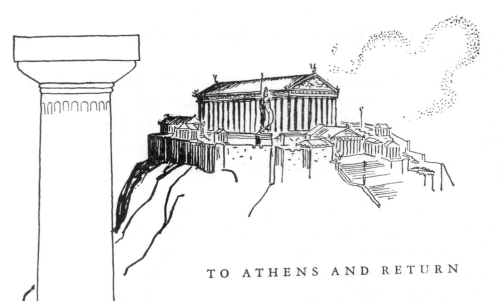

TO ATHENS AND RETURN

IN OCTOBER, when they had been married a year, Antony asked Octavia how she would like to go to Athens. Another winter of her brother's company, with that everlasting good gambling luck of his, was more than Antony could stomach. The Egyptian also kept whispering to him that his Genius would be better off, away from Rome and Octavian. So he had thought of Athens. Athens was not so exciting as Alexandria, but it was interesting and surely far more beautiful than this town made of brick.

Athens also was so much nearer to Asia. He could keep in closer touch with Herod and his affairs in Palestine. He might go himself and help his Roman troops fight back the Parthians. He might even make an invasion into Parthia next spring.

With the possibility of a dangerous campaign ahead of him, Antony made out his will before they left. Octavia kept delightfully busy with traveling arrangements for the baby and the packing. She did not see the will. Antony took it to the Temple of Vesta

ATHENA

for safekeeping. There, in the most sacred spot in Rome, protected by the holy virgins, he knew it would be safe from prying eyes. It contained this sentence: "When I die, let my ashes be taken to Alexandria to be buried by Cleopatra."

Octavia was flushed with excitement as they set out for Athens. Although Athens had now been under the rule of Rome for fifty years, in her mind, the famous old city was still glowing in the light of its Golden Age, four centuries ago.

The Acropolis was just as she had pictured it—a rocky hill rising above the city. But when she had climbed the marble steps leading to the top, she found the Temple of Athena, the pale, pink marble Parthenon, far more beautiful than in her imagination.

And no one could possibly have described the mystery and wonder she felt as she stepped into the half lighted interior and looked up at the magnificent statue of the virgin goddess! Towering thirty feet or more from her ivory feet to the crown of her helmet, Athena seemed truly alive in that dim shifting light—a supernatural being watching over her city.

Not until Octavia was out again under the clear blue sky, could she realize that it was not the guardian goddess of Athens that she had seen, but a wooden statue carved four hundred years ago by the great sculptor, Pheidias.

"She must have been a gorgeous sight," Antony was saying, "before all the gold that covered her draperies was stolen."

Octavia smiled up at him.

Antony was looking very handsome that day, wearing the short white gown and white shoes of the Greeks. He was also in the highest of high spirits. Good news had come from one of his generals left in Palestine of a successful battle against the Parthians, who had now been driven out of Jerusalem and back to their own borders. So he was happy, and, therefore, Octavia was happy.

When Spring came, at the end of a carefree winter, Antony took a run over to Palestine, to see what he could do to help Herod get possession of Jerusalem. Though the Parthians had been driven out, the young Maccabean, supported by his party of wealthy Sadducees, was still in control of the city. Up in Samaria, where Herod had large estates and properties, he had been well received, and found many supporters. Most of the people, Antony saw, had been sensible enough to see that, backed up by the Romans, Herod would win out in the end. But the people of Judaea were stiff-necked—a stricter kind of Jews than the Samaritans—whom they despised. Difficulties would increase as Herod went south along the Jordan River.

On his return to Athens, Antony may have mentioned to Octavia that Herod had very wisely arranged to marry into the Maccabean family, which should make him more acceptable to the Jews, since that was their royalty. The young princess to whom he was betrothed was the granddaughter of the old High Priest, Hyrcanus, and from all accounts she was extremely beautiful.

A second carefree Athenian winter began, but was soon interrupted by desperate cries for help from Octavian. His sister's peace of mind was shattered, but Antony paid no attention.

Octavian wrote that he had been defeated in a naval battle against the pirate Sextus because he was lacking in ships.

Antony had a fleet of three hundred vessels which were lying idle, but he would send none of them to Octavian's rescue, though his wife begged and pleaded with him.

"Think," she said. "In exchange, you may be able to get soldiers from Octavian to use against the Parthians!"

Drawing on every possible argument, including tears, Octavia finally persuaded Antony to return to Italy and offer Octavian part of his fleet, but then it was almost too late.

Sailing into Tarentum, they found the shipyards noisy with hammers, and saw hulls in every stage of construction. Octavian was building his own fleet.

He had no use for Antony now, and wanted nothing to do with him. Antony was for taking him at his word, by Hercules, but Octavia begged permission to go ahead and talk with him.

She found her brother with his two good friends, Agrippa and Maecenas. Agrippa was in charge of building the fleet.

Maecenas had come down from Rome to help with negotiations. He had made the trip he said, in most delightful company. The poet Virgil had come with him, and also another poet, by the name of Horace, to whom Virgil had introduced him, and who had written a most amusing account of their little journey.

Octavia drew the two men aside, begged them to use their influence with Octavian, and then she pleaded with her brother.

"I am utterly miserable. Everyone looks to me to keep peace between you, and if you two remain unfriendly, I shall have utterly failed—failed perhaps to protect Rome from another war!"

Her tears melted Octavian, for he loved his sister. To please her, he agreed to dine with Antony that night, and, at length, with her help, they came to an agreement. Antony would leave one hundred warships for Octavian to use in conquering Sicily.

In return, Octavian promised to send two legions for Antony's future use against the Parthians.

Then, with Octavia smiling upon both of them, the two men parted as nearly friends as they could ever be.

Antony left for the east again. Octavia went only part way with him. Kissing her on the cheek, telling her to wish him good luck, to be happy and take good care of the babies, he sent her back home. Octavia returned to Rome to mother a houseful of children, Antony's and Fulvia's, besides her own—five-year-old Marcellus, his sister, and his little half sisters, Antonia and the newest baby.

And Octavia was not unhappy. She was glad to care for them all, and to keep the home open and ready for Antony's return, not knowing then that, having neatly slipped through the knot that bound him to Octavian, Antony never intended to return.

LIVIA

DRUSUS

TIBERIUS

THE FUTURE EMPRESS

THIS IS LIVIA, who had now become the wife of Octavian, and who was to live with him happily for over fifty years.

Livia already had a husband, a very fine gentleman, by the name of Tiberius Nero, when Octavian first laid eyes on her and determined to marry her.

Marriage not being looked upon as a sacred bond, but merely an arrangement to be made convenient and pleasing to all parties concerned, no difficulty was encountered. Seeing that the desire of his young wife coincided with that of her admirer, Tiberius Nero obligingly gave her a divorce, and the new nuptials were celebrated.

Her two sons were to stay with their father until his death. DRUSUS was a mere infant.

TIBERIUS, a sandy haired boy of four, was later to be adopted by his stepfather and eventually become the second emperor of Rome.

IN THE SPRING OF 37 B.C. Herod's long siege of Jerusalem began. In the dusty heat of midsummer, it was far underway. Herod's forces and the Roman legions had cut off all supplies, encircled the city and, encamped in the surrounding valleys, were waiting for it to surrender. Battering rams were pounding at its ancient walls.

In that same dusty valley, almost 1,000 years before, David, the warrior king, had stood gazing up at that rocky fortress, then the last unconquered stronghold in the land of Canaan. From the top of their thick walls, the native Canaanites had looked scornfully down upon the Jewish army and mocked at them, but David's men had scaled the heights, slaughtered the defenders and taken for their own the primitive city of crude huts. Thus old Jebus-salem of the Canaanites had become the City of David.

Thereafter, for almost 500 years, until the tragic exile into Babylon, descendants of David had ruled in Jerusalem, and had cherished the memory of that great chief or king who had first united the twelve wandering tribes into a nation. When the exiles returned from Babylon, expecting a new king or Messiah, they believed, according to the prophet Isaiah, that he, too, would be of David's line.

Another 500 years had passed, and while the Jews still kept looking for that promised king, for the past hundred years the Maccabeans, descendants of another hero, had served as High Priest, or King.

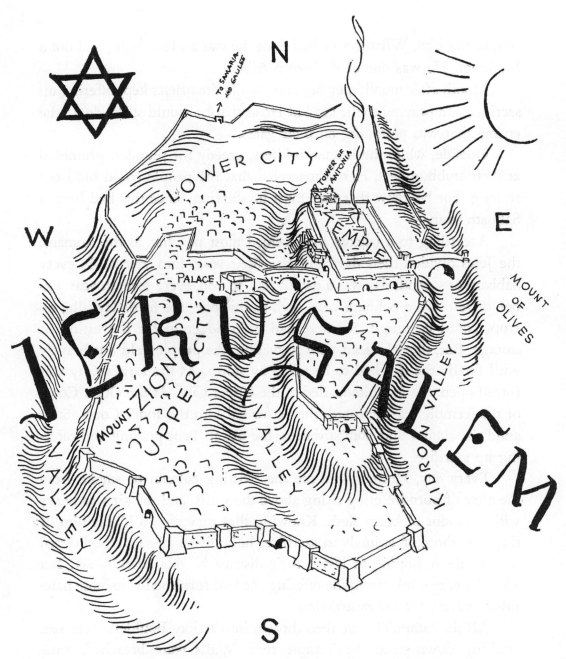

So, although this Maccabean who now held the city was not of David's line, though he had savagely mutilated his uncle and stolen from him the office of High Priest, though he had called in the Parthians and caused all manner of bloodshed, still the people of Jerusalem were supporting him. Whatever he had done, he was a Maccabean, and not a foreigner. He was one of their own tribe.

Month after month they held out, while the priests kept offering up sacrifice and praying to the God of Hosts that he would strike down the enemy that was pounding on their gates.

Outside, while the Roman soldiers, greedy for plunder, grumbled at their stubbornness, Herod marveled that the people could hold out so long. For he knew that they must be starving, since this had been a Sabbath year.

According to a custom that seemed most peculiar to the Romans, the Jews divided their days and also their years into sevens. As every Sabbath or seventh day was a day of rest, so, too, every seventh year was one of rest. On a Sabbath year, such as this one, the fields lay idle, no crops could be raised. So there had been no grain for harvesting or storage. But, though faced with starvation, the people held out bravely until finally the city had to be taken by storm. As the Lower City was forced open, the inhabitants fled to the Upper City. As the Outer Court of the Temple was captured, they crowded into the Inner Court. Still, amid the clamor and bombardment, the priests kept praying and offering up sacrifice.

Every day, Herod could see the twisting column of smoke from the altar of burnt offering rising above the walls, and the air was heavy with the odor of burnt flesh. Knowing that they would blame him, if they ran short of animals to sacrifice, he allowed more to be hoisted over to them, hoping to lessen their distrust by this friendly act. But with the very smoke from the offerings he had furnished rose more hate-filled prayers for his destruction.

All the catapults were then thrown into action. Boulders were sent crashing down upon the Temple roof. Walls were breached, gates broken open. Roman soldiers and Herod's men rushed in, crowded the steep narrow streets of the Upper City, fighting hand to hand with the defenders. Enraged to have been held off so long, thirsty for revenge, the Romans murdered, robbed and plundered, splashing in the blood.

Herod cried aloud, tore his hair and protested. This was no way for a King to enter his capital city! But they were beyond control. By way of this bloody siege, Herod entered the City of David to be King of Judaea for over thirty years.

The siege had lasted five long months. It was now autumn.

And autumn, for the Jews, was the end of one year and the beginning of the new year. On their calendar, it was the year 3,723 from the creation of the world. The priests were preparing for the great new year festival of Rosh Hashana. It would be followed by the most solemn fast day of the year—the Fast of the Atonement, one for which crowds of pious worshippers from all over Palestine would soon be gathering in Jerusalem.

From the windows of the Maccabean palace looking east, Herod could see the Temple, whose courts were still heaped with rubbish from the siege. Standing beside the new King, in the palace window, as six years ago she had stood with her small brother watching the winter sun set, was his bride and queen, the lovely Mariamne.

More lovely did she seem to Herod, more tantalizing in her fragrant beauty than a rose, more irresistible, more precious than any possession he had ever owned.

And more necessary, for now he, Herod, might have sons of royal Maccabean blood. And they would be safe on this throne which he had been obliged to seize with bloody hands.

Or would they be safe? Could they, any more than he, be safe, so long as other Maccabean princes lived to covet that throne and gain a following among the people? And were there not always daggers, poison, and jealous enemies to guard against? Intently and suddenly, with a quiver of fear, he searched the proud though lovely face of this Maccabean princess.

Feeling his eyes upon her, Mariamne turned, smiled, half opened her lips to speak. Then she closed them again, and continued to stand quietly watching the endless column of smoke rising from the altar and trailing up into the autumn sky.

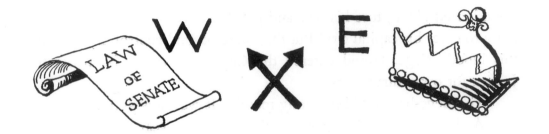

A TURNING POINT

AFTER BIDDING FAREWELL to Octavia, Antony had let his unruly heart lead him back once more to his beloved Cleopatra. He had sent to Egypt for her, and she had come to meet him again in Asia Minor. At the first touch of their hands and lips, the four years that had separated them seemed to melt away. Their plans for the future came to life again—plans for ruling the entire world!

"And in no foolish Roman way," said Cleopatra, "but like gods on earth, absolute and supreme, as kings were born to be."

"First, I must conquer Parthia," said Antony, who, after all, preferred conquering to ruling. At his suggestion, Cleopatra furnished gold and supplies, and went with him as far as the Euphrates River, there to see him off on that long talked of campaign.

In return, he presented her with a number of the richest Roman provinces in Asia Minor, a generous gift, indeed, had they been his to give! Cleopatra also received a coveted strip of Herod's property, along the Jordan River, near Jericho, valuable for its palms and balsam. That threw Herod into suc ha murderous rage that he was tempted to have Cleopatra waylaid and killed, as her gorgeous retinue came trailing back through Palestine. But not daring to do so, he had had her conducted safely home, along the ancient highway, to the border of Egypt.

There she waited for good news from Parthia. None came. The campaign had turned into a hideous disaster, from which Antony had come staggering back in remorse and sunk into a drunken stupor.

Cleopatra had rescued him. The easy pleasures of Alexandria had soon revived his spirits, and the next year he set out a second time to conquer those unconquerable Parthians. That time, although he still failed to reach Parthia, Antony got as far as Armenia. He marched on the capital, put the King in chains, and sent him back to Alexandria, where his victory was celebrated by a most magnificent Triumph!

When the Romans heard of that, they were dumfounded. "A Roman Triumph in Alexandria!" they exclaimed. "Why on earth should Antony hold his triumph in Egypt, instead of here in Rome?"

To that question Octavian had a ready answer. "Antony intends to make Alexandria, instead of Rome, the capital of the Roman empire," he told the Senate. "Antony is bewitched by Cleopatra. Has he not bestowed upon her provinces which belong to you, as Romans? Has he not deserted Octavia, his faithful wife, for that accursed female?"

"You should leave his house!" Octavian then told his sister.

But Octavia, only wishing not to be the cause of any trouble, would not leave, until Antony, offended by her brother's slander of Cleopatra, sent a bill of divorce to her, and requested her to move. By this harsh act, Antony lost much sympathy in Rome.

He still had, however, many staunch defenders in the Senate, who now attacked Octavian. They accused him of cheating Antony's soldiers out of their fair share of land, and cited other grave mismanagement, to which Octavian made a quick reply.

"Any and all Senators," he announced, "who wish to support Antony are now requested to leave Rome at once."

Four hundred, almost half of the Senate, packed up and left Italy. All were firmly determined to persuade Antony to break away from Cleopatra. It was the only way, they agreed, that he could save himself from ruin. They found Antony in Athens, but with no desire to be saved. Newly wed to Cleopatra, he was spending his honeymoon, carefree and deliriously happy.

Octavian, back in Rome, however, was a very worried man. What if, for once, he had acted too hastily? What if the Senate could not be made to declare Antony a public enemy? He was almost ill with nervousness until he heard about the will—the will which Antony had made out just before leaving Italy.

In the safe keeping of the Vestal Virgins, it was a sacrilege to touch it, but Octavian was desperate. He had it seized, and when to his relief he found what damning evidence it contained, he had it read aloud before the Senate.

In the will, Antony named his children by Cleopatra as his only heirs, and declared that Caesarion, Cleopatra's son, was the only rightful heir of his father Julius Caesar. Could more proof be needed, Octavian asked, of Antony's treacherous intentions?

Yet he did not follow up the reading of the will by requesting the Senate to declare war on Antony. He was too shrewd for that. Very cleverly, he threw all the blame on the Queen of Egypt, and pictured her as such an artful, dangerous enemy of Rome that the Roman Senate felt obliged to declare war on Cleopatra.

Octavian was satisfied. "That means Antony, too," he thought. "He'll never break away from her." And in that he was right.

Antony could not bring himself to part with Cleopatra, though he grew quarrelsome and edgy over the bad omens that now began to occur. First, the statue of Bacchus, the god he represented, was knocked over in a cyclone. That was in Athens. In the town of Patras, the Temple of his divine ancestor, Hercules, was struck by lightning. And there, too, the swallows that lived in the rigging of Cleopatra's flagship were driven away by a strange flock of birds!

Patras, where they had then moved, was a port on the west coast of Greece. The Egyptian fleet and Antony's two hundred battleships were at anchor in the gulf. There they stayed until word came that Octavian had landed with an army on the point of a small bay farther to the north. Antony then moved north to that same bay, and went into camp on the opposite point, which was called Actium.

Antony stationed his soldiers around the shore of the bay in such a way that Octavian's men could not move inland without a battle. On the other hand, once inside the bay, the fleets of Antony and Cleopatra could not move out, because Octavian's ships were lined up across the mouth. There were four hundred of them, most of them light, swift ships which Agrippa had built for use against the pirates.

"Don't risk a battle against these ships," Antony was advised by the Roman generals. "Draw Octavian inland into a land battle."

"We are not sailors," begged the centurions. "Let us fight on land, where we know how to fight, not on rotten timbers."

Cleopatra, on the contrary, kept begging Antony to make it a naval battle, urging him and pleading with him in a tone of voice that he could not resist. On September 1, he announced to his men that the next day they would engage in a battle at sea.

Then, having decided to make it a naval battle, having set the day, and forced the Roman soldiers to fight on water instead of land, Antony did not even wait to see how the battle turned out. It seems unbelievable, but it is true.

At first, when the ships were rowed out of the harbor, Cleopatra had been watching them from her flagship anchored near the shore. Antony saw her there as the battleships, loaded with foot soldiers and archers, left the narrows for the open sea. She was still there as Octavian's light ships moved in swiftly about Antony's huge ones and began to attack them as they would a fortress. But then, suddenly, while the battle was still undecided, Antony noticed that Cleopatra's ship was moving. It was sailing away!

Forgetful of the battle, forgetful of those thousands of men who were fighting and dying for him, forgetful of everything except that Cleopatra was leaving him, Antony, ruled as always by his emotions, and now completely swept away, turned and sailed after her. . . .

Two hours later, the fleet surrendered, and the battle of Actium was over. One of the very important battles in the history of the world was this battle of Actium, for it was more than a contest between two ambitious men.

It was a struggle between two ways of living—the age old despotism of the East, where rulers had power of life and death over their degraded subjects, and the new western ideals of justice according to law and order which the Roman Republic had developed. It was a turning point in history. The decision had been made. The world was going forward.

THE LOVE STORY ENDS

FOR THREE DAYS and nights, after Antony was taken aboard the Egyptian flagship, Cleopatra stayed below in her cabin and refused to speak to him. For how could she? What was there to say to that crazy man who had thrown away their future?

Alone, in the prow of the ship, Antony sat with his head in his hands, deep in remorse over what he had done, and torn with agony because Cleopatra would not see him.

When her ladies, Iras and Charmian, were finally permitted to bring him to her, Cleopatra felt truly sorry for him. His eyes were like those of a whipped dog. But there was no time to waste in mourning over what was past. The battle had been lost. They must now plan to defend themselves as best they could with what forces were left to them in Egypt. She had already begun turning over various plans in her clear, active mind.

Antony was of no help to her. Never having learned to control his emotions, it was now too late; they had made a wreck of him. He could only agonize and groan and threaten to kill himself as they neared Africa. At a small fort, three days west of Alexandria where they stopped for water, he refused to go any further. He wanted to stay right there on the edge of the desert and die! A few weeks later, however, the two men who had stayed with him persuaded him to go on to

Alexandria, where he could at least have a decent burial, if he was still determined not to live.

"I am," he insisted dramatically. "I am through with life." And upon reaching Alexandria, he shut himself up in a small house on the harbor, at the far end of the breakwater, where he need look at nothing but the open sea, and the great lighthouse. He stayed there all winter, then he returned to life to enjoy what little there was left of it before Octavian should arrive.

For now, it was learned that Octavian had landed in Asia Minor and was marching south with a huge army along the ancient highway toward Egypt. Egypt being the only country still holding out against him, Antony knew that the end could not be far away. Why not eat, drink and be merry, then, for what time was left? Returning to the palace, he rounded up old friends, organized a club called the "Die-Togethers" and spent every night with them in wild carousal.

Cleopatra was still busy trying to prepare for the emergency in case Alexandria should fall and the capital have to be moved to a port on the Red Sea. She was having a number of Egyptian battleships dragged through some ancient canals on the Isthmus of Suez, or, where the channels were filled up with sand, hauled overland from the Nile to the Red Sea.

To avoid capture, she planned also to have her two sons leave the country. Julius Caesar's son, who was now seventeen, was to go with Egyptian merchants on their summer voyage to India. Alexander, "the Sun," ten years old, was to be sent to Media. His twin sister, "the Moon," Cleopatra felt could be safely kept at home.

For herself, in case of need, she was pushing forward the work on her unfinished tomb, or mausoleum, near the Temple of Isis. Also, she was experimenting with various poisons, trying them out on criminals, to see which death was the least horrible.

Had she followed Octavian's advice, she would have used the poison on Antony, for by secret messenger Octavian had sent word that he would treat her kindly if she would kill Antony. But if Antony had followed the advice sent to him by Herod, he would have taken Cleopatra's life, in order to save his own. Neither one was tempted, for they still loved each other, though their lives and their love story were almost at an end.

By June, although Antony had led out the forces and tried to defend it, Octavian had seized the fort on the eastern border of Egypt, and was camped close to the walls of Alexandria.

The last night of July, his last night on earth, Antony spent drinking with the "Die-Togethers." The following day, up at sunrise, and dressed in his armor, he was preparing to lead his men in a last fight against Octavian. Then, from a rise of ground where he was standing, he saw first his fleet in the harbor and then the cavalry desert and go over to the enemy. Blind with rage, believing she had betrayed him, Antony rushed back to the palace, tore through the halls, howling, cursing and damning Cleopatra.

Terrified, Iras and Charmian ran to protect their mistress, hurried with her to the unfinished mausoleum, bolted the door, and breathless and trembling ran to the upper floor. From a window they called down to some workman or servant on the ground below.

"Run! Tell Antony, the Queen is about to kill herself!" The man ran. But, too excited to get the message straight, he told Antony that Cleopatra was already dead. At once, but too late, Antony realized that his rage had been without foundation.

"Cleopatra?" he moaned. "O, my beloved Cleopatra. To think that I, a famous soldier, should have been slower in courage than a woman! But I shall soon be with you!" Seizing a sword, he plunged it into his side, and fell back, unconscious.

Anxious faces were bending over him when he regained conciousness. Learning that Cleopatra was still alive, he begged to be taken to her, and was carried to the mausoleum.

There the bolts were jammed so tight that the women could not open the door. But there were ropes, used by the workmen, hanging from the roof. With them tied to the stretcher on which Antony had been carried, Cleopatra and her two women hauled him up through the window into the upper room. There he died, his head in Cleopatra's arms, her tears falling on his face.

Shortly after sunset, Octavian entered the city, visited his beautiful prisoner, coolly appraised her charm with his steady calculating eyes, and left, promising her that she would be treated honorably. Cleopatra listened in despair, for the words rang false to her. Later when she learned that he was secretly planning to display her in his Roman Triumph, she broke down completely.

"No!" she cried. "No! No! No! I will not be taken to Rome to be exhibited in his Triumph! No, not that!" Pacing the floor, beating her small fists against her breast, tearing frantic fingers through her hair, she finally threw herself on her couch in a paroxysm of sobbing, to lie there delirious for several days. Recovering her composure, one day, near the end of that unhappy month, she begged permission to visit Antony's tomb. There, she bent down and kissed the cold marble slab that lay above him.

"O Antony, dearest Antony," she whispered. "If the gods below with whom you are now dwelling can or will do anything for me, since the gods above have betrayed us, hide me, bury me here with you. For amongst all my bitter misfortunes, nothing has been so terrible as this short time that I have lived without you!"

Covering the gravestone with flowers, she then ordered a table set as for a feast. Among the delicacies brought in, was a basket of figs, in which lay a small, but very poisonous asp.

No one was in the tomb with Cleopatra when she died, except Charmian and Iras. They had dressed her that morning in her most lovely and royal garments, that they might go proudly with their Queen into that unknown shadowy land beyond the gates of death.

Iras was already dead when the soldiers of Octavian broke open the tomb and entered it. Charmian was dying, but with her last breath, straightening the crown of her beloved Queen, who lay on a golden couch, quiet and peaceful at last, and half smiling, as in sleep.

Cleopatra's children by Antony were spared. Taken to Rome, they were made welcome and mothered by Octavia.

Caesarion, however, was seized and executed—the last of the Ptolemies and the only son of Julius Caesar.

Octavian now stood alone, and without a rival, sole master of the Roman world, of which ancient Egypt had, at last, become a province. It was the year 30 B.C. The month was Sextilis, the same month in which thirteen years before he had first been made consul—the month which would later be named AUGUST.

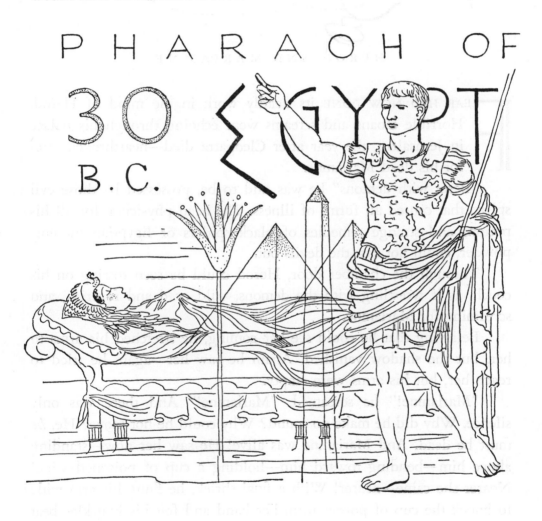

PHARAOH OF
30 EGYPT
B.C.

HEROD AND MARIAMNE

FEAR HAD NOW DONE its deadly work in the mind of Herod. Horrible moans and screams went echoing through his palace in Jerusalem, the year after Cleopatra died—heartbroken cries for his dead Mariamne.

"Beset with demons" he was said to be, possessed by those evil spirits that caused all forms of illness. The head physician, for all his potions and strange remedies of black spiders or Egyptian mummy powder, could not cast the devils out.

Through the chamber door, Herod could be seen tossing on his couch, as if wrestling with the demons, wild eyed and feverish, and screaming for Mariamne.

Believing that he could see her coming, he stretched his arms to her, but the shadow vanished. Again he saw her—again he tried to reach her, but his arms were empty.

"Mariamne!" he screamed. "Mariamne!" And there was only silence. Why did he make no sound? Why could he not move? He, *he* must be dead. And Mariamne was alive! He saw her now—standing above him—bending toward him—holding a cup of poisoned wine! Nearer she came—nearer! With a final shriek, he flung his arm wide to knock the cup of poison form her hand and felt his knuckles beat against the wall. Then at last he woke from his delirium. Cold and exhausted, his head clear, Herod woke to face the truth. Mariamne was dead—lost to him forever; he himself had had her killed.

This dreadful deed, this tragic death of Mariamne had followed closely upon Herod's first meeting with Octavian, after the battle of Actium. Upon hearing of Antony's defeat, Herod had wasted no time before presenting himself to his new overlord. As soon as he learned that Octavian was on his way to Egypt, he had set forth to meet him on the island of Samos.

He had feared, however, to go so far, and leave Mariamne behind him in Jerusalem. What if some other man made love to her while he was gone? What if he were killed? What if he did not return at all, and she should then become the wife of another? The very idea sent the wild blood pounding in his throat, and he contrived a mad scheme to prevent it.

"The Queen must not be allowed to live," he said, taking his chamberlain aside. "If I do not return, she is to die also. But she must never suspect it. You understand, the Queen must not suspect it." Searching the man's face, and seeing no reason to distrust him, Herod had set forth on his uncertain mission.

Nine years had now passed since Herod had been crowned in Rome. But from his recollection of the younger man Herod judged that Caesar Octavian, as he now called himself, was one with whom plain facts and simple bearing would be most effective.

Therefore, before entering the presence of this all powerful Roman, who could now make or ruin him, Herod had removed his crown and all of his royal ornaments. He had then stated his case briefly, with the result that when he left, not only was his crown secure, but his kingdom had been greatly enlarged.

Octavian had recognized in Herod the kind of strong, capable king that Rome needed to protect the border against Parthia. So he had restored to him all the lands which Antony had given to Cleopatra, and added much more territory. Proud and exultant, Herod rode back to

Jerusalem, eager, above all else, to report his success and share his triumph with his beloved Queen.

He found Mariamne as he had left her, alone without her children, locked in a fortress, under guard, safe but greatly changed. Cold and disinterested, she turned away and had no word for him. When he tried to touch her, she shrank away in horror.

Herod saw at once that Mariamne had learned of his plot to have her killed if he did not return. Then came the ugly thought. How had Mariamne teased the secret from the disloyal chamberlain?

Herod's mean-minded sister now fed his fears and suspicions. Glad to get even with Mariamne, whom she hated for her haughty manner, the evil girl hinted of secret meetings between the Queen and the chamberlain. She suggested that it was no longer safe for Herod to trust Mariamne to pour his wine for him, as had been his habit. To prove it, she bribed a servant to help her carry out a devilish plot.

A day or so later, a cup of wine was set before Herod which the cup bearer told him was a love potion prepared for him by Mariamne. He advised the King, however, to test its effect first on someone else. A prisoner, condemned to die, was sent for. Given the wine to drink, the man fell dead of poison. Terrified, Herod sent for Mariamne, begged her to deny her guilt.

Mariamne, white with anger at being accused of such a crime, refused to speak. Nor did she deign to utter a word in her own defense when later she was brought to trial. In proud silence, she stood and heard herself condemned to death.

Herod had no heart to order the sentence carried out. For weeks he kept sending messages of love to her prison cell, pleading with her to say that she was innocent. He paced the palace halls waiting for a single word from her which never came.

Outside in the streets could be heard the harsh, shrill voices of the Jewish people, an angry mob, furious at the unjust treatment of this Maccabean princess.

"Maccabeans" stormed Herod. "Maccabeans!" Always these Mac-

124

cabeans! Would he never be rid of them? Must he kill them all? Young Aristobulus was dead, and old Hyrcanus—the boy and the old priest—both of them. He had had them both killed. Wasn't that enough? Must he kill all of the Maccabeans to be free of fear? If so, he would wipe out the whole family, root and branch. Then perhaps the rebellious Jewish people would settle down, then perhaps they would be terrified into silence, and let him be King in peace.

So Mariamne had been sent to her death on the scaffold, and other suspected enemies wiped out.

No sooner had Mariamne been beheaded than Herod had gone mad with grief. In time the demons and evil spirits left his tormented body, but his mind was poisoned forever.

Never again was Herod to be free of fear.

TRIUMPH AND PEACE

THE HIGHEST MILITARY honor in the Roman state was a Triumph. Octavian now returned to Rome from Egypt to enjoy a Triple Triumph. Not one—but three days in the middle of August 29 B.C. were set aside for the celebration of his victories.

The first day was for the victory at Philippi, when the death of Julius Caesar had been avenged.

The second day was in honor of his two naval victories, the one at Actium and one against the pirates of Sicily.

The third day, greatest and most magnificent of all, was the celebration of his victory over Egypt.

Each day the streets were lined with crowds echoing the thrilling

IO TRIUMPHE IO

VICTORIOUS IMPERATOR IN HIS TRIUMPHAL CHARIOT

cry of Io Triumphe High-o! the Triumph! But on the third day, hours
before the first strains of music could be heard, there was no standing
room left along the streets or on the housetops. And as the procession
started to move along the Sacred Way, in the direction of the Forum,
the excitement was intense.

First to appear, following the musicians, were the two sleek milk
white oxen to be used in the sacrifice, their horns gilded and hung with
garlands of flowers.

Next, trundling by on heavy wheels, came the carriages heaped
high with trophies and spoils of war. Before the crowds ceased marvel-
ling at the riches, the captives were led by in chains, most of whom, on
this day of mingled tragedy and joy, would soon be strangled to death
on the steps of the dungeon.

And now a triumphal car rolled by, high on top of which, dazzling
in its life-like beauty, was to be seen an image of Cleopatra, lying on
her golden couch, as she had in death.

Next, walking, two by two, in clean cut precision, came a company

126

IO TRIUMPHE IO

LICTOR WITH HIS FASCES · BULL DECKED FOR SACRIFICE

of twelve lictors carrying fasces decorated with laurel, followed by more musicians and dancers.

And then—ah then! in all his glitter and glory came the hero of the day, the victorious imperator (general of the armies). Standing in a golden chariot, drawn by four white horses, rode Octavian, looking most majestic—and unnatural. Dressed in a purple cloak embroidered in gold, he was wearing a gold crown of laurel leaves, and his face was painted vermilion like that of the statue of Jupiter on a festival day. In his right hand he held an ivory sceptre topped by the Roman eagle.

Riding with him were two boys, their faces radiant as his own had once been on a similar occasion. The small, dark one was pointed out as being his sister's son, Marcellus. The taller one, with sandy hair, was his stepson, Tiberius.

Following on foot, with their white togas and broad crimson stripes, came the two consuls and several hundred Senators, their faces florid in the heat, but their manner full of dignity, despite their unsuccessful effort to keep in step with the music.

At sight of them, a faint murmur of shocked surprise ran through the crowd. It was the first time in the history of Rome that the Senators had followed, instead of preceded, the general. It could only mean that the first place of authority in the Roman state had been taken from the Senate and given to a single man.

Rome was no longer a Republic!

The victorious army brought up the end of the parade, cavalry clattering by on their high-stepping horses, foot soldiers in shining armor crowned with laurel, decorated for valor, singing songs, cheering, and shouting the contagious cry of Io Triumphe!

Winding through the Forum, up to the Capitoline, the procession halted there before the statue of Jupiter, Greatest and Best. There the white oxen were slaughtered and their blood spilt in sacrifice on the burning altar. Octavian then stepped forward. Removing his crown of laurel he laid it upon the knee of Jupiter as a mark of gratitude to Heaven for his victories.

Descending the marble steps again, all returned to the Forum, where with great pomp a new Temple was dedicated by Octavian, a new building opened, lavish gifts presented to leaders of the city. Additional rewards and special medals were accorded veterans and heroes, all with appropriate and impressive oratory.

But, a little apart, on the fringe of the Forum, there was seen something that indicated the true importance of that day—a great gate, no longer standing open. Solemnly, and for but the third time in the history of Rome, the Temple of Janus had been closed.

Peace had come at last to the Roman world.

Civil war, Octavian promised them, and wars of conquest were over. From now on, the only battles fought would be to protect the empire from the uncivilized barbarians, not to extend its borders.

And so it was to be. For 200 years, longer than at any time before or since, the world around the Mediterranean was to be at peace. That famous and unequalled era of peace, known as the great PAX ROMANA, had now dawned.

III

AUGUSTUS

PEOPLE WHO WERE LIVING

(in ROME)

dressed to perform a sacrifice

27 B.C.

OCTAVIAN

WAS HONORED BY THE ROMAN SENATE WITH THE SACRED TITLE OF "AUGUSTUS"

AUGUSTUS HAD MANY

TEMPLES

AND SHRINES TO THE ROMAN GODS REPAIRED AND BUILT WITH THE HELP OF AGRIPPA,

VIRGIL

TRIED TO HELP AUGUSTUS RESTORE FAITH IN OLD ROMAN GODS, BY WRITING HIS POEM THE "AENEID"

They burned the YULE log in midwinter

DRUIDS

THE ANCIENT PRIESTS OF GAUL WORSHIPPED IN THEIR SACRED OAK GROVES

FARMER   SOLDIER   CHIEFTAN

GAULS

AND SOME EVENTS THAT TOOK

WHEN HE BECAME AUGUSTUS

(in J E R U S A L E M)

18 B.C.
THE NEW

HILLEL

THE GREAT RABBI WAS
STUDYING AND TEACHING
THE LAW IN JERUSALEM
HE HAD A GRANDSON, GAMALIEL, who
became the teacher of the Apostle, PAUL

TEMPLE

WAS DEDICATED WHICH
HAD BEEN BUILT BY

HEROD

AGRIPPA

MARRIED JULIA, BY REQUEST
OF AUGUSTUS. HE WENT TO
SYRIA AS THE GOVERNOR
AND VISITED HEROD,

Gaius   Lucius

he was killed
3 years later

He dug a canal
from the Rhine
to the North Sea

He married
ANTONIA

They went
with men
to battle

12 B.C.

WARRIOR   PRIESTESS

GERMANS

DRUSUS

FOUGHT AGAINST THE GERMANS
AND WON THE HONORARY TITLE
GERMANICUS

AUGUSTUS

WAS MADE A GOD
DRUSUS BUILT THE FIRST
ALTAR TO HIM IN GAUL,

PLACE BETWEEN 27 AND 12 B.C.

131

AUGUSTUS

AUGUSTUS CAESAR!

I T WAS IN JANUARY, 27 B.C., that Octavian became Augustus Caesar.
The gates of Janus were still closed. Peace, prosperity and order
seemed to have returned to Rome. And on the first day of that
month named for the old god who watched over all gateways and
beginnings, the Senate voted that the statesman's crown of oak leaves be
accorded Octavian as a mark of his service to the state, and also the
special title of honor which had been selected for him.

None of the names or titles by which he was then called had

133

seemed to them sufficiently distinguished. Although in time, Caesar, Imperator, Princeps, all of them, were to become titles of royalty they had no such meaning then!

CAESAR, which was to become CZAR and KAISER, was but a personal name which Octavian had inherited from his adopted father.

IMPERATOR, which was to become EMPEROR, was the title given any victorious Roman general-in-chief.

PRINCEPS, which became the word PRINCE, meant simply "first citizen." In the Senate his name stood first on the roll call.

Some more distinctive title should certainly be found, the Senators believed, for this man who was now looked upon as the second founder of the State. But what? Romulus, the name of the first founder of Rome, was suggested as appropriate, but turned down because Romulus had been a king, and "Rex," or king, was still an evil-sounding word in Roman ears.

AUGUSTUS met with approval. It was awe inspiring and suggested a leader especially chosen by the gods and acting under divine guidance and protection. Since that was what Octavian sincerely believed about himself he was most gratified by this choice. On the Ides of January, 27 B.C., therefore, by vote of the Roman Senate Octavian was given his new title of Augustus.

By vote of the Roman Senate—that was an important point! The Republic had not been destroyed. Octavian had presented Rome with a new constitution, which preserved all the outward forms of the old Republic. But it was only an empty shell, within which he himself could actually control the Roman world. To reach this unique position, Octavian had followed a middle course, cleverly combining the conflicting advice of Agrippa and Maecenas.

Two years before, immediately after his military triumph, Octavian had started to put the long disorganized Roman world in order. He had asked his two friends for their opinion as to how to go about it. Should he continue to keep the power in his own hands, or should he let the Senate have control again, and so bring back the Republic?

Which in the long run did they think would be the best for Rome?

Agrippa was in favor of the Republic; Maecenas against it.

"Consuls elected every year are far safer for a country than a king," said Agrippa. The son of a good king often turns out to be a tyrant. Rome had begun with kings, he continued—six of them. But the seventh had been such a tyrant that the kingdom had had to be overthrown. The Republic had then been established, and as a Republic Rome had flourished and grown strong.

Maecanas disagreed. For the past hundred years, he pointed out, the Republic had been so weak, and the Senate so corrupt, that one military leader after another had tried to overthrow the government, and kept Rome constantly in civil war. The Republic had worked well enough, he admitted, while Rome was a small city state, of the size for which that kind of government had been planned. But it was not suited to the great empire of many provinces and conquered peoples that Rome had now grown to be.

Octavian had listened to both arguments. He wished truly to do what was best for Rome. There were many plans made by Julius Caesar, many of his own that he wished to carry out. But to do so, he knew that he must avoid Caesar's mistake of making too much show of his authority. Therefore, he proceeded cautiously.

First he won the confidence of the Senators by treating them with utmost respect and submitting his every plan for their approval, as if it really mattered. Then, by insisting that the powers he held be voted to him for a limited time and not renewed unless agreeable, he dispelled any fear they might have had that he wanted to make himself king. Therefore on the first of January, 27 B.C., when he dared to make the supreme test of offering to give back all the powers which he held, he was not disappointed. The Senators did not accept his offer. Instead, they insisted that he keep all the power he had, and gave him more, voted him the title of honor, and even decreed that from then on the name Augustus Caesar should be included in the formal prayers which the priests offered for the welfare of the Senate and Rome. Thus it was, within the hollow shell of the old Republic, that the Roman Empire took form and grew.

Meanwhile, enlisting the help both of Agrippa, a patron of architecture, and of the diplomatic Maecenas, Octavian had gone ahead with improvements in Rome. A great building program was begun. The Senate membership was revised, and by 27 B.C. the government of Rome itself was in smooth running order.

The time had then come, Augustus Caesar thought, to consider his empire at large. All over the empire everywhere he wanted law and order established. The people within its borders must live in peace and prosperity. The barbarians without must be fenced out securely.

A huge, wall-sized map of the empire was suggested and designed by Agrippa. It would show the length, breadth and population of every province from the Euphrates River to the Rhine, and all the Roman highways connecting them with one another and with Rome. It was to be painted later on the walls of a portico in the Forum. Plans were also made to set up on the Forum a Golden Milestone, on which the names of all the chief cities in the empire and their distances from the capital could be engraved.

To collect the necessary data, four geographers were hired to travel through every country, make observations and send back reports and figures. These would also form a basis upon which each province might properly be taxed.

In the east, the provinces were old, long civilized countries, well under the control of subject kings like Herod of Judaea, who would protect their borders and collect their taxes.

In the northwest, the provinces were very different. The tribes of Gaul had never been entirely united. No accurate census had ever been taken of the people. There was much that needed to be done in that most primitive portion of the empire.

So while Agrippa was left to take charge of affairs in Rome, Augustus, himself, planned to go to Gaul, the land that was to become France —land of the Druid priests.

136

THE DRUIDS

THE YOUNG MOON was rising again, above a grove of sacred oaks, somewhere in Gaul. Watching it from a hilltop on the outskirts of a nearby village was one of Gaul's ancient priests, a venerable Druid, leaning on his staff. Bent and old he was; his eyes almost too dim to see the stars. But he could see the moon slip-

137

ping above the black treetops into the open sky. And it still filled his heart with wonder, as it had on those nights when he, too, like the moon, was young.

He shook his head. Ah, when he was young! Ah, then! Life had been very different for a Druid. In those good old days before the Romans came to Gaul to be a Druid priest meant to have honor and power. It meant to go each spring to the Great Court, and sit in judgment over delegates from every tribe and canton.

How proud he had been when his father, who had been one of the chiefs of Gaul, had sent him as a boy of ten to live with the Druids and become skilled in their wisdom. Twenty years it had taken to commit to memory all that they had had to teach him about the stars and the planets, the nature of man, and the meaning of the universe. The old priest shook his head sadly at the thought of the changes that had since taken place.

Now that the Romans had come into this land of the Gauls, to conquer and rule over them, the Druids had been robbed of their rightful power. They were no longer allowed to be judges. They had been degraded. Many of his fellow priests had taken to practicing low forms of magic, to hold a following among the foolish people.

Bah! Far better, he thought, to stand alone—alone with his old thoughts as he did now, upon this hilltop, watching the new moon. Alone he was, and old. Old and bent and worn, his eyes grown dim, his fingers stiff and crooked like small branches of an oak. But not for long, he said, would it be so.

Not much longer now would he be old and useless and alone. Soon the day must surely come when he could die. And then he would become YOUNG again!

For what was death but passing like an old moon through a few nights of darkness into a new life?

Younger Druids also took special notice of the moon that night, for it was five nights old. And one among them, searching for healing herbs, had found a plant of mistletoe growing, as it rarely did, upon a sacred oak. The sixth night of the moon was the one on which to cut that mystic bough.

The next night, then, the Druids, clad as always in their long white robes, summoned the people to attend the ceremony and the sacrifice. Leading two young white bulls, yoked for the first time, they moved in slow procession out through the quiet fields, along the misty marshland to the grove of oaks, which was their only temple. In among the dark trunks and interlacing shadows they wound their way, until they came to the one tree that had nourished in its rough bark the seed of the mistletoe.

Solemnly then, while the people watched with upturned faces, a priest ascended the tree and cut away the mistletoe with his golden sickle. In his outspread cloak he carried back the precious bough, never letting it touch the ground, for fear that the earth, mother of all growing things, might take back unto herself its life giving power. The white bulls were then sacrificed to the one great god, whose spirit lived within the oak tree, and so had passed also into this branch of mistletoe which had grown upon it.

As a charm to be cherished against evil, each follower carried back a twig, and the procession returned to the village. Later each young woman would drink a potion brewed from the white berries, that many strong sons and beautiful daughters might be born to her.

Centuries later, when Christian priests were to bring a new religion into Gaul, they would find it wise to nail the cross or image of the Virgin to the trunk of the sacred oak, that the new belief might blend into the old, and the old be gradually forgotten.

How long the Druids had been in Gaul, or where their ideas came from, no one can be sure. Their belief in immortality was like that of the early Greeks. And the name Druid is said to have come from the Greek word for oak.

Their knowledge of the stars may have come from the Chaldeans, or native priests of ancient Babylon, brought to them, perhaps, by the Phoenicians, who had sailed the Mediterranean long before Rome was founded, back in the days of the Trojan war. On these coins, used by the Gauls, may be seen crude signs of the zodiac. On the first one the symbol of the year is shown between the sun and the moon. On the other, the year, represented by a horse, is prancing between Cancer (midsummer) and Capricorn (midwinter).

Midsummer and midwinter were both celebrated with fire.

Each winter when the sun reached the sign of Capricorn, and they knew that the shortest day and the longest night of the year had come, the Druids lighted a log, a Yule log. They kept it burning through that longest night as a symbol of the sun's light and warmth, which would begin to grow stronger on the following day. It was the time of the Saturnalia in Rome.

In midsummer as the sun entered Cancer, the sign of the crab, and daylight was at its peak, the celebration in Gaul was far from the simple burning of a log. The fires of midsummer filled the air with cries of agony and scorched the treetops with their sheets of flame. In a gigantic wicker basket, woven in the shape of a human being, men, criminals most of them, were burned alive as a wholesale sacrifice to the gods for the benefit of the nation.

This horrible rite, which was also perhaps a way of purging the land of its criminals, had been described by Julius Caesar in his book about Gaul. It was a custom of that province most shocking to the Romans. They had long since forgotten the fact that, like all other early races, their ancestors too had once practiced human sacrifice.

It may be possible that the Druids themselves had found it a custom of the more savage natives, when they had first come to Gaul, but had not been able to do away with it. For people cling to old customs and beliefs. They are slow in dying.

However, it was one custom which Caesar Augustus, as emperor of Rome, now intended to eliminate.

Any Gaul who wished to have the honor of being made a Roman citizen must be forbidden to participate in that savage sacrifice.

TALES OF THE WILD NORTHWEST

S O AUGUSTUS WAS GOING TO GAUL. He made the announcement one afternoon to his family and friends, reclining at dinner. To the children, seated as usual at a nearby table, going to Gaul meant excitement and adventure. "Going to Gaul!" exclaimed ten-year-old Drusus in an excited whisper to his brother Tiberius. Their stepfather was going to Gaul!

Just that morning Drusus had been reading Julius Caesar's War in Gaul, and had imagined himself with Caesar fighting the wild tribes and conquering the country.

Many centuries later American boys would be reading, with the same thrill, of pioneers and Indian fighters on what would then have become the frontier of civilization. For Gaul was the wild west to the Romans, as far as their civilization had penetrated. Beyond the Rhine, which marked the border of Gaul, there were no permanent towns, but deep, dark forests through which roamed the wandering tribes of war-like Germans. These people dressed in skins, lived by hunting and fishing, raising only occasional fields of corn around their temporary villages. Across the water to the north of Gaul was the almost unknown island of the Britons—people no less primitive than the Germans. And beyond that, what? No one knew.

Drusus turned again to his brother.

How far into Gaul was their stepfather going, did Tiberius think?

Up into Germany and over to Britain as Julius Caesar had done?

Tiberius did not answer. He wanted to hear what else Augustus himself was saying about his plans. Motioning Drusus to be quiet, Tiberius leaned forward to listen, a deep frown between his large near-sighted eyes and his mouth half open, which unfortunately made him look almost stupid. Actually, this solemn, silent, sandy-haired boy, who was to become Rome's second emperor, was extremely intelligent, and so unusually level-headed for a boy of fourteen, that his schoolmates often called him the "old man."

For the past five years, since the death of their own father, the two brothers, Tiberius and Drusus, had been living with their stepfather Augustus in his home on the Palatine.

There they were under the ever watchful eye of Livia, who was a most ambitious mother, constantly on the alert to promote the future of her boys.

Livia was watching Tiberius now, as he sat listening to the conversation between Augustus and Agrippa. The two men were talking about the walled towns of Gaul, and the need of replacing the muddy trails connecting them by well paved Roman roads. Livia was pleased to see how absorbed Tiberius was, but wished he would sit up straight and not squint so, comparing him, as she always did, to Marcellus, Octavia's

handsome son, who always appeared to better advantage. Forever charming and agreeable, Marcellus was too great a favorite with his uncle Augustus to please Livia. Augustus looked upon him, she feared, as a future husband for his twelve-year-old daughter, Julia, who was now sitting between Marcellus and Tiberius.

Young Julia, spoiled and saucy, with her curls piled up in a much too grown-up fashion, and her pretty full lips painted much too red, was trying to flirt with both of the boys at once. Unable to distract their attention from Agrippa, however, who was describing the mining towns of Gaul and the skillful metal workers, she was obliged to listen. But she showed no interest, until Agrippa mentioned jewelry.

Then Julia jumped up and ran to her father. Throwing her arms about his neck, she made him promise that he would bring her necklaces and bracelets from Gaul, before she would return to her place at the table.

On the other side of Marcellus was his half sister, Antonia, as gentle and sweet in manner as her mother Octavia. Beyond her were the twins, Cleopatra's attractive children, to whom Antonia (through their father, Antony) was also a half sister. The twins were being brought up by Augustus, as were also a couple of mysterious-eyed young eastern princes. (Subject kings of Asia Minor had a habit of sending their sons to Rome, either as hostages, or to keep them from being murdered by their jealous relatives.) They completed the circle at the children's table, and brought Livia's eyes back to her own sons, Drusus and Tiberius.

Tiberius continued to listen to the adults. The rest of the young group began comparing notes as to what they themselves already knew or had heard about the Gauls. All of them had seen Gauls from the backwoods, wandering about the Forum dressed in their scarlet or plaid cloaks, and long peculiar trousers. Several had seen tall blond Germans dressed in wolf skins staring up at the strange buildings, but none of them had ever seen a Briton. It was believed that few Britons if any had ever come to Rome.

"And yet tin comes to Rome from Britain, all the time," remarked Tiberius, unexpectedly. He found it interesting to think how many things like tin traveled from place to place, trying strange, far-off countries and unknown people together. Wheat came from Egypt; purple dye from Syria; spices from India; tin from Britain. He might have told the others how the tin was brought on pack horses and by barges down the rivers, but he didn't. The others, he saw, were more interested in the fact that the Britons fought in chariots and painted themselves blue.

"They use some kind of plant called woad," said Drusus. "Julius Caesar wrote about it, and said they looked terrible in a fight."

Drusus was very much disappointed to find that Augustus did not intend to go to Britain or into Germany, as Julius Caesar had done, or even far enough up into Gaul to see the chieftains who still wore helmets decorated with the horns of animals.

Augustus was merely going to sail across to Marseilles or Narbo which were perfectly civilized cities where people lived and dressed just as they did in Rome! The important chiefs of Gaul were going to meet him there.

Augustus was going to divide Gaul into four parts instead of three, have the people counted, open schools to teach them to speak Latin, and set up Roman law courts. But what excitement was there in that? Dull, humdrum business, it seemed to Drusus, compared to conquering a country the way Julius Caesar had done and exploring unknown islands and fighting the barbarians across the Rhine. Caesar had been almost shipwrecked on the coast of Britain, but just the same he had gone into the river called the Thames. And he had found that there were Druid priests there, too, just as there were in Gaul. Before that he had crossed the Rhine to terrify the Germans. It was to help the Gauls drive out a tribe of Germans who had crossed into their territory that Caesar had first gone to Gaul.

"That's what I'll do, when I grow up," thought Drusus. "I'll go up into Gaul. And if those wild Germans ever come over the Rhine again, I'll go over into their country, and keep on going as far as I can go, and conquer it, the way Julius Caesar did in Gaul!"

Only part of Drusus's wish was to be fulfilled.

The Germans were never to be conquered and brought under the rule of Rome. Yet while he was still young, Drusus was to lead many expeditions through the swamps and into the dark forests of Germany. And for his daring and bravery, he would be given the honorary title of "Germanicus."

That was still far in the future. Now it was not ten-year-old Drusus but his stepfather Augustus who was going to Gaul.

A WEDDING

JULIA AND MARCELLUS were married while Augustus was in Gaul. It was a typical Roman wedding, held in the atrium of the bride's home, with Julia in wedding veil of red and a woolen girdle tied with the "knot of Hercules," and Marcellus wearing a wreath of flowers on his head.

After the proper auspices were taken, the two joined their right hands before a married woman acting as priestess. The sacred cake was offered to Jupiter by the Pontifex Maximus, then shared by the bride and groom. Prayers were said to the goddess of marriage, and a sumptuous wedding feast enjoyed by all the guests.

In early evening came the wedding procession. To the music of flutes and by the light of flaming torches, the young bride was escorted to her future home. She was led by three young boys, one ahead, one holding each hand, while others followed her, carrying a distaff and spindle. At the door of his house Marcellus, the bridegroom, was waiting. After Julia had smeared the door posts with fat and oil, he lifted her over the threshold and carried her into the atrium.

On the hearth there was wood laid for a fire. Julia kindled it with her wedding torch and then put out the torch and threw it to be caught by one of the guests.

The next day came another feast, this time in the new home.

The feasting was the best part of the whole affair to young Drusus, who was no more interested in weddings than any other eleven-year-old boy. Drusus liked soldiers and excitement. And when, not long after Augustus left, word came that there had been an uprising among the Spanish tribes, and his stepfather had gone with the Roman legions into Spain to restore order, that was something after his own heart.

And when Tiberius his own brother was sent to Spain, to have his first experience as a soldier, Drusus wished with all his heart that he, too, were old enough to go. Instead he had to stay home, with his school books, and keep on learning Greek and all the other things his mother said he had to know to be an educated gentleman.

In Spain, during the campaign against the Spanish tribes, Augustus became dangerously ill. By the time he had completely recovered, the uprising had been successfully put down and order restored among the rebellious mountain tribes.

In 23 B.C., at the end of three years, Augustus was back home in Rome again, pleased with the new son-in-law of his own choosing, and eager to see what buildings had been completed under Agrippa's supervision, during the time that he had been away.

PANTHEON

AS IT STANDS TODAY

AFTER BEING REBUILT

M.AGRIPPA.L.F.COS.TERTIUM FECIT

ORIGINALLY BUILT BY AGRIPPA

"FECIT" MEANS "HE MADE IT"..

M.AGRIPPA·FECIT

THE PANTHEON

ONE OF THE buildings which Augustus was most pleased to find completed was the PANTHEON, the great temple to all gods, which had been built and donated to the city by Agrippa. He went with Agrippa to see it one day, shortly after his return to Rome and found it more than gratifying.

147

The Tiber was flooding its banks, as usual in early spring. As they proceeded northward from the Capitol, a damp wind blew across the marshes, causing Augustus to cough frequently and shiver with the cold, although he had taken the precaution to wind his bare legs beneath his toga with warm strips of wool. But no physical discomfort could dull his enthusiasm at first sight of the new temple. Of all the buildings that were now fast turning Rome from a city of brick into a city of marble, none stood higher in the esteem of Augustus than the temples.

For years past, the religious rites had been neglected, the temples allowed to fall into ruin and decay. And it was for that very reason, Augustus believed, because their bargain with the gods had not been properly fulfilled, that the Roman state had grown so weak and so corrupt. Now that he had restored the state, he wished also to restore the old religion.

Over eighty temples to the various individual gods had already been repaired, rebuilt or built anew. And now, in his honor, this great temple, dedicated not to one but to all the gods had been built by his loyal friend, Agrippa.

Against the deep blue heaven, it rose before them, that spring morning, clean and shining in the bright Italian sunlight. Through the columns of the portico, and crossed by their slanting shadows, could be seen the gleaming entrance doors of gold-plated bronze. Carved above the columns on a panel of stone they read the words:

M. AGRIPPA L. F. COS. TERTIUM FECIT

which meant "Marcus Agrippa, son of Lucius, in his third consulate, made it."

Today that same inscription still marks the entrance to the Pantheon, keeping alive the name of the capable, trustworthy man who built it. The bronze entrance doors are the same ones through which Agrippa and Augustus entered that spring morning twenty centuries ago. Though the original temple was to be partially destroyed in the following century, it was soon rebuilt, just as it stands today. All the other temples built

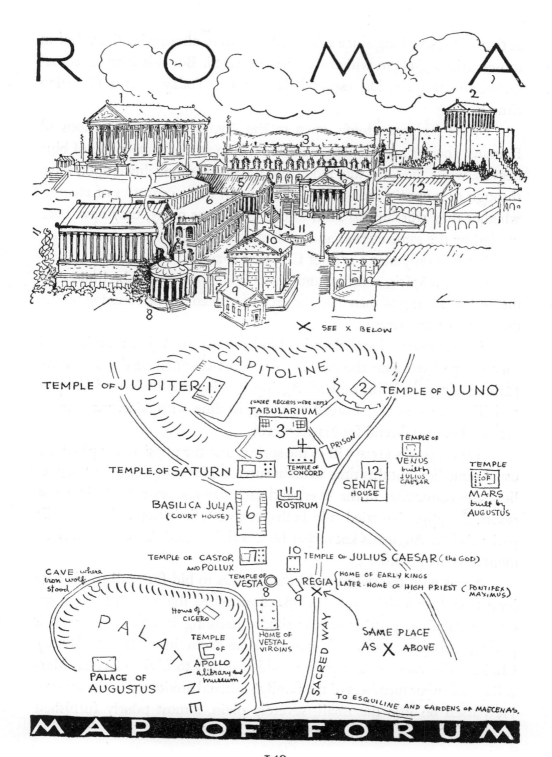

ROMA

TEMPLE of JUPITER 1. CAPITOLINE 2 TEMPLE of JUNO

(WHERE RECORDS WERE KEPT)
TABULARIUM 3

PRISON

TEMPLE OF VENUS built by JULIUS CAESAR

TEMPLE OF MARS built by AUGUSTUS

TEMPLE of SATURN 5 4 TEMPLE OF CONCORD 12 SENATE HOUSE

BASILICA JULIA (COURT HOUSE) 6 11 ROSTRUM

TEMPLE of CASTOR and POLLUX 7

10 TEMPLE of JULIUS CAESAR (the GOD)

CAVE where Iron wolf stood

TEMPLE of VESTA 8 9 REGIA HOME OF EARLY KINGS
LATER HOME OF HIGH PRIEST (PONTIFEX MAXIMUS)

Home of CICERO

HOME OF VESTAL VIRGINS

SAME PLACE AS X ABOVE

PALATINE

TEMPLE OF APOLLO a library and museum

PALACE OF AUGUSTUS

SACRED WAY

TO ESQUILINE AND GARDENS OF MAECENAS.

X SEE X BELOW

MAP OF FORUM

at that time have long since crumbled into ruin, along with the belief in those various gods to whom they were erected. But this temple, consecrated to all gods, has escaped destruction. Today it is a Christian church.

Under its great dome, open to the sky, countless generations of Romans, ancient and modern, have looked up at that same circle of blue heaven, while the same sun, moon and stars have shone down upon them through that open window. And through all those centuries of change, whether they worshipped Him as one God or as many, they have been guided by the same eternal and unchanging spirit.

For it is only man's *idea* of God that changes.

God is a Spirit, constant and unchanging, no more to be limited by the understanding of men than the arch of heaven can be confined within the dome of any temple.

As the bronze doors closed behind the two men that morning and they stepped out into the portico, Augustus coughed again, and complained of a pain in his midriff. Agrippa, seeing that he looked feverish and ill, suggested that instead of going to dine with Maecenas, he go directly home and send for his physician.

Augustus was always ill in the spring, and the physician applied the usual remedies, but this time without success. Hot compresses did not relieve the congestion in the liver, and each day the fever rose. As a last resort, the physician tried cold baths, but with little hope of saving his patient's life. Augustus knew that he was dying, and Agrippa was summoned to his bedside.

It was with the sad thought that he was to bid farewell to his life-long friend, that the loyal Agrippa approached the home of Augustus on the Palatine. (An extremely simple building it was,—not at all a palace, although the word was to come from its name Palatium.) Choked with memories, Agrippa nodded briefly to Livia, Octavia, Marcellus and other members of the family gathered anxiously in the atrium. He passed on into the small, severely plain, almost poorly furnished room that Augustus always occupied.

Stepping to his low, flat, cot-like bed, he bent down to hear the last words of the dying man.

"My one hope," said Augustus weakly, "is that the foundation which I have laid for the government of Rome will stand firm."

He then removed his signet ring and handed it to Agrippa. That ring was the seal of authority. As Agrippa returned to the atrium, the eyes of every member of the family were fastened on it. The air was vibrant with hostility.

Livia resented him because he stood in the way of her son, Tiberius. Octavia felt aggrieved that her son Marcellus, young though he was, should have been passed by. Marcellus, himself, was completely astounded by the oversight.

"Had he not been adopted by his uncle? Was he not the husband of his daughter Julia? What else did that mean but that he was to inherit the political power as well as the private fortune of his uncle Augustus when he came to die?"

But Augustus did not die. Not on that spring day of 23 B.C. Very shortly it was announced from the sick room that the dying man had rallied. By summer he was well again.

That, however, did not remedy the attitude of the family toward Agrippa. Even though Augustus protested that, having no legal rights to do so, he could not actually appoint anyone as his succesor, their jealousy and distrust of Agrippa continued. So marked was it that Augustus was made miserable, and Agrippa, never ambitious for himself, was disgusted.

There was work for the empire to be done in either Armenia or Syria, and with that as the real reason or excuse for a hasty departure, Agrippa left Rome and went East.

Taking up life again where he left off, Augustus turned his thoughts to another important part of his plan to restore the old Roman religion.

At his request, a long poem was now being written which was to serve the Roman people as a Bible, or sacred book of their religion . . . he was eager to read it . . .

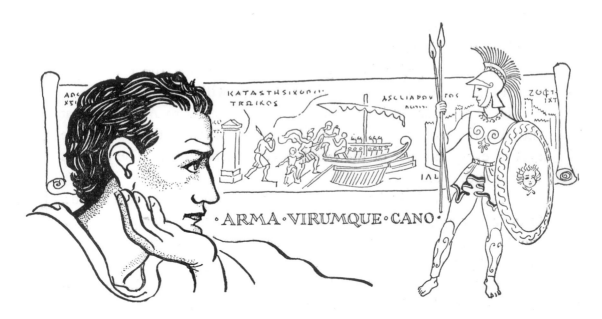

A BIBLE FOR THE ROMANS

VIRGIL, THE GENTLE POET, was writing the poem that was intended for the Roman Bible. Long before he left for Gaul, Augustus had conceived of the idea and convinced Virgil of the need for it. It was well known, he had pointed out, that the Roman people had degenerated. The early Romans had been hard working, law abiding and god fearing. Now they had grown soft and immoral. Something was needed to bring them back to the sturdy virtues of their forefathers. Some great poem should be written, Augustus felt, that would inspire them with pride in their race, their history and their old religion.

The Greeks had such a book in the Iliad of Homer, which kept alive the memory of their old gods and heroes. The Jews had a sacred book which told of their god and the ancient days of their race. Why should not the Romans also have such a sacred book or poem?

It was to Horace that Augustus had first spoken about writing it. But Horace, content now, and happy on a farm in the hills which Maecenas had given him, was not to be tempted into any such long and arduous task. Virgil, more hard-working and conscientious, had been persuaded to undertake it. And so plans had begun for that famous Latin poem, the Aeneid. It was decided that the theme of the poem should be the old, well known legend of Aeneas. He would show how difficult a task it had been for Aeneas to found the Roman race, and how he had been able to do it only because he had given instant obedience to the gods, by whom he had been guided.

Almost from the moment Virgil had consented to write the poem Augustus had been impatient to read it. While away in Gaul, he kept writing so many letters to Virgil to inquire about his progress, that the gentle poet was driven to mild desperation.

"Upon my honor," he had replied, "if I had anything worth your listening to, I would gladly send it. But the subject is so vast that I almost think I must have been beside myself to undertake it, especially as I am devoting part of my time to more important studies."

From the first line to the last, the poem was to be for Virgil a difficult undertaking. But he worked on industriously, and by the time Augustus returned to Rome, he had six books, or half of it, written. He had come up to Rome from Naples with the manuscript, expecting to read it to Augustus only to learn from Maecenas that Augustus was ill and not expected to live.

Now that Augustus was well again, Virgil was again preparing to read the poem to him, when illness once more intervened. This time it was young Marcellus who was stricken, and this time death was not to be cheated. In the summer of 23 B. C. Marcellus died, leaving sixteen-year-old Julia a widow. His mother, Octavia, was prostrated with grief. All Rome was shocked by his death. In mournful silence the crowds listened to the funeral oration and watched the procession winding out past the theatre named for the boy (which is still standing in Rome) to the Campus Martius where his body was to be cremated. Augustus was stunned by the loss, and could scarcely believe that the ashes of young Marcellus and not his own were the first to be laid in his newly completed tomb. (That tomb may also still be seen in Rome.)

After the funeral, Virgil, returning to his home on the Esquiline, felt that, before reading it to Augustus, he must now add another verse to his Aeneid. The name of Marcellus, he thought, ought now to be included among those of future Roman heroes mentioned at the end of the sixth book.

So a day or so later, the poet was sitting at his desk, with the parchment unrolled before him, writing the words, "Thou art Marcellus." Then searching for more words to fit the metre, he sat staring into space, one long leg twisted about the other in the ungainly fashion of the country boy he had never quite ceased to be. Nearby in the gardens of Maecenas, he knew that Horace and other congenial friends were engaged in delightfully idle conversation with their wealthy patron. But he was determined not to join them until he had mastered the verse upon which he was at work. Finally it was perfected. And then, seven years after Virgil had begun work on it, the day was set, and this part of the Aeneid was read for the first time.

The sun shone down into the peristylium, touching Virgil's dark head and casting his shadow on the marble table before him, as he modestly unrolled his manuscript. The circle of listeners waited expectantly. Julia was there, and Octavia, heavy-eyed from weeping. Augustus nodded and Virgil began to read. His voice trembled at first, for he was very shy, but soon the sweeping rhythm of his own words carried him along. And for the time being, his hearers lost themselves and their own sorrow in listening to the hardships and sorrows of the ancient hero, Aeneas, and his Trojan followers.

The Aeneid, as Virgil scarcely needed to explain, had been patterned after the Greek poem the Odyssey, sung by Homer about 1,000 years before. As that told of the Greek hero, Ulysses, and his adventures after the siege of Troy, the Aeneid told of the Trojan hero Aeneas, from the time he escaped from the burning city of Troy until he founded a new home on the Tiber.

This, in brief, is the song or story of the first six books of the Aeneid, from which Virgil was now reading.

THE STORY OF AENEAS.

AS THE STORY OPENS, Aeneas and the Trojans have already been travelling seven years since leaving Troy. Aeneas has suffered untold hardships, brought upon him by the spiteful goddess Juno, because Venus, his mother, had beaten her in a beauty contest, and she wished for revenge.

BOOK I

The Trojans are at sea. Their ships are being buffeted about by a terrific storm that Juno has caused. Hearing the commotion, old Neptune raises his hoary head above the waves, to see who has dared stir up the sea without his permission. To put the guilty Juno in her place, he calms the storm. This makes it possible for poor Aeneas and his exhausted followers to reach the nearby shore of Africa. There they land not far from the site of a new city, called Carthage, which they find is being built by Dido, a beautiful Phoenician queen. Dido, however is a pet of Juno. Therefore, Venus, looking down from on high, suspects that Juno is up to more mischief. Seeking out Jupiter, Lord of Heaven, Venus asks him, why and for how long he will allow her dear son Aeneas to be persecuted. Jupiter soothes Venus by telling her of the wonderful future in store for Aeneas, as founder of the Roman race, and forefather of the illustrious tribe of Julius. Jupiter then sends Mercury flying down to Carthage to make sure that Dido will receive the Trojans with hospitality. Aeneas has been welcomed and feasted by the beautiful Dido, and is being begged to tell her the story of his wanderings, as the first book ends.

BOOK II

Aeneas tells the story. "After the Greeks had besieged our city unsuccessfully for many years," Aeneas is saying, "the goddess Athena helped them build a tremendous wooden horse, which they left standing outside the city gates. Then apparently they sailed for home. We Trojans, suspicious at first, were finally tricked into dragging the horse inside the city walls, only to find that it was filled with Greek soldiers who opened the gates to those outside. Though we fought desperately to save it, our ancient city fell. As I stood aghast, Venus, my mother, appeared to me, told me to take my family and flee. At first Anchises, my aged father, refused to leave, but suddenly, there came omens from heaven. The soft tuft of hair on my small son's head was seen to glow with light, and a star shot through the sky, marking a path for us to follow. Then my old father picked up the household gods and the sacred hearth fire and was ready to leave. I spread a tawny lion skin across my shoulders, and carrying my father upon it, holding my small son by the hand, escaped from the burning city. Somewhere on the way, my dear wife who was following became separated from us and lost. I went back alone to search for her, but met only her ghost, and knew that I must go on without her. Near Mount Ida, I was joined by these, my companions, who were determined to go with me wherever I should go. With tears, I left the shores where Troy once stood . . . An exile, I launched forth into the deep, with my associates, my son, my household gods and the great gods of my country."

156

BOOK III

Dido is still listening. Aeneas tells her how they landed at one place after another, but were never allowed to settle. Always he had been driven on by dreams, prophets and oracles to fulfill his destiny. On the island of Sicily, his old father, Anchises, had died. "This was my finishing disaster," says Aeneas, "this the end of my long tedious journey. Parting hence, a god directed me to your coasts."

BOOK IV

The Trojans are still at Dido's court. Dido has fallen deeply in love with Aeneas, and this is their love story, manipulated, interfered with, watched over, by the gods and goddesses. It ends when Aeneas, obeying the command of Jupiter, deserts the broken hearted Dido, and sails away again hoping this time to reach Italy to fulfill his destiny.

BOOK V

The Trojans are at sea. Looking back, Aeneas sees the smoke rising, and the flames above the walls of Carthage, and suspects the truth, that in her grief and despair, Dido has taken her own life. Just out of sight of land a storm arises and drives the Trojan ships back to Sicily. And there where his old father Anchises had died the year before Aeneas, as a devoted son, celebrates the anniversary with appropriate funeral games. Then again he sets sail for Italy.

BOOK VI

Aeneas visits the land of the dead. Landing in Italy, at last, Aeneas finds himself not far from Cumae, a city of Greek colonists, and near the mouth of a cave, where Sibyl the priestess delivers the mysterious oracles of Apollo. Approaching her, Aeneas begs her to take him to visit his father in the land of the dead. "Easy is the path that leads down to hell," says she, but none may ever return from there, who has not first found and plucked the Golden Bough. Searching for it in the forest, Aeneas is guided by two white doves, sent by Venus, to a tree on which there is a bough that looks exactly like mistletoe. Returning with it, he follows the priestess to the mouth of a hideous black cave. After sacrificing black bulls to Pluto, god of the underworld, they enter the night black opening. Passing by Grief, Fear, Disease, War and all those spectres that lie between Life and Death, they finally reach the River Styx. There, Charon, the grim boatman, is persuaded by sight of the Golden Bough to ferry them across the water. Pacifying Cerberus, the hideous three-headed watchdog, on the other side, Aeneas and the Sibyl pass through his well guarded gate and along a pathway until it divides. To the left it leads down to a pit, twice as deep as heaven is high, where the wicked are being tortured and punished for their sins. To the right, it leads into the green fields of the Blessed. And there Aeneas finds his father. There too the old man points out to his son the souls of future Roman heroes, waiting to be born. Romulus is there, and all the clan who are to take their name from Iulus, son of Aeneas. Julius Caesar, the god, is there, Augustus Caesar, King of a new Golden Age, and last of all that youth of promise who was to die so young, that pitiable youth, Marcellus!

As Virgil read those last lines, Octavia fainted. Later, in appreciation of the lasting honor he had paid her beloved son, she gave the poet a handsome reward.

Augustus was deeply moved, and gratified by the entire poem. He was sure that when the next six books had rounded out the story, all that he had hoped for would be accomplished.

Virgil was not satisfied. Though he was to work on it for eleven years conscientiously and devotedly and finish the twelve books, its author was never to be satisfied with the Aeneid.

Perhaps it was because he was a lover of truth and he was forcing himself to preach of old gods in whom he no longer believed.

WHO WERE THE ROMAN GODS? And what was the old Roman religion which Augustus now wanted to revive? In the beginning, when the early Latins (or future Romans) had been but semi-savages wandering in the forest, just as all races of people must have been once upon a time, their gods were spirits of the forest. Ignorant and fearful, they felt a power in the strange world about them that they did not understand— a Great Spirit moving through their forest! Spirits were everywhere— in every crackling stick—in every stone, in the howling wolf, the wind, in lightning—thunder. Water—fire—trees—all held spirits that could harm them or perhaps be made to help them.

To force or bribe or persuade these spirits to be friendly they thought up strange taboos, magic formulas and made human sacrifice, trading one life to save others. And, as if binding themselves into a bargain, they called what they felt and did

RELIGIO

(from the word meaning to bind fast)

And that is what Religion is: "Man's desire and effort to bind himself fast and secure to the Great Spirit of the Universe."

MARS

MARS, it is believed, was the first spirit to be given a name by these wandering Latins. Every spring, when the winter was over, they set out to fight their neighbors for new fields to plow and plant. So, that first month of the new year, when they were filled with the spirit of war, became sacred to Mars, god of both war and seedtime.

When these wandering Latins finally settled down and became farmers, they found spirits of the countryside to worship—PAGAN spirits, for "country" is what the word "pagan" means.

JOVE was the sky spirit who would send the rain.

SATURN was the spirit of the plentiful harvest.

TERMINUS was the guardian of the boundary stones . . . and there were many others. It was a simple family religion, with no temple

JOVE   TERMINUS   SATURN

but the home, no priest but the family father. Above the hearth, the father's guiding spirit or GENIUS, represented by a small figure, stood between two other figures, guardian spirits of the well filled storehouse. These three, representing the spirit and welfare of the household, were its LARES and PENATES.

VESTA, spirit of the hearth fire, was the heart and center of the home, and was tended by the sisters of the family.

JANUS, the guardian of the house door was paid his due respect by the brothers, that he might keep out enemies and all evil spirits.

To all these spirits of the home and field—and they were many—the father saw that, with the help of his sons and daughters, the proper sacrifices were paid. No task, however small, was undertaken without recognizing the unseen spirit that was behind it. Their religion was part of everything they did.

In time, the Latins joined with another tribe, the Sabines, to form Rome, and the country spirits of both tribes were adopted by the little town or city. The city-state then became like an enlarged family. The king, as father of his people, became the high priest, or Pontifex Maximus. Lesser priests, called brothers, were appointed to assist him. Six Vestal Virgins, or sisters, tended the city's sacred hearth fire. And Janus guarded the city gate. Sacrifices became very formal, and were carried out strictly according to the letter of the law. The people themselves no longer took part in them, so the old spirit was gone.

The Etruscans, another tribe, then came down from the north, established themselves in Rome, and brought their gods to be accepted by the Romans, and worshipped by them.

VESTA   VENUS   JANUS

JUPITER

JUPITER was the greatest and best, the king and father of heaven. He took the place of the old sky spirit JOVE. The Etruscans built a temple for him on the Capitoline. In it they placed a huge image of him, looking like a man. That was the first time the Romans had ever imagined a god or spirit as having the shape of a human being.

Meanwhile, before Rome was founded, pioneers from Greece had landed in southern Italy and established colonies and towns. As Rome grew larger, the Romans began to trade with these Greek cities, to the south of them, and gradually one by one they adopted the Greek gods. They carried back their images and set them up in Rome, and in most cases gave them the names of the old Roman spirits with whom they seemed to correspond. In time all of the twelve Greek gods who were supposed to live on Mt. Olympus had arrived in Rome and been accepted. And all the myths which the imaginative Greeks had made up about these marvelous creatures had been learned by the practical minded Romans, who could never have invented them.

According to these myths, in the beginning of the world there had been only FATHER HEAVEN and MOTHER EARTH.

They had children—huge, forceful, gigantic creatures, called the TITANS.

Two of the Titans, CHRONUS (or Father Time) and Rhea were married. They had six children:

PLUTO   NEPTUNE   Juno   Ceres   Vesta   JUPITER

Chronus swallowed the first five of his offspring. So the mother fooled him when the sixth one was born.

She wrapped up a stone and gave it to her husband to swallow, and so saved the baby Jupiter.

Jupiter promptly gave his father a strong drink and made him up-swallow his five brothers and sisters. Then, after building himself a fortress on Mt. Olympus, Jupiter drove away old Chronus, his father, and set himself up as king of heaven, with his sister Juno as queen. Jupiter had five children:

MERCURY   MARS   Venus   Athena   HERCULES

JUPITER'S DAUGHTER VENUS WED THE TROJAN ANCHISES AND AENEAS WAS THEIR SON

IULUS HIS SON, WAS THE ANCESTOR OF JULIUS CAESAR

One day, Venus, this beautiful daughter of Jupiter, came down to earth, married a Trojan, and so became the mother of the hero Aeneas. Aeneas, in turn, was the early ancestor of Romulus, who became not only the first king of Rome, but also another Roman god.

Just how this came about—how Romulus came to be a god—is told by Livy in his history. For now, while Virgil was writing the Aeneid, Livy was at work on his famous history of Rome. He began it with his long loved story of Aeneas, even though he now knew it to be legend or myth, rather than actual history. Livy began where Virgil ended his sixth book. This is his story:

After Aeneas had finally landed in Italy at the mouth of the Tiber River, he found himself in territory inhabited by a tribe of natives known as Latins. The king received him, and he married the king's daughter, whereupon her former suitor declared war upon him. After many mighty battles, in which the Etruscans came to the help of the Latins and the Trojans, Aeneas was finally victorious. Upon the king's death, he inherited the Latin throne. After his own death his son became king and built a new capital for the Latins, which he called Alba Longa, the long white town. Eight generations later, Aeneas's seven times great-grandson was king in Alba Longa.

This king had a very evil and jealous brother who drove him from the throne, expelled his sons, and, hoping to wipe out the family, forced

AENEAS HAD ANOTHER DESCENDANT

THEIR CHILDREN WERE THE TWINS,

RHEA SILVA, WHO MARRIED **MARS**   **ROMULUS** AND **REMUS**

the king's daughter to become a Vestal Virgin. But Rhea surprised her uncle! She became the mother of twin sons whose father was Mars. In spite of their evil uncle's attempt to drown them, these famous twins, Romulus and Remus, grew up, drove away their uncle and put their grandfather back upon his throne.

Then they went northwest to found a new city for themselves on one of seven hills overlooking a yellow river.

There, on a date supposed to be April 22, 753 B.C., Rome was founded and Romulus became the first king.

After telling the principal events of his reign, which included stealing the women of the Sabine tribe because the Romans were in need of wives, Livy tells how Romulus, that first mythical king, came to be made a god.

"One day, a sudden storm arose," he said, "accompanied by violent thunder and lightning; the king (Romulus) was enveloped in a thick cloud which hid him from the eyes of the assembly, and was never more seen on earth. The senators who had been standing close to him said that he had been snatched away to heaven by a whirlwind. Then, a few setting the example, the whole multitude hailed Romulus as 'a god, the son of a god, the King and Father of the city of Rome.' "

After his death, Julius Caesar, another so-called descendent of Aeneas, had also been made a god.

Who now would be the next one?

165

GOLDEN EAGLES COME HOME

ONE WINTER DAY, early in the year 21 B.C., Augustus, munching with peculiar relish a small sour apple, and carrying in his left hand a letter from the king of Parthia, climbed to the small study at the top of his house, which was his favorite retreat. There he could consider this annoying matter of Parthia without interruption.

It was high time, Augustus thought, for Rome to settle accounts with that irritating and still undefeated rival. At the winter capital of Parthia on the Tigris River, there were still Roman standards—golden eagles of Rome, which had been there on display for thirty years. In all those thirty years, to Rome's shame and humiliation, no general had been able to recapture them. Julius Caesar had been killed before his campaign against Parthia could be carried out. Antony's attempt had met with miserable defeat.

Now the king of Parthia, it seemed, did not intend to fulfill his latest agreement. Augustus reread his evasive letter. Nine years ago, on his return from Egypt as master of the Roman world, Augustus had brought home with him a young son of the Parthian king, as a pledge of his father's good intentions. He had kept the boy in Rome for six years and then had sent him back to Parthia on condition that the king, his father, would send back the Roman standards. The handsome young oriental prince had long since arrived in Parthia, but the golden eagles had not yet appeared in Rome.

Instead Augustus had received this letter in which the king suggested that ransom be paid for the return of the Roman prisoners who had also been held captive in Parthia.

Augustus shoved the letter aside, and scraped his small teeth thoughtfully along the core of his apple.

Most people in Rome, he knew, expected him to take up the unfinished work of Caesar and Antony, undertake a campaign, annihilate Parthia and push on the boundary of the Roman empire to the border of India. But he himself had no such idea.

He was a statesman—not a warrior. He preferred to accomplish his purpose by peaceful means if it were possible.

In this case, Armenia, he believed, might prove the key to the situation. He drew toward him and bent over a map of that eastern part of the Roman world, sent him by one of the travelling geographers. There was Armenia, like Syria, lying on the border between the empires of Rome and Parthia. Herod, whose kingdom included much of Syria, and whose two sons by Mariamne were now also living in Rome, would remain a loyal subject. Augustus felt sure of that. But the king of Armenia was a slippery fellow, very likely to switch his allegiance to Parthia, if it seemed to his advantage.

Fortunately, he had been such a bad king that the Armenians themselves were dissatisfied and wanted a change of rulers. A brother of the king had been living in exile in Rome. The thing to do, Augustus decided, was to march into Armenia with an army and crown this brother king. That would show Parthia and any other possible friends of Parthia that Rome meant business, and that a promise made to Rome had better be kept.

He would go East himself, Augustus thought, and take Tiberius. Tiberius could lead the army into Armenia, while he stayed on the island of Samos and directed operations from there. Tiberius was now twenty-one, level headed, and quite capable of managing the whole affair. And it would please Livia, who would also go with them.

Then, with the thought of leaving Rome, it suddenly occurred to Augustus that there was no Agrippa now to leave in charge while he was gone. How he needed Agrippa! Rolling up the map, he reached for his pen and ink, carefully adjusted a piece of horn which acted as a brace to his limp forefinger, and wrote to Agrippa, asking him to return from the East at once, as soon as possible.

That night, seated on the edge of his bed, with his right shoe taken off first for luck, what he considered a very bright idea struck Augustus. It concerned Agrippa and his daughter Julia, who was now fast becoming much too merry a young widow. Upon his return to Rome Agrippa must divorce his wife and marry Julia! So Julia at nineteen became the wife of Agrippa, who was then forty-two, old enough to be her father. Augustus was highly pleased, and hoped upon his return from the East to find a baby grandson, another heir of his own flesh and blood to fill the vacant place left by Marcellus!

The trip to the East was a major success. All plans worked out and not a drop of blood was shed.

In Armenia Tiberius found that the bad king had been conveniently murdered by his own relatives. So all he had to do was to crown the new king and seat him on the vacant throne.

The Parthian king, properly alarmed by such speedy action in Armenia, hastened to fulfill his bargain with Rome. Tiberius went to Syria to receive the standards as well as the prisoners, who were all allowed to return home without ransom.

The winter spent on the island of Samos was most enjoyable. Envoys from all the neighboring kings came to pay respect to the emperor of Rome. Even from faraway India came one delegation, with friendly greetings to this powerful ruler of the West, and bringing curious gifts, among them a tiger, an animal unknown to the Romans.

In the summer of 19 B.C. the imperial family were on their journey home. Stopping in Athens on the way, they found Virgil, still working on his poem. Since he was not feeling well, Augustus urged him to return with them to Rome. The poet only reached Brundisium. There, on September 22, Virgil died, after making a request which was not to be granted. His request was that the Aeneid, on which he had spent eleven years, should be destroyed and never published.

The carrying of the standards into Rome was the signal for great rejoicing! They were placed in the Temple of Mars the Avenger. Rome's shame and disgrace were now wiped out. The golden eagles had returned from Parthia!

Augustus also, to his great joy, saw his first grandson who, as he hoped, had been born during his absence. This baby boy, the first son of Julia and Agrippa, was named Gaius.

OUT OF PERSIA

MANY OF THE ROMAN prisoners who had lived for thirty years in Parthia, were contented there, and had no desire to leave when they were given permission to do so. Many who did return found that the ways and gods of Rome now seemed very strange to them. They had much to tell of the more familiar customs of the Parthians.

They told of Mithra, the Persian Sun God, whom they had learned to worship. They described the fire altars, which were kept forever burning, and tended by the Persian priests or Magi. They told of miracles and wonders that they had seen performed by those celebrated wise men of the East, those Magi, whose fame had long since spread to Rome, and whose name and skill today live on in our word "magician."

ZOROASTER

On December 25th, about the time of the Saturnalia, when the Roman streets were thronged with merrymakers, those who had lived in the East thought of how the people there would be celebrating the birthday of the Sun God, Rejoicing in his yearly triumph over the darkness of winter, they would see in that victory promise of the final triumph of Light and Goodness over all Darkness and Evil. For that was the teaching of the old Persian prophet, Zoroaster, who had founded the wisdom of the Magi.

Zoroaster, one of the great prophets of the world, had lived and taught in Persia about 600 B.C. when Rome was but a village. In those early days, the Persians, like the Romans, had worshipped spirits in the world about them—the sky, the fire, the thunder, the earth and the sun, whom they called Mithra. But while the Romans had continued to add more and more gods, the Persians had been led by Zoroaster to the worship of One God, a Spirit of Light and Goodness, to whom he gave the name AHURA MAZDA.

All the world, said Zoroaster, was a battleground between Good and Evil, and every man born in this world must choose on which side

171

of the battle he would fight, that of Ahura Mazda and his angels of light, or that of Angra Mainyu, the Devil, and all darkness and evil.

Good Thoughts, Good Words, and Good Deeds were the weapons of those soldiers who would fight for the Good Spirit, and work was the way in which they served him best. A man's daily work was his prayer and every act of his life was part of his religion, as all living should be.

In the Avesta, the sacred Bible of the Persians, may still be read the teachings of Zoroaster. There it is told how the reward for a good life on earth comes to a man after he is dead:

"On the third night (after death) when the dawn appears and the sun is rising, the soul enters the way made by Time, open both to the wicked and the righteous. At the head of the Chinvad bridge, the holy bridge made by Mazda, they ask for their reward. Then the fiend carries off in bondage the souls of the wicked Devil worshippers who have lived in sin.

"But it seems to the soul of the faithful one as if a wind were blowing from regions of the south, a sweet-scented wind, sweeter than any other wind in the world.

"And it seems to him as if his own conscience were advancing to him in that wind, like a maiden fair, white armed and beautiful.

"And the soul of the faithful one addresses her, asking: 'What maid art thou, who art the fairest maid that I have ever seen?'

"And she, being his own conscience, answers him, 'O thou youth of good thoughts, good words, good deeds, of good religion, I am thy own conscience.'

"I was lovely and thou madest me still lovelier; I was fair and thou madest me still fairer through this good thought, this good speech and good deed of thine.'

"And so, following the maiden, the soul of the faithful one rises above the Chinvad bridge, through one Paradise after another until he enters the seventh heaven of endless Light, and into the presence of Ahura Mazda himself and his holy angels!"

Zoroaster had been killed by one of the jealous priests of the old religion, which he had tried to purify. Left without their leader, the Magi had let the religion slip from the high standards which Zoroaster had set. They had loaded it with mysterious rituals, added star lore learned from the Chaldean or native priests of Babylon, and brought back the worship of Mithra, the old god of the sun.

Mithra was now to be worshipped as the son of Ahura Mazda, who had been sent to earth to help win the war against Evil and save mankind from being overcome by Darkness and Death.

This is Mithra, shown by a sculptor, in the act of slaying the mystic bull, whose life-giving blood was supposed to have fertilized the good earth and caused it to bring forth fruit and grain.

Mithra seemed nearer and much more real to ordinary people than the pure Spirit, Ahura Mazda. They were eager to be baptized in the blood of the bull, become his soldier in the war against evil, and so earn life everlasting in Paradise, that seventh heaven of bliss. So Mithraism had grown popular and spread beyond the limits of Persia, into Armenia, Syria and all of Asia Minor. Now it was being carried to Rome.

Within the next hundred years Sun Worship would become the leading religion of the Romans. Only with difficulty would it be made to give way to the next and last oriental religion to be adopted by them. But as the fire on its altars died away, this Persian religion was to leave behind as a heritage to future generations their Christmas holiday and Sunday.

For in years to come, when the early Christian fathers were uncertain on which day of the year to celebrate the birth of Jesus, it was to be decided that it would be wise to use that day, long held sacred to the sun.

"And we do rightly so?" St. Chrysostom was to say. "The worshippers of Mithra call this December 25th the birthday of the sun, but is not our Lord the Sun of Righteousness?"

And so, a new way of life was to blend into an old, and the old be gradually forgotten. That is the way the world grows, one civilization after another, layer upon layer.

WE STILL CALL IT SUNDAY

SUNDAY, THE FIRST DAY of our week, also came to us in that same way from the religion of the Persians. One day out of every seven was kept sacred by them to the Sun. It was the Sun's day. And like the Sabbath of the Jews, it was a day of rest. On the Sun's day all work was forbidden—except what was necessary in the fields. For cultivating the good earth was, in itself, a sacred duty, as taught by the great prophet, Zoroaster.

The second day was the Moon's day.

And each of the other days was named for one of the planets, and so for one of the old Babylonian gods, since it was from the priests of Babylon that Persian Magi had learned the study of the stars.

This chart shows the old Babylonian names, and how they were to be changed into those of the Roman gods, and then into the gods of the Germans and Norsemen, names we still use today:

BABYLONIAN	ROMAN	GERMAN AND NORSE
————	Sol	Sun's Day
————	Luna	Moon's Day
Nergal	Mars	Tiu's Day
Nabu	Mercury	Wodan's Day
Marduk	Jupiter	Thor's Day
Ishtar	Venus	Freya's Day
Nibib	Saturn	Saturn's Day

Tiu, or Teut, who gave the name to Tuesday, was the great god of the Germans. He was the god of war, supposed to be the divine ancestor of the race, who were also known as Teutons.

Wodan, or Odin, whose name became shortened to Wednesday, was the sky or heaven father, who had but one eye, the sun. He was the lord of Valhalla, that heaven to which went all dead warriors, who were fortunate and brave enough to have been slain in battle.

Thor, whose name is in Thursday, was a powerful god of the storm, making himself heard in the roar and rumble of the thunder, while

175

lightning flew from his hammer as he pounded it against the clouds.

Freya, who was Odin's wife, the goddess of love and beauty, gave her name to Friday.

There was also a god named Frey, who was Freya's brother. Frey was the sunshine. He wielded his sword, shaped like a sunbeam, against the wicked Frost Giants, who kept those lands of the north locked in ice and snow for so many months. And Frey rode a boar with golden bristles, radiant as the sun.

On the year's shortest day, when the Persians were celebrating the victory of their sun god over the darkness of winter, the people of the far north were feasting and revelling in honor of Frey, who had defeated the Frost Giants again. Filling their drinking horns, they tossed off the foaming mead, and then feasted on a wild boar, carried in by the hunters with shouts and cheering, roasted whole, and carved by the bravest man.

But of these gods and this celebration the Romans, in these days of Augustus, knew nothing.

They were beyond the border line of civilization.

HEROD AND THE TEMPLE

AFTER HIS RETURN from Parthia, Tiberius was sent by Augustus northwest, to be governor of Gaul. Agrippa, no longer needed in Rome, went east to be the governor of Syria, taking Julia with him, and their small sons. For now they had two little boys—Gaius, who was between two and three, and the baby brother whose name was Lucius.

Upon his arrival in Syria, Agrippa was looking forward to seeing the many beautiful new buildings which had been erected by Herod in Palestine and also in Syria. They were said to rival in number and magnificence those which he and Augustus had been building in Rome. Especially beautiful, visitors said, was the new Temple in Jerusalem.

Herod had now been king of the Jews for twenty years. The outside world, admiring his accomplishments and ability, had begun to speak of him as Herod the "Great." But to the Jews he was "Herod the Terrible." Every year their hatred of him had increased.

Hoping to please them, he had built them the new Temple, one to be proud of, but they hated him none the less for it.

Their old Temple, which it replaced, had stood for five hundred years. Poor and dilapidated, it was the one which the exiles had built when they returned from Babylon. It had been stormed so many times since, that the walls were zigzagged with wide cracks and in places ready to crumble. But when Herod proposed to tear it down and build a new one on the site, fear and horror possessed the people.

They did not trust him. What if he planned to build some heathen temple on that sacred site! For years the Jews had been watching Herod erect buildings of which they did not approve—temples, baths, palaces, race tracks, all in the Greek and Roman style. In or near every city of his kingdom, there were now amphitheatres for games and chariot races and the degrading combats of gladiators. Just outside Jerusalem, Herod had built a theatre in honor of Augustus, where indecent plays about the immoral Greek gods and goddesses were staged. These tempted the young Jews, who were forbidden to attend. Within Jerusalem itself there had long been a gymnasium where athletes wrestled naked, in Greek fashion, shocking and forbidding to the pious Jews.

The princes and high priests, or Sadducees, accepted the foreign ways. But not the majority of the nation. They followed the strict teachings of the Pharisees. And they were horrified when Herod proposed to tear down their sacred Temple.

Augustus, himself, had advised Herod not to touch it. "If the old temple is not destroyed, do not destroy it," he had said. "If it is, do not rebuild it."

But Herod would not be turned aside from the one thing that he hoped might overcome the stubborn hatred of his people.

Solomon, the son of David, had built the first Temple. It had been magnificent and splendid. Herod was determined to build a temple even larger and more splendid than that old one of Solomon, which had been destroyed.

The outer court of his Temple would cover the entire hill, from one valley to the other. It would be surrounded by colonnades of white marble, roofed with sweet smelling cedar. It would have walls and ceilings of beaten gold, gates of gold, gates also of Corinthian bronze. And before the Most Holy Place would hang a curtain, woven in the most beautiful colors of earth, air, sea and fire. Thus Herod had planned his Temple.

And in the building of it he had taken utmost care to see that no hated Gentile, as the Jews had feared, was permitted to work on any sacred part of the Temple and so pollute it with his "unclean" hands.

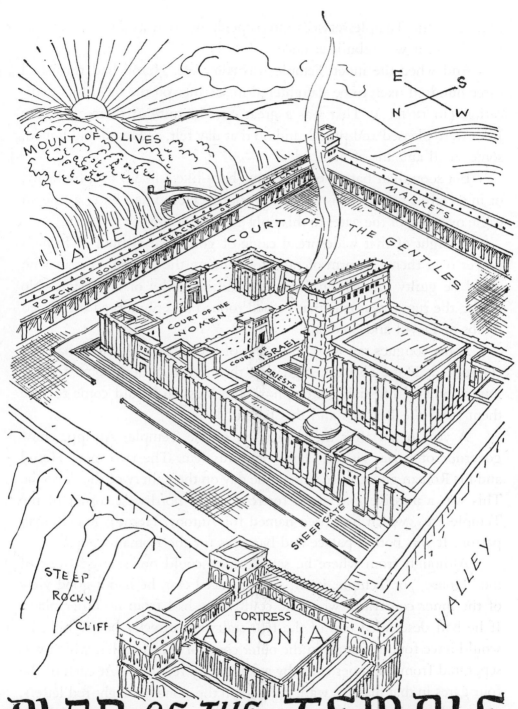

PLAN OF THE TEMPLE

Nor were the Temple services interrupted. As soon as any section was torn down, it was rebuilt at once.

And when the inner Temple was complete, Herod had furnished three hundred oxen to be slaughtered in sacrifice on the day of its dedication (in 18 B.C.). That was a great day. In spite of themselves, the Jews were pleased and proud, and on that day felt, as Herod had hoped, some small amount of gratitude.

But soon their hatred of him came back like a flood. For, foolishly, or in an effort to flatter his Roman overlords, Herod had hung a Roman eagle over one of the gates to this holy Temple of the Jews.

At sight of that widespread eagle of gold, that symbol of Rome's power over them, a storm of rage rose among the people. A man who could be guilty of such an outrage could be guilty of any crime. No doubt, the rumor was true that he had robbed and plundered the sacred tombs of David and Solomon.

Loose tongues ran wild with tales of crimes Herod had or had not committed. Hope also ran high that the time had now come for the long promised Messiah. Surely, now, the Messiah would come to save them from the Romans and this hateful king.

A year or so after the dedication of the Temple, Agrippa, now governor of Syria, visited Herod in Jerusalem. The two men, Herod and his Roman guest, were seated one day on the gallery of the Antonia. This was a massive gray stone fortress, at the northwest corner of the Temple area, which had been named for Antony, Herod's first Roman patron. It was both a palace and barracks for the Roman troops.

Although from where he sat Agrippa could not see the front of the "House," or Temple, itself, since it faced east, he had a good view of the inner courtyard, which he could have had from no other place. If he had descended one of the two stairways directly below him, he would have found himself in the outer court of the Gentiles, which was separated from the inner court by a wall, sixty feet high. At each of the four gates in that massive wall, painted on the stone in bright red letters, were glaring signs warning foreigners in three languages, Greek, Latin and Hebrew, not to enter the sacred court under penalty of death. Only Jews might climb the twelve steps and pass through the gates.

Directly inside, as Herod pointed out, was the court of the Jewish women. Only men, no women, were allowed to climb the next flight of steps and pass through the next gate into the court of Israel. That court of the men, as Agrippa saw, was separated by a low balustrade from the inmost court of the priests.

As Herod spoke, a sudden loud bleating mingled with his words. Looking down, Agrippa saw directly below them a new flock of sheep which were being driven in through a gate in the north wall, and were about to be admitted to the court of the priests.

Just inside that court, Herod explained, were tables for washing and skinning the animals, and hooks on which to hang the carcasses. An underground cistern furnished water to wash the livers before examining them for omens, and also to flush away the filth from the entrails, and the blood, though most of the blood was used to fertilize the gardens of the High Priest.

"And the meat," Agrippa added. "I suppose the High Priests also get all of that vast amount of meat?"

Herod nodded. "All except a fragment which, with the fat and a basin or two of blood, is burned on the altar."

Agrippa inquired about the House itself. Only priests, Herod told him, were allowed to enter. Even while it was being built, he himself had never gone inside. But in the first room were the golden lampstand and the altar of incense and twelve loaves of bread. Beyond that, separated by a veil, was the Holy of Holies, which no one but the High Priest ever entered, and he only on one day of each new year—the Day of the Atonement.

"And what was in that place?" Agrippa asked, knowing that the Jews made no "graven image" of their God.

Herod merely shook his head and shrugged his shoulders.

Then quite suddenly his dark eyes narrowed sharply, his body grew tense and he pointed with a trembling finger to a crowd below gesticulating and talking in wild excitement in the Temple courtyard.

"More of those troublemakers from Galilee," he hissed. "Prattling about the coming days of the Messiah, when they expect to rid themselves of you hated Romans—and of me!"

Herod's face now turned a sickly yellow. He whirled about sharply, as if fearing a hidden dagger might stab him in the back. Rising abruptly, he motioned to Agrippa, and, with hasty step, disappeared into the doorway of the Antonia—out of sight of the Temple which he had built—out of sight of those ungrateful people for whom he had built it, and who still hated him.

HILLEL, THE GREAT PHARISEE

IT WAS LATE AFTERNOON. The low sun threw a long shadow of the Temple across the altar and the inner courtyard. In the far porch of Solomon, to the east, from which one could look out over the valley to the still sunlit gardens on the Mount of Olives, the Pharisees were bringing to a close their endless arguments and discussions. The groups which had listened all day to learn from the various teachers how to carry out the sacred Law to the most minute detail were thinning out. Many were still confused on certain points.

Just what kind of knot might one tie on the Sabbath without com-

182

mitting a sin? And was it or was it not considered sinful to eat an egg which a hen had laid on the Sabbath day? But there was no time to hear more discussion about that now.

The markets were also closing in the wider portico to the south. Crates of pigeons and doves for sacrifice, spices, incense and jars of oil were put by for another day.

The money-changers were clearing their tables, and those who collected temple taxes were drawing the shirr strings in their bags of jingling coins.

On that late afternoon, a man with firm but unhurried step might have been seen making his way toward the western portico and the outer gate—a man of more than middle age, but one whose calm face and shining, alive eyes showed that he had found peace within himself. Over his turban hung a black and white prayer shawl, fringed about the edge, and fastened to his forehead was a small black box. For he was a Pharisee and a rabbi, one of the teachers of Israel, and one of the truly great ones. His name was Hillel.

Passing the Hall of Hewn Stone, behind the Temple, where the Sanhedrin met, that Court of which he was a member, Hillel crossed the viaduct which bridged the deep valley separating the Mount of the Temple from the Mount of Zion and the upper City. And there on a stone step at the foot of the street, he saw a small boy waiting for him. At sight of his grandfather, the little boy ran to meet him, eager to tell how much of the Torah, or Law of Moses, he had memorized that day, for he, too, was to become a rabbi. He was Gamaliel, the future teacher of the Apostle Paul.

"Today, I could recite more than any other boy in the synagogue," he began, then quickly stopped, and corrected himself. "I know, I know," he said. "One should learn and love the Torah, but not wear his learning proudly like a crown."

The rabbi nodded gently, and then bidding the child recite what he had learned, slipped the boy's small hand in his, and together the two of them, the man with his head bent to listen, the small boy with

183

his piping voice, climbed the crooked street, turning under an archway, mingled with the crowd and disappeared.

The next morning found Hillel again at the Temple teaching a circle of eager pupils how to apply the ancient Law of Moses to their modern life.

One must study the Torah constantly, he told them, to learn the will of God. An ignorant man can never be truly righteous.

"Do not say, 'I shall study when I have free time from other work' because," he added with a smile, "that time will never come."

Patiently he taught and answered the questions of his pupils until the sun was low and it was late afternoon again. Again as he crossed the bridge over the valley to the west, the small grandson was waiting for him at the foot of the street of steps. A woodcutter with a bundle of faggots passed them as, hand in hand, they started up the hill. Seeing him, the boy begged Hillel to tell again the story of his early life, when he too, had been very poor and earned his living by cutting wood. So this time as they turned the corner and passed out of sight, it was the man who was talking, while the small boy's head was turned up eagerly to listen.

According to stories, or legends which are told of him, Hillel had been born in Babylon. Perhaps his ancestors had been among those ancient captives who, like the Romans of this later day, had chosen not to return after the Exile. His older brother was a merchant, and took care of young Hillel while he went to school in his native city. But as soon as he had learned all that the Jewish schools in Babylon could teach him, he set out for Jerusalem in order to study further. There, to earn his food and pay his teacher, he had been obliged to become a wood-cutter.

One winter day he had failed to earn the necessary fee to be admitted to the school. He could not bear to miss the lesson, so he climbed up on the flat top of the house, and tried to listen through the window in the roof. It was snowing. He lay quiet, heeding only what was going on below, until suddenly he found that he was covered with snow. His feet and legs were frozen. Fortunately the teacher had seen his shadow from inside and rescued him. From then on, he had been allowed to attend school without pay.

All the years of his life, Hillel had been studying the Law of Moses, or the Torah, seeking to extract every kernel of truth to be found in it. But he had never confused trivial details with what was truly important, or placed the letter of the Law above the spirit.

One day a Roman, interested in the religion of the Jews, which taught righteousness and justice, but puzzled by the endless number of Laws and rules that it seemed necessary to observe, approached Hillel.

"I am ready to accept your religion," he said, "provided that you can tell it to me simply, and in as short a time, let's say, as I can stand on one foot."

Perhaps he expected to be turned away rudely as he had been by Shammai, another prominent but less broadminded rabbi of the day, whose studies had made him sharp and irritable and intolerant of all foreigners. If so, the Roman must have been surprised, and converted, no doubt, by the answer he received.

Simply and quietly Hillel replied: "Our religion can be put into one sentence:

WHAT IS HATEFUL TO THYSELF, DO NOT UNTO THY NEIGHBOR. That is the whole of the Law; the rest is but explanation."

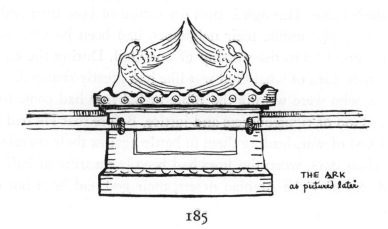

THE ARK
as pictured later

THE LAW

THE LAW OF MOSES

THE TORAH, OR LAW OF MOSES, the law which the Pharisees studied day and night, was the only law which the Jews had ever had. It is found in the first five books of the Bible. This sacred book was already old when Virgil began writing the Aeneid. Most of this ancient tradition was put into written form about four or five hundred years before—or shortly after that unhappy time when the Jews had been taken to exile in Babylon.

Fearful that in that strange land the history of their race and all of its past glory might be forgotten, they had gathered together what remained of old histories written several hundred years earlier, as well as all of the myths, legends, stories, songs and psalms which had been handed down by word of mouth for generations. And these formed their Bible. Through it runs the record of how time and again the Jewish people, unlike their neighbors, had been brought back by their great prophets to the worship of one God. During the centuries, however, their idea of what God was like had greatly changed.

Those who were writing the Bible in Babylon had come to think of Him as God of righteousness and justice. Before that He had been a vengeful god of war, leading them to battle against their enemies. And in the earliest days, when the Jews had been but a tribe of half-savage shepherds roaming the Arabian desert, their god had been but one of

186

the many strange spirits which seemed to people the desert world about them. Then, as they had led their herds of sheep and goats from one oasis to another, they made bloody sacrifices to the chosen god of their tribe for his protection, burning on the altar their first-born children, as later they were to offer up each first-born lamb and goat.

In time these ragged shepherds pushed north out of the barren desert into the fertile valley of the Babylonians, and later from there on into Palestine, the land of the Phoenicians, or Canaanites.

Fearing that their desert god would have no power in this land of green pastures and villages, they adopted the local gods of the Canaanites. Later driven by famine into Egypt, they accepted the gods of the Egyptians. There in Egypt they remained, oppressed by the Pharaohs until rescued by Moses, their first great prophet and leader.

Leading his people out of Egypt back into the desert, Moses brought them to the worship of one God whose name was Jahveh "the thunderer," whose dwelling place was the volcano Mt. Sinai, and whose power could be seen in the pillar of flame by night and in a pillar of cloud by day. Allowing them to make no idols or images of their God, Moses had them build an ark in which the spirit of Jahveh might be carried with them over the desert, as they journeyed on toward Canaan.

This is the story of those earliest days of the Jews up to the death of Moses as told in the first five books of the Bible: GENESIS, EXODUS, LEVITICUS, NUMBERS, DEUTERONOMY.

בָּרוּךְ יְיָ

IN THE BEGINNING the Spirit of God was waving over the face of the waters and heaven and earth were created. And on the sixth day God created man in his own image. Of the dust from the ground he formed him, and breathed into his nostrils the breath of life and man

187

became a living being. And on the seventh day God rested from his work. And thus he blessed the seventh day and sanctified it.

Then the Lord God planted a garden in Eden, to the eastward and there he put Adam, the man whom he had formed. And while Adam slept, he took one of his ribs and from it he made a wife and helpmate for him. Now Eve, the woman, beguiled by the serpent, ate of the forbidden fruit of the tree of life which stood in the midst of the garden, and gave also unto her husband. And because he had forbidden them to eat of this tree, God sent Adam forth from the Garden of Eden, and condemned him to till the ground, until he should return to the dust from which he had been taken.

And in time Eve bore sons to Adam, Abel and Cain. Abel was a keeper of sheep, but Cain was a tiller of the ground. And Cain rose up against his brother Abel and slew him. Therefore the Lord sent Cain forth to be a fugitive and vagabond on the earth forever.

And it came to pass when men began to multiply and God saw that the wickedness of man was great, He said, I will bring a flood upon the earth and destroy both man and beast whom I have created. But Noah built an ark as God commanded him, and in went his sons and his wife and his son's wives, and of every living thing there went in two by two. And the rain fell upon the earth forty days and forty nights and all in whose nostrils was the breath of life died. And when the waters were abated and the earth dried, Noah went forth out of the ark. And the Lord said, never again will I smite the earth as I have done. And God blessed Noah and his sons, (Shem, Ham, and Japeth), and said unto them, be fruitful and multiply, and of them was the whole earth overspread.

And after many generations, from Shem was descended Abram. And Abram went forth with his father from the land of his birth in Ur of the Chaldees into the land of Canaan. Now the Lord said unto Abraham, Get thee out of thy country and from thy father's house unto the land that I will show thee, and I will make of thee a great nation. Walk before me and be thou perfect, and I will give unto thee and thy seed after thee all the land of Canaan for an everlasting possession. And Abraham did as the Lord commanded. And when he was a hundred years old, a son Isaac was born to him.

Isaac had twin sons, Esau, who was red and hairy all over, a skillful hunter—a man of the field, and Jacob, who was a quiet man, dwelling in tents. And when he was grown, the Lord appeared unto Jacob and said unto him, Thy name shall not be called any more Jacob, but ISRAEL shall be thy name.

Now the sons of Israel, or Jacob, were twelve, but he loved Joseph more than all of them, and he made him a coat of many colors. And therefore his brothers hated Joseph. And it came to pass when they went to feed their father's flock, and Joseph came unto them, that they stript him of his coat, and sold him for twenty pieces of silver to merchantmen, on the way to Egypt.

And in Egypt, Potiphar, an officer of Pharaoh, bought Joseph and made him overseer over his house and all that he had. And for seven plenteous years, Joseph gathered and stored up food in the cities. And when seven years of want followed, there was famine in all lands but in the land of Egypt. And Jacob, seeing that there was corn in Egypt, sent Joseph's brothers down to buy. And Joseph knew his brethren, but they knew him not. And he said, I am Joseph your brother, whom ye sold in Egypt. Haste ye, go up to my father, and bring him down unto me, and thou shalt dwell near unto me, and I will nourish thee. And Jacob and all his seed brought he with him into Egypt. And Joseph dwelt and died in Egypt, he and his father's house.

And the children of Israel multiplied and the land was filled with them. Now there arose a new King over Egypt, and said, Behold the people of Israel are more and mightier than we. Therefore he set over them task masters and made their lives bitter with hard labor in mortar and in brick. And he gave instructions that every man child born to a Hebrew mother should be killed.

Now the wife of a man of the house of Levi bore a son. And when she could no longer hide him, she made for him an ark of bulrushes and laid it on flags by the river's brink. And the daughter of Pharaoh came down to wash at the river. And when she saw the child, she had compassion on him, and he became her son. And she called his name MOSES.

And it came to pass when Moses was grown up, and he saw an Egyptian smiting a Jew, that he smote the Egyptian and hid him in the sand. Now when Pharaoh heard this, he sought to slay Moses but Moses fled and dwelt in the land of Midian. And he led the flock of his father-in-law back of the desert unto Horeb, the mountain of God. And God called to him out of the midst of the burning bush, and said I am the God of Abraham, of Isaac and of Jacob. I am that I am. I will send thee unto Pharaoh, that thou mayest bring forth my people, the children of Israel, out of Egypt.

And when the time came, the Lord spoke to Moses and Aaron, his brother, saying, In the tenth day of this month, let every man of the congregation of Israel take a lamb for each house. They shall kill it in the evening. And they shall take of the blood, and strew it on the side posts and upper doorpost of the houses. And they shall eat of the flesh in that night, roast with fire, and unleavened bread, and with bitter herbs they shall eat it. It is the Lord's PASSOVER. For I will pass through the land of Egypt this night, and will smite all the first-born in the land of Egypt, and when I see the blood, I will pass over you, and the plague shall not destroy you. And this day shall be unto you for a memorial; and ye shall keep it a feast to the Lord forever.

And when Pharaoh had let the people go, God led them about through the wilderness of the Red Sea. And the Lord went before them by day in a pillar of cloud and by night in a pillar of fire. And the heart of Pharaoh turned and he made ready and took all the chariots of Egypt and pursued after the children of Israel. And the Lord said unto Moses, lift up thy rod, and stretch out thy hand over the sea and divide it. And the children of Israel went on dry land through the midst of the Red Sea. And the Egyptians pursued and went in after them and the sea returned to its strength and of the host of Pharaoh there remained not one of them.

In the third month when the children of Israel were gone forth out of the land of Egypt, they came to the wilderness of Sinai, and there camped before the mount. And the Lord came down upon Mount Sinai, and called Moses, and Moses went up, and was there with the Lord forty days and forty nights. And the Lord said unto Moses, Hew thee two tablets of stone.

And he wrote upon them the words of the TEN COMMANDMENTS: Which God spoke, saying:

  I. I am the Lord thy God, Thou shalt have no other gods before me.
  II. Thou shalt not make unto thee any graven image.
  III. Thou shalt not take the name of the Lord thy God in vain.
  IV. Remember the sabbath-day to keep it holy.
  V. Honor thy father and thy mother.
  VI. Thou shalt not kill.
  VII. Thou shalt not commit adultery.
  VIII. Thou shalt not steal.
  IX. Thou shalt not bear false witness against thy neighbor.
  X. Thou shalt not covet thy neighbor's house or anything that is thy neighbor's.

(Different versions vary slightly as to wording and numbering).

The books of Leviticus, Numbers and Deuteronomy are the record of many more laws given to the people of Israel and of their troubles, as they struggled on to the edge of the Promised Land.

And there Moses went up from the plains of Moab, unto Mount Nebo, that is over against Jericho. And the Lord said to him, This is Canaan. This is the land which I swore unto Abraham, unto Isaac, unto Jacob. I have caused thee to see it with thine eyes, but thou shalt not go over thither. So Moses died there in the land of Moab: but no man knoweth of his sepulchre unto this day.

And there hath not arisen a prophet since in Israel like unto MOSES, whom the Lord knew face to face.

DIVUS

AUGUSTUS, THE GOD

AUGUST, 12 B.C., an altar was erected to Augustus Caesar in Gaul, and he was made a god of the Roman Empire. That was the most outstanding event of the year, although it was an eventful twelve months for the entire family. In the first place Agrippa died. Julia was again a widow. And now she had four children, and a fifth was soon to be born. Gaius and Lucius, the two small boys, who were now about six and eight, had been adopted by their grandfather, as his heirs. He adored them, and was also fond of their little sisters, Julia and Agrippina. As for Julia herself—she was still young and lively, and, Augustus thought, needed another husband to look after her.

Casting about for a suitable third son-in-law, Augustus chose his elder step-son. This was a blow to Tiberius. He had never cared for Julia. He was already married, truly in love with his wife, and most reluctant to divorce her. But he was obliged to comply with the request of Augustus.

Tiberius and Julia were wed. The marriage was to go fairly well for a short time, but Tiberius was too sober and silent for the lively Julia. While he was away in one of the provinces, she found wild companions and more exciting lovers, and began to seek pleasure in ways that were eventually to lead her to a tragic end.

Drusus, Livia's second son, the younger brother of Tiberius, was now married to Antonia, the gentle daughter of Octavia and Antony. Ruddy and full of enthusiasm as ever, he came back for his brother's wedding from the border of Germany. His boyhood dream of crossing the Rhine into German territory had now been realized. Each year, for the past three years, Drusus had led an expedition into the deep German forests. He had also been in charge of building fortifications along the Rhine, as a protection against the German tribes, who had again invaded Gaul and crucified Roman citizens. Pushing through the morasses and marches in the north, he had dug a canal from the Rhine through the Zuyder Zee into the North Sea.

Now this year of 12 B.C. Drusus was made governor of Gaul, and he and Antonia went to live in Lyons, which was the Roman capital. It was an old town of the Gauls, and a great meeting place of the tribes. There, every spring, the Druid priests had held court, judging and settling all disputes that had arisen among the people, divining the will of the gods, and offering sacrifices.

The power of the Druids had now been broken; their rule replaced by Roman law, and those Gauls who had become Roman citizens forbidden to take part in the old sacrifices. As a substitute, the Gauls were now given a new god to worship—Augustus, the Emperor of Rome—Augustus Divus. Divus is the Latin word meaning god-like, or divine.

The first altar to him was built by Drusus at Lyons. On the first day of August, 12 B.C., it was solemnly unveiled. Delegates from sixty of the old Gallic tribes were present for the ceremony. A priest was ordained "High Priest of Rome and Augustus." And from then on, on the first of August, each year pilgrims were to come from everywhere in Gaul to worship at that altar.

Similar altars were also erected in many other towns of Gaul. On one of them the following inscription was engraved:

"The people of [the city] have dedicated this altar to the divine Augustus, and have vowed him an annual feast forever. May this be to the honor and glory of the emperor Caesar Augustus, son of the divine Julius, father of our country, sovereign pontiff, and to the honor and glory of his wife and children and of the Senate and the Roman people and of [this town] which dedicates and devotes itself forever to the worship of his divinity."

This declaring Augustus a god did not mean that there was any thought of him as God, the creator of the universe. Making him a "god" was more like making him a saint in the Roman Catholic Church of today. He was patron saint of the Roman empire.

The change grew more or less reasonably out of the old Roman religion. When the death of the former High Priest left that office vacant, Augustus had become Pontifex Maximus. There had always been a law that the Pontifex Maximus must live in a public residence. But Augustus did not care to move into the one provided for the other High Priests, so he presented part of his palace to the state, that it might be considered a public residence.

His hearth fire was then looked upon as a public hearth fire, as sacred and important as the one in the temple of Vesta. His Lares and Penates also became those of the state. And as in every Roman household, the Genius, or guiding spirit of the family father had been worshipped, it did not seem strange for the Genius of Augustus to be worshipped as the guiding spirit of the empire.

Although Augustus allowed no altars to be built to him in the city of Rome, altars for his worship were built in all the army camps and also in all the provinces of the East, where it was a long established custom to bow down before kings and rulers, as being gods on earth.

In all his world, one people only refused to worship at his altars. They were the Jews. They would pray *for* him if they must but they would not pray *to* him. Proud and intense in their obedience to the law of Moses, they worshipped but one God, Javeh, God of their nation, and they would have "no other gods before him."

Everywhere else, in every great city of his empire, temples and shrines were erected for his worship. Natives of every subject land from the Euphrates River to the Rhine added him to their other gods and offered prayers to him, and in this one act the empire was united.

Thus it was that Augustus Caesar, supreme magistrate of the Roman Empire and its first emperor, also became its god—Augustus, Divus.

IV

DIVUS

PEOPLE WHO WERE LIVING

IN

EGYPT

THE WORLD'S TALLEST
LIGHTHOUSE STOOD
IN THE HARBOR OF
ALEXANDRIA,

STRABO

THE GEOGRAPHER WAS
SIGHT SEEING IN EGYPT
WITH THE ROMAN GOVERNOR,

AUGUSTUS HAD TWO
ANCIENT OBELISKS
SHIPPED TO ROME,

PHILO-JUDAEUS

A BOY IN ALEXANDRIA WAS
STUDYING BOTH THE TORAH
AND THE GREEK PHILOSOPHERS

IN

AMERICA

IN

CHINA

THEY LOOKED BACK TO
ITZAMNA
AN EARLY HERO

9 YEAR OLD
PING-TI

THEIR DATES
WERE CARVED ON STONES,

THE MAYANS WERE BUILDING THEIR
PYRAMID TEMPLES,

EMPEROR OF CHINA I A.D
WAS THE LAST OF THE
EARLY HAN DYNASTY
WHICH BEGAN IN 202 B.C

AND SOME EVENTS THAT TOOK

WHEN AUGUSTUS WAS A GOD

4 B.C.

HEROD DIED

THERE WAS REBELLION OF THE JEWS AGAINST THE ROMANS IN BOTH JUDAEA AND GALILEE

6 B.C.

JUPITER SATURN AND MARS WERE CLOSE TOGETHER AND SHONE LIKE ONE LARGE STAR

JESUS

OF NAZARETH WAS BORN,

TIBERIUS

WAS MARRIED TO JULIA, BUT LEFT ROME TO LIVE ALONE IN EXILE ON THE ISLAND OF RHODES,

8 B.C.

JUNONALIS
JULEUS
SEXTILIS
AUGUSTUS
SEPTEMBER

TO HONOR AUGUSTUS THE ROMAN SENATE RENAMED THE MONTH OF

AUGUST

VARUS

ROMAN GOVERNOR OF SYRIA, PUT DOWN THE REBELLION, BURNED THE CITY OF SEPPHORIS AND CRUCIFIED TWO THOUSAND,

A DECREE

"WENT OUT FROM CAESAR AUGUSTUS THAT ALL THE WORLD SHOULD BE TAXED"

PLACE BETWEEN 12 B.C. AND 1 A.D.

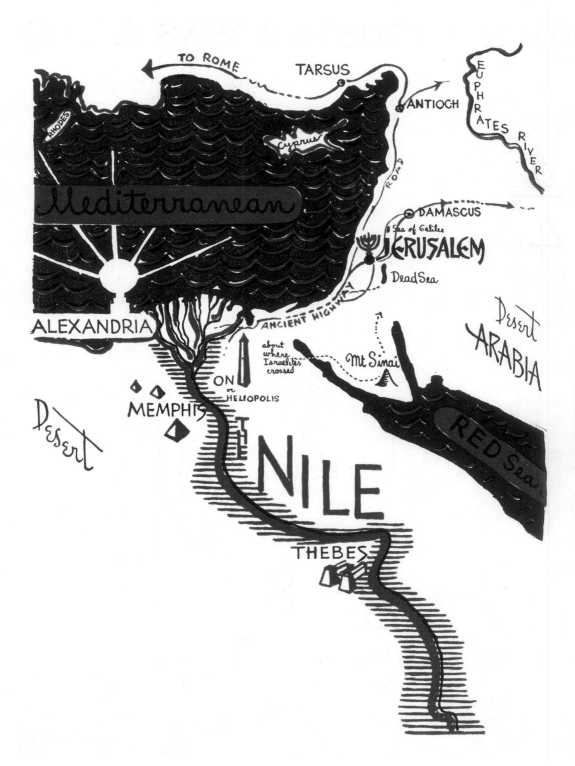

A ROMAN PHARAOH

HAIL NOW to Augustus Caesar, Pharaoh and God of Egypt. Behold him like an ancient Pharaoh, holding in his hand an image of Maat, the symbol of truth and justice and wearing the head-dress of Horus, god of the rising sun. For Egypt now belonged to Rome, and as emperor of Rome, Augustus Caesar was also ruler or "pharaoh" of Egypt.

In this August of 12 B.C., just eighteen years had passed since that morning in another August when Cleopatra had fled in terror to her

199

tomb near the temple of Isis, Antony had died in her arms and young Octavian had entered Alexandria conqueror of Egypt and master of the Roman world.

What could be more natural, then, than for Egypt's new ruler to be regarded as a god, just as Egypt's pharaohs had always been, and also pictured as Horus, god of the rising sun? Here, as Horus, Augustus is seen adoring the holy mother Isis, the goddess with whom Cleopatra had been identified. Both belong to Egypt's most sacred myth, the strange but beautiful story of Osiris, the most beloved god of the Egyptian people, one who had died and risen to new life again.

Once, it seemed, the god Osiris had lived and ruled in Egypt as a king, a good king, fair and just, and beautiful as a palm tree, or as fields of wheat growing by the Nile. Isis, his wife, was also fair and beautiful. But he had a wicked brother by the name of Set who was all darkness and evil. Set plotted against his good brother and killed him, just as the darkness of winter kills the green things of this earth. And Set put the body of Osiris in a coffin and threw it into the Nile, and it floated off to sea. Isis, the loving wife of Osiris, was heartbroken. Weeping bitterly, she set forth and searched the world over for the dead body of her lord. At last on the shore of Syria she found the coffin cast up by the waves, and from it a small green tree was growing.

Isis carried the coffin back to Egypt and hid it. But Set, the wicked one, found the dead body of Osiris and hacked it into fourteen pieces, and scattered them hither and yon. Over valley and desert, the faithful Isis searched again, until she had found the pieces and buried them.

And then Horus was born—her child and son of the dead Osiris. And Isis hid her new born son in the rushes by the Nile. There she raised him, nursing him tenderly while he was weak and feeble like the rays of the winter sun, until he was strong enough to contend with his wicked uncle. Then, grown to young manhood, Horus rose in all his power and conquered the evil Set, just as the warm spring sun rising above the rushes of the Nile conquered the darkness of winter. And as the warm rays of the spring sun also brought forth to new life the vegetation of the earth, so also Horus raised his father Osiris from the winter of death.

And Osiris, the good king, lived again. But from then on, he ruled and judged, not on earth, but in the Kingdom of the Dead which lay somewhere beneath that earth which seemed to hold within it the seeds of eternal life. There in that shadowy land below the horizon, into which the sun sank each night and rose again each morning, the souls of the dead came before Osiris to be judged.

For death must come to all men. But if, like Osiris, they have been good and true in their life on earth, they too will pass through death into a new life.

On the next page is a judgment scene from the Egyptian Book of the Dead.

Seated at the left is Osiris, Lord of Truth. At the far right is the man who has just died and whose soul is being judged.

"Hail to thee, great god, Lord of Truth!" he is saying. "I have come to thee my Lord, led hither in order to see thy beauty. Behold, I bring to thee righteousness!"

Meanwhile in a jar on the scales, his soul is being balanced against the image of Maat, the goddess of truth and justice, who herself stands facing him as he enters the judgment hall. Horus with his falcon head is there beneath the scale. The jackal-headed god is the god of embalming who superintends the great care given to preserve the body of the dead. Thoth, the god with the ibis head, is writing down the record of the man's life on earth.

There were forty-two commandments which a truly righteous Egyptian must keep, and to these the dead man now swears to the assembled gods that he has been true.

"I have not done evil in place of truth. I allowed no one to hunger. I caused no one to weep. I did not murder. I did not commit adultery. I did not steal. I did not revile the King. I did not blaspheme the god. I gave bread to the hungry, water to the thirsty, clothing to the naked, and a ferry to him who was without a boat. I made divine offerings to

the gods, and food offerings to the dead. Save me, protect me, ye gods who are here in the Hall of Truth. Enter no complaint against me before the great god—Osiris."

How old this sacred story of Osiris may be, no one knows. It must have been told long before the Egyptians began to write, for originally Osiris was the Nile. Her life-giving Nile and her glorious sun were Egypt's earliest gods.

Back in that dim past when the Egyptians had been only hunters roaming and paddling through the reedy marshes, the sun that rose each day, warm and glorious above the river, had seemed to them to be all-powerful, and they took it for a god. Their word for sun was RA. And they imagined RA as a hunter, like themselves, paddling himself across the river of Heaven in a boat of reeds.

In time these wandering Egyptian hunters settled down and began to cultivate the fields of wheat and barley in the valley of the Nile. Then the great river which flooded and enriched the earth at the beginning

of each season seemed also to have the power of a god. Life came from the Nile and from the Sun. Together they made the bare fields of winter green with new life again.

Now each morning as they saw the sun RA rising up from the horizon over their level fields of grain, the Egyptian farmers thought of him as a golden falcon or hawk, soaring with widespread wings on his daily flight across the heavens. So they began to picture RA with wings, then as a falcon, or as a man with the head of a falcon, and to call him Ra-Hor-Akt, sun of the horizon, or merely Horus, god of the rising sun.

The earliest pharaohs took the hawk of Horus as their symbol. And the principal festival in early times was the worship of Horus. It was centered in an old city known as On. There stood a great Temple to the Sun. Before that temple Joseph and his brethren and their father, Jacob, must have walked, for it was there in On that Joseph served as overseer in the house of the pharaoh, and took as his wife a daughter of one of the priests of the Temple. It was there, too, that young Moses learned the wisdom of the Egyptians, long before he led his people out of Egypt and gave them the ten commandments.

About one hundred years before Moses was born, one of the Pharaohs set up before the Temple to the Sun tall obelisks of reddish granite, long pointed shafts of stone, resembling the rays of sunlight. Now that the Romans had taken over Egypt, two of these obelisks had been moved away from the old city of the Sun, where they had stood for centuries. Roman engineers had hauled them up the Nile to Alexandria. And by order of Augustus Caesar they had been erected before the entrance to his newly completed palace or temple—one which Cleopatra had started to build for Antony.

Today, although those two old obelisks belong to a far earlier age than that of Cleopatra, we call them "Cleopatra's Needles," for they are still standing today—but not in Egypt. Less than one hundred years ago, they were moved from Alexandria, and one was taken to London, and one to Central Park in New York City.

two   obelisks   of   granite

Those two old obelisks—how many centuries have passed over them!

And yet for centuries before they were ever erected, when the people of Europe were in the Stone Age, and the Jews were but half savage shepherds of the desert, the Egyptians had been highly civilized. They had commandments to teach justice, good will and peaceful living. They were also telling a parable of eternal life, believing that, in the end, life and truth and goodness must triumph over evil and death.

It was there too in ancient Egypt that another great truth was first conceived and taught—the idea of One God.

AKH·EN·ATON

REMEMBER AKHENATON

BUT WHO WAS AKHENATON? A young Pharaoh of Egypt, who lived more than 1300 years before these days of Augustus. A frail, delicate young Pharaoh, with an ugly body, but a shining spirit, he stands alone, quite alone, in the history of the world. For he was the first man to come upon the truth that God is One—one single Spirit—the life-giving spirit of the entire Universe.

Akhenaton was born in 1388 B.C. And he was born too soon. Few, if any, of his followers in Egypt could understand his teaching. Like children in kindergarten trying to learn higher mathematics, they were not ready for it. It was beyond them. So when Akhenaton died, there was no one to carry it on.

Egypt went backward instead of forward, until now, thirteen centuries later, visitors who came to Egypt were very scornful of the Egyptian religion, and shocked by what they saw of it. Animal worship, they called it. And so it was, among the masses of the people. In the beginning, various animals, like the hawk, had been taken as symbols of a tribe or an idea, just as today, for instance, the bear and the tiger represent ball teams, and the bee is a symbol of "busy-ness." But in time, the idea and the symbol got separated. The idea was forgotten, and only the symbol was left—to be worshipped.

Animals of all kinds were held sacred in Egypt. The bull, the beetle, the cat, the ibis, the eagle, the frog, sheep, dogs, monkeys—even the hippopotamus and the crocodile. Some were kept in temples and tended by priests, and when they died their bodies were carefully embalmed and laid in cemeteries.

One visitor to Egypt was a Greek from Asia Minor, by the name of STRABO, who was soon to begin writing his famous geography. Strabo took a trip up the Nile with his friend the Roman governor of Alexandria; they stopped off at the town of the sacred crocodile.

"Our host," he said, "who was one of the officials, went with us to the lake (where the crocodile was kept) carrying from dinner a kind of cookie and some roasted meat and a pitcher of wine mixed with honey. We found the animal lying on the edge of the lake. When the priests went up to it, some of them opened its mouth, and another put in the cake, the meat, and then poured down the honey mixture" and the crocodile swam away.

At Memphis, the oldest capital of Egypt, the two travellers, Strabo and his friend, were taken to view the sacred bull known as Apis. He was kept in a sanctuary, but at a certain hour each day his priests led him out into the court so that the people might gaze upon him, and then led him back into his stall.

The bull was black, and had a square white spot on his forehead and other marks which were taken as proof that he contained the soul of Osiris! When the bull died, he would be embalmed and his mummy placed in a splendid marble mausoleum. All Egypt would go into mourning until a new bull calf had been found and declared by the priests to have the proper markings to show that the soul of Osiris had now entered his body.

Strabo and the Roman governor also visited Thebes, the last city to be used as a cipital by the native Pharaohs, and the birthplace of Akhenaton. There the visitors saw temples to Amen, the god of Thebes. These had been built by the same Pharaoh who had erected those obelisks of granite in the city of the Sun, which had now been shipped to Alexandria. His great-great-grandson was that young Pharaoh Akhenaton.

Originally, Akhenaton had not been his name. As a small boy, he had been called Amen-hotep, meaning "one in whom the God Amen was satisfied." At the age of twelve the boy, who was very delicate, had been married to a little girl of nine or ten, by the name of Nefertiti. When he was thirteen, he became the pharaoh, and also a priest in the Temple of the Sun God, Amen-Ra. For Amen, the tribal god of Thebes, had then been promoted to the higher position of the sun god of all

Egypt and was spoken of as Amen-Ra. The priests of Amen-Ra were rich and powerful, but they were worldly and corrupt, and this young pharaoh-priest, who loved truth and beauty above all things, became disgusted with them and with their god, Amen, and with all the other gods of Egypt.

As he studied the sun and pondered and thought about it, it came to this young Egyptian that just as there was only one sun in the world, there could be but one God! And as the sun did not shine upon any one land alone, but warmed and lighted the whole world, so God must not belong to any one race or nation.

A life-giving spirit, radiant, like the sun, he belonged equally to all people and creatures everywhere.

The young Pharaoh spoke of God as ATON, and changed his own name to AKH-EN-ATON, "beloved of Aton." This is from one of the beautiful psalms Akhenaton wrote in praise of God.

O living Aton, Beginning of Life!
Thy dawning is beautiful on the horizon of heaven.
Thou fillest every land with thy beauty; thou bindest them
With Thy love. How manifold are Thy works!
O thou sole God, whose power no other possesseth.
Thou didst create the earth according to thy desire.
Men and all cattle, large and small.
All that go upon their feet—all that fly with wings.
The foreign countries of Syria and Kush (as well as)
This land of Egypt.
Thou settest every man in his place. Thou suppliest their needs
(Though) their tongues differ in speech, their forms likewise
And the color of their skins (thou art)
Lord of them all.
How excellent are Thy designs, O Lord of Eternity!
Thou art in my heart, for Thou art the duration of Life
By Thee men live.

As a symbol of God Akhenaton took the disc of the sun, with rays ending in many little hands. And he wrote,

"Every day I behold Thy beauty.
Give me Thy hands, holding Thy spirit.
That I may receive it and live by it.
Call Thou upon my name unto eternity
And it shall never fail."

Using his power as Pharaoh, Akhenaton tried to establish the worship of Aton. He sent stone masons out to cut the name of the old god Amen from the temples and altars, and to chip off even the plural word "gods" wherever it appeared. Opposed by the old priests of Amen, he moved from Thebes and built a completely new and beautiful city, dedicated to the one God. There he lived, trying to reflect in his own spirit the beauty which he saw in Aton. He refused to hate or to make war on any other nation, even to protect his empire, which was then being attacked.

As frail and delicate in body as he was strong in spirit, Akhenaton died when he was barely thirty. As soon as he was gone, the old priests came back again, bringing the old gods. The next Pharaoh and his court moved back to Thebes, leaving the beautiful new city deserted. For years Akhenaton was referred to as "that criminal," then as time went on his name was no longer mentioned, and finally it was forgotten.

Now, in these days of Augustus Caesar, his poor fragile body and the beautiful songs which he had written had been hidden in the Valley of the Tombs for thirteen hundred years. There they were to remain lost and forgotten for nineteen centuries more.

Not until 1907 would the world discover Akhenaton, and learn that once in ancient Egypt there had lived a great soul, so far ahead of his age that he tried to teach a way of living that the world today is not yet ready to accept.

ΦιλΟ
PHILO · JUDAEUS

PHILO AND THE LIGHTHOUSE

LIVING IN EGYPT in the city of Alexandria in this year 12 B.C. was a little Jewish boy with the Greek name of Philo who was to become known as the philosopher Philo-Judaeus. One morning Philo, who was then only nine or ten years old, woke up with great excitement and much earlier than usual. As he slipped into his sandals and looked out of the window, he could tell that it was early because the sun had just tipped the statue of Poseidon that stood on top of the great lighthouse.

Pharos, the giant lighthouse in the harbor of Alexandria, was one of the "seven wonders" of the ancient world and a sight to be marvelled at by visitors. But it was an old friend to Philo. Every morning he looked out upon its tall white tower. Every night, with sleepy eyes, he watched its light shining in the dark square of his window while he whispered over once more to himself the verses of the Torah he had had to memorize that day.

Philo loved the Torah, and he loved the lighthouse. And he was glad that the Torah and the lighthouse and the long crooked sandy island on which the lighthouse stood were all connected in a way. He always felt very grateful to Ptolemy Philadelphus who had built the lighthouse and whose name was so easy to remember because it was like his own.

Philo meaning "love" was part of Philadelphus, which meant "one who loves his brother."

Philo felt especially grateful to that old Ptolemy on this bright

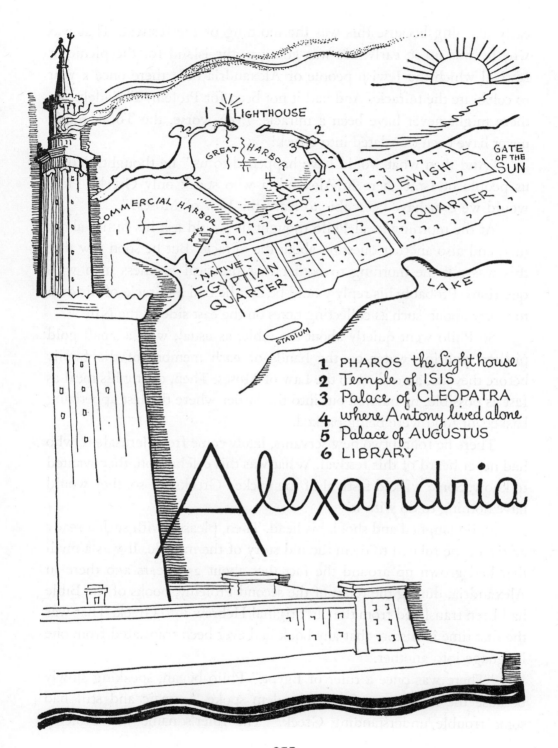

LIGHTHOUSE

GREAT HARBOR

GATE OF THE SUN

JEWISH QUARTER

COMMERCIAL HARBOR

DOCKS

NATIVE EGYPTIAN QUARTER

LAKE

STADIUM

1 PHAROS the Lighthouse
2 Temple of ISIS
3 Palace of CLEOPATRA
4 where Antony lived alone
5 Palace of AUGUSTUS
6 LIBRARY

Alexandria

early morning because this was the morning of the festival. That was why he was up so early. He was going to the island for the picnic or festival which the Jewish people of Alexandria held there once a year to celebrate the miracle. And had it not been for Ptolemy Philadelphus, there might never have been a miracle. Even worse, the Torah might never have been translated into Greek!

"And then what would have happened to us," he thought, "all of us people of Israel here in Alexandria who speak only Greek? How would we ever have been able to learn the Law of Moses?"

At the morning meal Philo thought he would ask his father about that, and also another question about the miracle. But he soon saw that this was not the morning to bother that practical business man with questions. Probably his reply would be that he had a miracle of his own to worry about, such as collecting taxes on the east side of the Nile.

So Philo went quietly about the table, as usual, with a small gold pitcher, pouring water on the hands of each member of the family before they ate, according to the Law of Moses. Then, eating his meal as fast as possible, he hurried out into the larder where the last appetizing baskets of food were being packed.

There he found two new servants, lately come from Jerusalem, who had never heard of this festival. What was this celebration, they wanted to know. Some wicked festival of the wicked Greeks? If so, they would have nothing to do with it!

Philo laughed and shook his head. Then, pleased with such a ready audience, he related to them the old story of the miracle. It was a myth that had grown up around the fact that about 250 years ago there in Alexandria, during the reign of the second Ptolemy, books of the Bible had been translated from the old original Hebrew into Greek. That was the first time in history that any book had ever been translated from one language into another.

"There was once a ruler of Egypt," Philo began, speaking slowly because the newcomers from Jerusalem spoke Aramaic and still had some trouble understanding Greek. "The ruler's name was Ptolemy

Philadelphus," he continued, "and he was a Greek. He thought it was a shame that his people were not able to read the laws given by Moses to the people of Israel. So he sent to Jerusalem for seventy or seventy-two elders to come here and translate them. This was a very hard thing to do, because they must not add or take away or change one single word. So Ptolemy had to find them the most quiet place to work. That was the island on which the lighthouse stands where they would hear nothing but the waves. There the seventy old men took the sacred book, and holding it up toward heaven, prayed that they might not fail. Then each one went off by himself and began to write, and they wrote for seventy-two days. And when they had finished, it was found that each one had written exactly the same thing, word for word!"

So that legend was the basis for this festival. It began early. Long before mid-morning the bridge to the island was crowded with people, laughing, singing, shouting, jostling one another—good natured Egyptians, light-hearted Greeks, joining with the Jews.

For Alexandria was a happy meeting place of the East and West, a city where the people and ideas and customs of Asia and Europe met and mingled.

Prayers and thanksgiving came first. Then, in tents erected on the beach, or seated on the sand, the open air feast was enjoyed by circles of relatives and friends. After playing for a while with the other children, Philo went off to sit by himself and think. He loved to think and to try to search out the truth about all sorts of questions. So he was really a small philosopher.

For that word Philo-sopher, which also contained his name, actually means "One who loves wisdom."

"Anyone who is curious to learn every sort of knowledge and is never satisfied, may be called a philosopher," said Plato, who was, himself, one of the greatest of them all.

Philo was certainly curious to learn. He was thinking this day about the world and the story of how it had been created, which he could never quite understand.

The world had been created in six days, they said. But how long was each one of those days?

Days were measured by the sun, but the sun itself had not been created until the fourth day. That was what he was puzzling over now, as he sat with his chin in his hand gazing across the harbor toward the city.

Edging the opposite shore, and reflected in the crystal clearness of the water, were the royal palaces. Almost directly across from him were the museum and the library, full of thousands of books. This was not the library built by Ptolemy Philadelphus. That, he knew, had been even larger. But in the days of Cleopatra when his, Philo's, father was a boy, that library had been set on fire accidentally by the soldiers of Julius Caesar. What a terrible thing! All those books burned to ashes before he had a chance to read them! But some day he was going to read all the books in this library. He wanted to read and find out what the old philosophers of Greece had said and thought about the world, and how it had been made. Then perhaps he could figure out how long those six days were supposed to be, and other things that puzzled him.

As he grew older Philo was to read many of those many books in the great library at Alexandria. And though he held fast to his own religion and the wisdom of Israel, he was also to understand and appreciate the great wisdom of the Greeks.

Surprised at first to find so much that was similar in their ideas, he made the mistake of thinking that they must have learned the truth from reading the Torah and the psalms and proverbs and other sacred books of his people.

He did not realize that Truth is the same wherever it is found, and that some part of it may be found by all who truly search for it.

And perhaps, too, he did not realize that the Greek philosophers had lived and taught long before the books of the Bible were translated into Greek, back in the time they were first being written down in ancient Hebrew.

Φιλο
σοφία

PHILOSOPHY

Φιλόσοφος

PHILOSOPHER

QUESTIONS AND ANSWERS

SINCE TIME BEGAN there have been three questions that people have always asked and tried to answer, and will probably keep on asking forever:

1   What is this world we live in and how was it created?

2   How can we live in it with other people and be happy?

3   What will happen to us when we die?

Back in the earliest days of their history, when these questions first puzzled the ancient Greeks, they used their imagination, and invented myths to explain what they did not understand.

For hundreds of years these myths about Father Heaven, Mother Earth, the Titans, and the great gods of Olympus seemed to satisfy the people. But long before the common people lost faith in them, these primitive ideas failed to satisfy the thinkers.

Beginning almost six hundred years before this Age of Augustus, there had been a Golden Age in Greece, when Athens became so full of these great thinkers as to be a veritable "thinking shop." All were trying to discover the true answer to at least one, if not all, of the puzzling questions. But as they searched for the Truth, their ideas of it varied, just as pure sunlight appears to be red, green, blue or violet when seen through different colored windows.

To the first question, for example, one thinker answered that WATER had been the substance from which the world was made; another said FIRE; another, AIR. Another said a mingling of WATER, FIRE, AIR and EARTH. One believed the universe was all MIND; another said no, that it was all MATTER built up from its smallest particle, which he called an ATOM.

All the answers and ideas, which have since been divided into different sciences, were then taken together and called PHILOSOPHY.

PYTHAGORAS

Pythagoras was one of the earliest of these Greek philosophers, and the first one of them to teach that the world was round. Interested in mathematics, he felt sure that NUMBERS were the key to everything. All things in heaven or earth depended on rhythm, music and harmony of numbers.

Pythagoras had been born on the island of Samos about 586 B.C., or about one hundred and fifty years after Rome was founded. As a young man he travelled and talked with priests and wise men everywhere around the Mediterranean, especially in Egypt, the main center of learning. There he studied astronomy, and became convinced that the earth was a globe or sphere.

Later, his followers taught that the earth revolved with the other planets around a central fire, or hearth of the universe. The planets, he knew, travelled at different rates of speed, and he believed that as they went, the slower ones, like Jupiter and Saturn, gave off deep low tones, and the swifter ones, like Mercury, clear high notes which blended together into beautiful music, "the harmony of the spheres." The reason we don't hear it is because the music never ceases, and we can't compare it to silence. And so, since the rates of speed and the notes of music could be expressed in numbers, he said that NUMBERS were everything.

Pythagoras himself, it is said, liked to set down numbers in various patterns and shapes and study them.

"How do you count?" he once asked a pupil.

"1, 2, 3, 4," the pupil began.

"Stop!" said Pythagoras. "I will show you how 1, 2, 3 and 4 make 10." Taking his crayon, he arranged dots in this way:

"This," he said, "is the holy triangle of four."

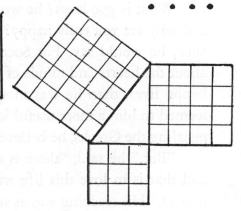

Working with triangles one day, he discovered one of the first laws we learn to use in Geometry. He drew a triangle like this:

Then he drew three squares, one on each side of the triangle:

These he marked off into small equal squares and, counting them, discovered that the squares on the longest side was equal to the sum of the squares of the other two sides. That is called the law of the three squares or Theorem of Pythagoras.

217

SOCRATES

More than a hundred years passed, and then, when the Golden Age was at its height, there might have been seen in the market place of Athens a short, ugly, thickset little man, with a bald head, a flat nose, and wearing an old wrinkled tunic. Surrounded by the finest young men of Athens, he would walk among them, talking to them, and training them to think for themselves by asking them questions.

What is goodness? he would ask them. What is happiness? When and why are you truly happy? When are you miserable? KNOW YOURSELF, he would say. For Socrates was more interested in finding out about the hearts and minds of men, and how they might lead good and happy lives, than he was in speculating how the world was made. It seemed to him a more useful kind of wisdom. As for the third question puzzling the Greeks, he believed the soul was immortal.

"But," he said, "there is only one way to prepare for immortality and that is to love this life and live it as bravely and as cheerfully as we can." His teaching was as simple and beautiful as his body was ugly.

"Life and its possessions are not of great importance," he told his pupils, "but a good life is. For no real evil can come to a good man either in life or death." And so he urged them not to strive for pos-

218

sessions, but for wisdom. "For goodness," he said, "comes with wisdom. Truth is the great possession, for truth and goodness are one."

Truth, the Spirit of Truth—that was the God of Socrates, the one God to whom he urged the young men of Athens to be faithful. And so he was condemned. Because he would not lead them back to the old gods of Olympus, whose evil conduct was worse than that of most human beings, the ruling citizens of Athens accused Socrates of leading their young sons astray. No doubt they called him an "atheist," a word that people today too often use to condemn someone whose idea of God does not agree with theirs.

Socrates was arrested, jailed and condemned to die by drinking a cup of poison hemlock. But Socrates bore no ill-will toward those who had condemned him. Nor did he have any fear of death.

"Be of good cheer," he said to his sorrowing pupils who were with him at the end. "You are burying only my body."

"Such was the end of the wisest, the justest, and best of all men whom I have ever known," said Plato.

Plato was twenty-six when his old teacher Socrates died. He was the greatest of all his teacher's pupils, and, many believe, the greatest of all philosophers. Plato was a handsome youth. Tall and strong, he had an outstanding record both as soldier and as athlete. It was because his shoulders were so very broad that he was called PLATO.

"Plato" means broad, like the word plateau. And like a plateau, which is both high and broad, was the philosophy of Plato. He was excited by almost every question concerning God or man, and he made his answers so dramatic and colorful that they became great literature. For, unlike Socrates, Plato put his ideas into writing.

His REPUBLIC is one of the world's great books. In it Plato imagines an ideal state, one that would so train its citizens to lead good and useful lives, that each one would be happy.

It was an ideal—an idea—but to Plato ideas were everything. Ideas, only, had real life. A tree is chopped down and burned, flowers fade and fall, a man dies. But there will always be men and trees and flowers. The IDEA lives on.

Once the world itself was only an idea in the mind of God, just as a vase was but an idea in the mind of the sculptor before he modelled it in clay—just as a poem was but an idea in the mind of a poet before it was expressed in words.

Plato had a most brilliant young pupil named Aristotle, one who had a most orderly mind, cold and calm and keen. Although he was Plato's pupil, he disagreed with his teacher.

Facts were more real and important to Aristotle than ideas. Actual facts about animals, minerals, vegetables—facts that he could observe and classify and arrange in logical order.

Aristotle had come to Athens a young stranger from the north. His father was court physician to the King of Macedonia, whose son was to conquer Greece, and whose grandson, Alexander the "Great," was to conquer "the world."

In 343 B.C., when Aristotle was about forty and the foremost philosopher in Athens, he was called back to the capital of Macedonia to take charge of the education of the high-spirited young Alexander, who was then thirteen. After Alexander had conquered Persia and Egypt and was hoping to spread the Greek learning through the old countries of the East, he remembered his old teacher, who was then writing a history of animals.

Alexander furnished money and a thousand men to go through Greece and collect specimens. With the animals they brought back, Aristotle established the world's first Zoo, and also the science of Zoology, though that was then still jumbled together with all the other sciences under the name of Philosophy.

This long standing disorder annoyed Aristotle. Gathering together all the knowledge that had been collected in the past, he classified and divided it into two parts, separating that which dealt with facts from that which dealt with ideas. And he then wrote what might probably be called the first encyclopedia.

Aristotle was the last of the great Greek philosophers. And he himself was not a native of Athens, but a Macedonian.

The Golden Age of Greece had long since passed. Rome was coming into power.

By 146 B.C. Rome had conquered the Mediterranean world.

Then, just as the Romans had imported the old myths and gods of Greece, they also carried home the Greek philosophy. All educated

Romans began to study Greek. The beliefs of the philosophers became the religion of such men as Cicero and Virgil.

But the average people of Rome had also lost faith in the old gods. And they were not able to read Greek, nor to understand Plato, most of them, even if they had been able to read his books. But, though they had not trained minds, they still had hearts and emotions. And they also wanted to know how to live in this world and to be happy. When life seemed unbearably wretched, they longed to believe that they might live again in a happier world.

So the Romans kept searching for a new religion that would give them hope. Some turned to the religion of the Jews, even though the laws seemed very severe. Others found comfort in the story of Osiris who had risen to new life, and flocked to worship in the temple of the holy mother Isis, there in Rome. Others gladly accepted Mithra as their savior, when the returning soldiers brought the Persian religion back from Parthia.

Many merely lived from day to day, with no religion at all.

It was to correct this unhappy lack that Augustus had rebuilt the old temples, requested Virgil to write the Aeneid, and tried in every way to restore faith in the gods of the Roman forefathers. It could not be done. People's minds can never be squeezed back into ideas which they have outgrown, any more than a growing boy can get his foot back into a baby's shoe.

Cicero, in his day, had also tried to fill the need of the Roman people. To him it seemed a shame that they should be deprived of the Greek philosophy, just because they could not understand the language. He decided to transfer some of the main Greek ideas into Latin. Just the year before Julius Caesar was killed, Cicero had written the book. It was dedicated to his friend Brutus, who, of all men, had tried stoically to live by what he believed was right.

In simple language, Cicero had attempted to explain the difference between the STOICS and the EPICUREANS. These were two schools of thought that had grown out of the older philosophies.

The STOICS, whose founder, Zeno, looked back to Socrates and Plato, believed that the world was ruled by a Divine Mind, or God, and that a spark of that same Mind was in each one of us, and that part was immortal. Therefore, the only way for a man to live, was to be guided by that spark of mind, or conscience, which was within, to try to understand and obey the divine law, and to know that whatever happened to him was the will of God.

EPICUREANS looked back to Democritus, who had said that there was no god, that the world, including man, was all matter—nothing but space and atoms. Death ended everything. Therefore, since this life was all we had, why not make the best of it, and be as happy as we can? Not caring too much about anything, doing nothing to excess, living reasonably—that was the way to be truly happy, said Epicurus, himself. But so many of his followers fell so far from that high standard, and took happiness to be just the opposite, that an Epicurean came to mean one who loved the best of food, the best of wine, and all the so-called joys of luxurious living.

That was why, perhaps, the poet Horace, who enjoyed the easy comforts of life, once remarked that he was a "pig from the sty of Epicurus" though he may truly have believed in the original teaching.

Most Romans were Stoics. Because the Romans had a genius for law and order it was but natural that they should feel and respect the divine law governing the universe.

The Greeks loved beauty, and saw the beauty in the world. And they reflected what they saw in music, poetry, drama, sculpture and beautiful philosophy and passed it on to the Romans. But the Romans, lacking that, were to pass on their great system of law and order to Europe.

For each nation, like each person in the world, has had something special to contribute.

No one person or race or nation has ever been or will ever be able to know all Truth or express all the Good to be found in this world.

TIBERIUS

GAIUS AND LUCIUS, the two grandsons of Augustus, were about the same age as Philo Judaeus, but not of the same turn of mind. They were far more eager to ride horseback or play games than to study Greek philosophy, especially as they were still struggling with the language.

When the boys discovered a book written in Latin that explained what their tutor, a Greek slave, expected them to know, naturally they pounced upon it, even though its author, Cicero, had been beheaded, they knew, as an enemy of their grandfather.

"Hide it!" whispered one of them, as Augustus suddenly came upon them reading it one afternoon. But too late. Their grandfather took it, and the boys watched him in frozen silence as he slowly unrolled the book, reading here and there. Then he handed it back.

"The man who wrote this book was a great orator," said Augustus simply, "and one who loved his country well."

He stood there for a few moments, with an odd expression on his face, before he came back to the present, and told the boys briskly that it would soon be time for them all to dine. They were to sit on the foot of his couch, as usual. Then they might go for a drive along the Sacred Way, or over to the Esquiline.

These two boys, these sons of his daughter Julia, appeared each day more dear and flawless in the eyes of their doting grandfather. To him they were the perfect combination of the gayety of their mother and the strength of their father, his old and loyal friend, Agrippa, whose loss he had never ceased to feel.

Now, in 7 B.C., Agrippa had been dead five years. Thirty-seven years had passed since that day in Apollonia when they had first visited the old astrologer.

Maecenas, too, was dead, Augustus's most trusted advisor; he had been gone a year. To fill his place, the now aging emperor had turned to his level headed stepson, Tiberius. He had given Tiberius a position of power and importance in the state, and had already come to depend upon his sound judgment and advice.

It was not this stepson Tiberius, however, but those two young boys, offspring of his own flesh and blood, whom Augustus looked upon as the future heirs to his power as emperor. Of this Tiberius was well aware, but it troubled him far less than it did his ambitious mother, Livia. She watched with increasing annoyance the preference shown by her husband for those two grandsons.

The chief source of annoyance to Tiberius was not the boys, but their mother, Julia, his wife, whom he had been forced to marry and whose scandalous conduct was now the common talk of Rome and had reached almost every ear but that of her adoring father.

Tiberius had now purchased the beautiful estate of Maecenas on the Esquiline, but he took no pleasure in living there with Julia. The gardens and villa were always filled with her fast friends, a dissolute noisy crowd of ne'er-do-wells, who drank too much, laughed too loud, and idolized to excess a clever but degenerate poet by the name of Ovid.

Tiberius had been wondering for months how much longer he would be able to endure the loathsome position he was in. Though disgraced by a wife who bestowed her favors on so many men that they

225

could scarcely be counted, he still could not stoop to tell her father the truth about her. Yet, if he did not tell, he must continue to live with her, if he lived in Rome.

The only solution, as far as Tiberius could see, was to leave Rome, to retire from public office. The island of Rhodes had always appealed to him as being an interesting place to live. Rhodes was a center for teachers and scholars of both East and West. There he could read, study and live the quiet kind of life that he enjoyed.

Livia begged him not to go. He was all she had—now—her only son. Drusus had been killed two years before in Germany.

Augustus was astounded at the proposition. Leave Rome! Why, pray tell, and for what reason? Retire from public office! Desert him, Augustus, now when he most needed his help and counsel? No. Flatly, no. He would not grant Tiberius the permission.

Tiberius closed his mouth, but firmly. He had made up his mind and he was not to change it. For four days he shut himself in and went without food until permission was grudgingly granted. Then quietly and quickly as possible, he prepared to leave. So secretly did he make his plans that almost no one in Rome knew that Tiberius had gone until the ship on which he sailed was well down the coast of Italy on the way to Rhodes.

Augustus was very bitter about what he termed Tiberius's unreasonable desertion of his wife and family. Livia could scarcely hold her tongue. She longed to open the eyes of Augustus then and there to the sins of his daughter, but decided that it was wiser to wait until she had an outstanding piece of scandal that was undeniable. So she bided her time, though impatiently.

Tiberius found life in Rhodes suited to him perfectly. He was away from Rome, but still in touch with the world. Almost all of the Roman officials in the East stopped there on the way back and forth. Ships from Alexandria often put in at the port made famous still by the remains of a once gigantic statue, known as the Colossus of Rhodes (and one of the world's "seven wonders").

Study of the stars was one of Tiberius's main interests, astrology as well as astronomy, for the two had not yet been divided.

In 6 B.C., the first year Tiberius spent in Rhodes, almost everyone must have been scanning the skies, exclaiming and pointing to what looked to them like an extremely bright star, but which astronomers recognized as three planets close together.

It was a very rare occurrence. Saturn, Jupiter and Mars were all shining together in that station of the Zodiac known as the Fish. This was most remarkable, for the three planets travel at such different rates of speed that it is but once in a hundred years that they happen to come close together. And it is only once in 800 years that the three are all seen in front of that particular star pattern known as Pisces, or the Fish.

In 800 A.D. Europe was to be in the dark ages, so its appearance then was not recorded. In 1604, it was to be reported again by an astronomer. In the year 2408, we are told, it is due to happen again. Probably no one in that year 6 B.C. who saw the strange and beautiful "star" ever quite forgot it.

Some think that it may be the one mentioned in the story of the three wise men, or Magi, from the East, who followed a star to Jerusalem and then on to Bethlehem. For Herod, the king whom they visited in the story, was still alive. In this year 6 B.C. when Tiberius went to Rhodes, Herod, the king of Judaea, had just two more years to live.

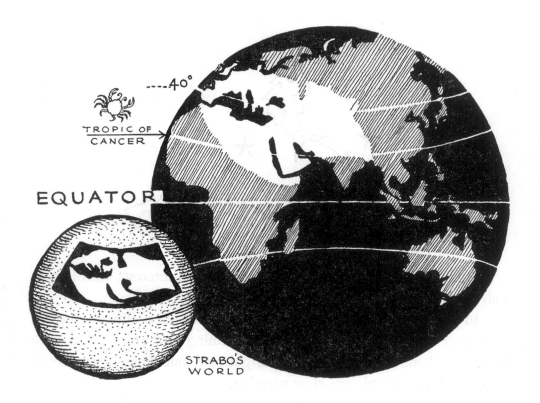

TROPIC OF
CANCER

----40°

EQUATOR

STRABO'S
WORLD

STRABO AND THE WORLD

SEVERAL YEARS, or possibly only a year, before Tiberius went to Rhodes, a ship sailed from the harbor of Alexandria, carrying an important traveller. A man in his middle fifties, with streaks of gray in his black hair, he stood in the stern of the ship until they were far out at sea, watching with peculiar interest the way in which the great lighthouse gradually disappeared below the water line, until only the tip was visible, and then that too was gone. A never failing source of interest to him was this constant proof that the surface of the sea was curved and the earth was round.

For this traveller was Strabo, the geographer.

After his trip up the Nile with his friend the Roman governor, on which they had gone as far as the borders of Ethiopia, Strabo had re-

228

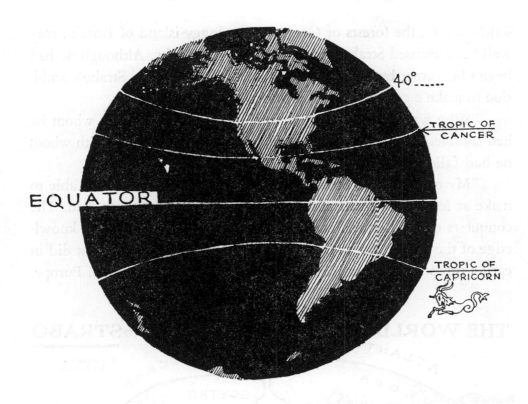

turned to Alexandria to study in the library. There he had pored over the works of all the old Greek philosophers who had written of geography in the past. Now, with many rolls of notes that he had made and with his mind full of the things that he had seen, Strabo was leaving Egypt for Rome.

This was not his first visit to that city of the West. He had arrived in Rome for the first time in 44 B.C., the year that Julius Caesar had been murdered. Strabo was then a boy of nineteen, having been born the same year as Augustus.

His birthplace was Amasia, a city in Pontus, not far from the border of Armenia. His parents, being wealthy and well able to do so, had sent their son to Rome, thinking, possibly, that a view of the West might round out his education. In Rome, young Strabo had studied with the sons of Cicero, under the same tutor. There he had also first read Julius Caesar's book about his war in Gaul. Caesar's description of the

229

wild country, the forests of Germany, the foggy island of Britain, may well have aroused Strabo's first interest in geography. Although he had begun his career by writing history, now, at fifty, it was Strabo's ambition to make a geography of the world.

"Why write another geography?" inquired someone to whom he had confided his purpose—someone, perhaps on shipboard, with whom he had fallen into conversation.

"My excuse," said Strabo, "is that I believe that I shall be able to make at least some small additions to what the others have said. The conquests of the Romans and the Parthians have added to our knowledge of the world, just as the campaigns of Alexander the Great did in earlier times. The Romans have opened all of the western part of Europe,

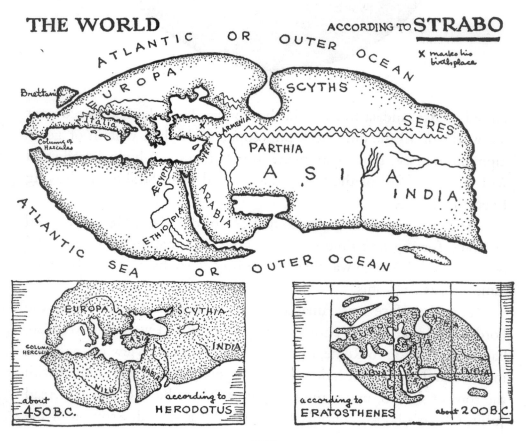

THE WORLD · ACCORDING TO STRABO

according to HERODOTUS · about 450 B.C.

according to ERATOSTHENES · about 200 B.C.

and the Parthians have increased our knowledge of the Scyths, who live in the northeast.

"Also, I believe, you could not find another person among the old writers of geography who has travelled more than I."

These are maps of the world by Strabo and by two much older Greek geographers, Herodotus and Eratosthenes, which Strabo had studied in Alexandria, and which, as you can see, he changed but little.

Herodotus had lived in Athens about 450 years ago, at the time of Socrates. As a boy, Strabo remembered hearing Cicero always refer to Herodotus as the "Father of Geography."

Eratosthenes had lived about 250 years later. He had been chief librarian at Alexandria. By measuring the length of the shadows thrown by the sun in different places on the earth, he had figured out for the first time the correct distance around the earth as being 25,000 miles.

On his globe Strabo showed all of the earth that he knew to be inhabited as "an island in the shape of a soldier's cape."

"We have learned by experience that the inhabited world is an island," he explained, in discussing it with a group of fellow travellers; "because, wherever it has been possible to reach the limits of the earth, sea has been found. And it is more than likely that that sea, which we call the Atlantic, or Outer Ocean, is one and continuous."

"In that case, you think it might be possible to sail around the world," surmised someone.

"I do, if the size of it were not such an obstacle," he replied. "We might easily pass out through the Pillars of Hercules into the Atlantic Ocean and sail from Spain to India."

"Has it ever been tried?"

"Yes. And those who undertook to sail around the globe turned back, they say, not because any continent stood in their way, but because of their want and loneliness.

"Yet, on the other hand," he continued, "it is quite possible that in the temperate zone there may be two or even more habitable islands, especially near the circle of latitude drawn through Athens."

231

"Another continent, perhaps, like that of ATLANTIS, would you say?" asked someone. He was referring to the old and familiar story of a long lost continent which had been related by Plato, and which Plato had learned from the priests of Egypt when he studied there.

Once in most ancient days, according to a tradition handed down by those old Egyptian priests, there had been a continent in the Atlantic Ocean, west of Africa, known as Atlantis. But an upheaval had occurred in the bed of the ocean, and the continent had sunk completely and disappeared beneath the surface of the sea.

Was the story true? Had such a continent ever existed? Had all the inhabitants perished, or did some of them escape? Was it a myth, or was it history? Those and other such questions kept the travellers on that ship in the Mediterranean speculating and surmising till the night was bright with stars.

"Strictly speaking, as a geographer," concluded Strabo, "it is not my business to inquire whether or not there may be other inhabited continents. The object of a geographer is to describe known countries. Also it would serve no purpose to be well acquainted with such distant places, especially if their inhabitants can neither injure us nor benefit us by their commerce."

And yet Strabo had shown that he found much the same fascination in wondering about it that people today find in wondering whether Mars may possibly be inhabited.

"What if, instead of turning north," thought Strabo late one afternoon as their ship was changing its course, "what if our captain should steer directly west, and we should go out through those Pillars of Hercules, and keep sailing on and on into the west, till we could go no farther? Where would we land? What would we find?"

Where would they land? What would they find? Those were questions to which no one in Europe would know the answer for 1,500 years. Not until 1492, when an Italian named Columbus, believing, as Strabo did, that it would be possible to sail around the world, was to set out from Spain to sail for India, and land instead upon another continent.

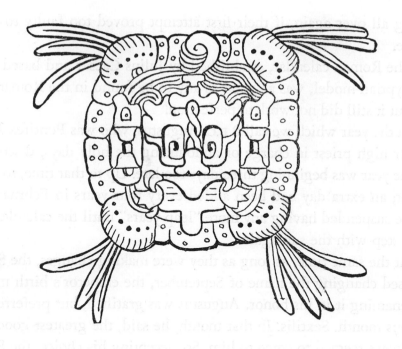

OF CALENDARS AND THE MAYANS

ONE LAW THERE IS in this world of ours, which all nations and all people, no matter how far apart, or how unknown to one another, have always recognized and respected. That is the eternal law and order of the universe, written where all may read it—in the skies.

From every spot on earth where they have lived, people have looked up in awe and wonder to watch the sun, moon, and planets travel their unchanging pathway through the heavens. They have noted how the seasons followed in their regular order, seed time, summer, harvest time, and winter, and have regulated their lives accordingly.

And, as they advanced beyond the state of savages, all people have tried, as best they could, to divide time according to the moon and sun, and mark off the seasons in what we call a calendar. This they have done with varying degrees of success, correcting their mistakes if possible, or starting all over again, if their first attempt proved too faulty to be of any use.

The Roman calendar, established by Julius Caesar and based upon the Egyptian model, was as good as any to be found in the Roman Empire, but it still did not work to perfection.

In the year which we call 8 B.C. Augustus, who was Pontifex Maximus, or high priest in charge of announcing the holy days, discovered that the year was beginning three days too late. Up to that time, to make it right, an extra day had been added every four years in February. So now he suspended having any more "leap years" until the calendar year got in step with the sun again.

At the same time, as long as they were making changes, the Senate proposed changing the name of September, the emperor's birth month, and renaming it in his honor. Augustus was gratified, but preferred the previous month, Sextilis. In that month, he said, the greatest good luck had always seemed to come to him. So, accepting his choice, the Senate passed this resolution:

"Whereas the Emperor Augustus Caesar, in the month of Sextilis, was first made consul, and three times entered the city in triumph, and in the same month brought Egypt under the rule of Rome, and put an end to civil war, and, whereas, for these reasons, the said month has always been most fortunate to this empire, it is hereby decreed by the Senate that said month shall be called AUGUSTUS."

So it was that Sextilis became August, in honor of Augustus Caesar, as the previous month had become July, in honor of Julius Caesar. But the following month was to remain September, because Tiberius Caesar was to cut short what seemed to him a silly practice, when as Emperor a similar honor was proposed to him.

"There are only twelve months," he remarked dryly. "What will you do when you have thirteen Caesars?"

It is small wonder that the Romans were having trouble with their calendar. To make a calendar that works perfectly is no easy task. It takes both a knowledge of astronomy and skill in mathematics. One difficulty lies in the fact that the number of days in a year, measured by the earth's journey around the sun, cannot be divided evenly by the number of days it takes the moon moving around the earth to make a month. Even the Greeks, with all their philosophy, evolved only a confused and muddled system.

And yet there was a calendar in existence, in this August of 8 B.C., that had been running perfectly for over six hundred years. On a day corresponding to August 6, 613 B.C., when Rome was still a village, this calendar, it is believed, had been established, and by people so advanced in astronomy and skilled in mathematics that it was to run for more than 2,000 years without the loss of a single day. Then, in the year 1561, it was to be deliberately destroyed by their mistaken Spanish conquerors, who would declare it a work of the Devil.

For they were American Indians, these people who had made the wonderful calendar. And they were living on that unknown continent across the Atlantic Ocean. They were the first civilized Americans.

They called themselves MAYANS.

Though the Spanish conquerors who followed Columbus knew of the Mayans, Christopher Columbus did not. On his first voyage in 1492 Columbus was to land on nearby islands where the Indians were primitive and uncivilized. But, on his second voyage, if he had steered less to the south and more to the west, he might have landed on the peninsula of Yucatan where the Mayans built their many beautiful cities, the most beautiful of them all the sacred city of Cheechan Itza.

But even if he had happened to land in Yucatan, Columbus would not have seen these Mayan cities in their glory. They were then in ruins. The tropical jungle was beginning to cover the great pyramids like those of the Egyptians which the Mayans had built. Wild, bright birds were flying through the deserted temples and palaces, which had been as truly beautiful in their own way as those of ancient Greece. White roads of stone, broad and smooth as those built by the Romans, Colum-

but would have found overgrown with vegetation and no longer in use.

Nor would Strabo have seen these cities in their prime, had he been able to sail through the Pillars of Hercules and southwest across the Outer ocean.

For it was between these days of Augustus and the voyages of Columbus that the Mayan civilization had flourished.

In this year 8 B.C. the Mayans were in Honduras and Guatemala, and had not yet moved up into the peninsula of Yucatán which was to be their final home. Yet they had a long history behind them.

They had set up their calendar in 613 B.C., but they had looked back to and begun to count by days, many scholars believe, from a mythical date which we would now call October 14, 3373 B.C. That, if true, would leave over 2,000 years unaccounted for.

Where had they been all those years between?

What had happened on that date from which they started counting?

236

EAST

FOOD

FOOD

ITZAMNA

Where had they come from, these Mayans, and who were they?

Those are questions yet to be answered by scientists who, today, are still digging in those jungle covered ruins. All we know is that they were the greatest of all the Indian people. Unlike the cruel, warlike Aztecs, who were to come later, the Mayans were peaceful builders and tillers of the soil, creators and not destroyers. Otherwise the Mayans are still a mystery, as mysterious as they are marvelous.

According to one myth which the Mayans told, their ancestors had come over the ocean from the east under the leadership of a god-like hero, or hero-god, ITZAMNA.

He was the god of light and life, creator of the world, father of them all, inventor of their system of picture writing, founder of their calendar and their civilization.

Sometimes they pictured Itzamna as the rising sun paddling across the water from the east in his magic skiff.

237

Unknown ages ago, according to the myth, a strange ship had appeared on the shore of Mexico, near what is now the city of Vera Cruz. (The same story is also told by other Indians of Mexico.) The sides of the boat glistened like the scales of a serpent. In it were people of fair skin, dressed in strange clothes, and wearing on their foreheads the symbol of the Sacred Serpent. They were known as Chanes, people of the serpent. And because they were wise, they became the teachers of the darker skinned natives whom they found in their new home.

But they had separated, these fair skinned people, some going north into Mexico to become the Toltecs, some south to become the Mayans though later they had been united again.

Is that tale a myth, or is it founded on actual history? Were the Mayans originally fair skinned people from the east? If so, from where did they come?

From the lost continent of Atlantis? Some say so, and claim that the date from which they count may be the date when their old home sank beneath the ocean.

Others laugh at that idea, as preposterous. There was never such a continent as Atlantis, they declare. All the people who inhabited America before the Europeans came, had come from Asia thousands of years before by way of Bering Strait, over the stepping stones of the Aleutian Islands. There, since remains of great tree trunks have been found, some scientists believe that the two continents may once have been joined together by a forest belt of redwoods.

Other scientists pooh-pooh both of these theories. The Mayans came from neither east nor west, they claim, but originated on the western continent, had always been there, and were truly and actually Americans. Still the question remains unanswered.

Who were these Mayans who built pyramids, wrote books, carved stones, studied the heavens, and invented a calendar as perfect as the corrected Roman one which we are still using today?

Who were these marvelous, mysterious Mayans?

CHILDREN OF THE SUN

I T WAS WHILE Strabo was still in Egypt that Augustus Caesar had ordered the two obelisks moved from the sacred city of the sun to his palace in Alexandria. Two other obelisks had been loaded on boats and shipped to Rome. On his arrival in Rome, Strabo was curious to see what had become of them. One he found standing in the Circus Maximus. The other one, topped with a golden ball, had been erected in the Field of Mars, to be used as a colossal sundial. Inlaid into the pavement upon which it stood were lines of bronze radiating from its base, to mark the progress of its shadow cast by the sun.

On the ninth of August, the Romans held a public sacrifice to the Sun, on the Quirinal, which Strabo may very possibly have attended. Though he, himself, was a Stoic, worship of the sun was a commonplace to him. He had been born in a country where worship of Mithra, the Persian sun god, was the state religion, and the King was often named Mithra-dates, "Child of the Sun."

So it would probably not have seemed at all strange to Strabo, if he had known that people were living on the other side of the world, to find that they also called themselves "children of the sun."

They were of two different races, these people, living in two lands as distant from each other as they were from Rome. One inhabited the high plateau of Peru, on the west coast of South America, looking out upon that great ocean now known as the Pacific. The other was diagonally across the Pacific, off the northeast coast of Asia on the island we now call Japan.

Peru and Japan. In both lands the people were semi-savages. They could neither read nor write. Nor were they advanced enough to make any kind of calendar. But they could feel the glory and power of the radiant sun as it shone down on their mountain peaks and islands, and both races had made it their greatest god.

The people of Peru were Indians. In time to come, about twelve centuries later, there were to arise among these Indians of Peru ambitious lords or chiefs who, in their language, were called INCAS. These Incas, or lords, were to unite all the surrounding Indian tribes into a great empire which they were to organize and rule so well as to be likened to that of the Romans.

According to ancient legends, these Indians who were to be known as Incas were all "children of the sun." The first creator of the world and its men was a boneless man, child of the Sun and Moon, who had come down from the north. Disgusted with men after he had made them, he had turned their land into a desert and deserted them. Then had come another son of the Sun and Moon, known as Pacha-camac, the "earth creator." He had turned the deserted people into pumas, apes and birds, and created a new people, and taught them agriculture.

Another story said that the sun, sending down its life giving rays, had created a new race of people out of metal eggs. From the gold eggs came the chiefs or Incas, from the silver eggs came their wives, and from the copper eggs came the common people.

These were the old myths, told much later when these now primitive Indians of Peru had become known as Incas.

Each day, as the red sun set in Peru, sinking behind the black rocks in the Pacific, it was the dawn of a new day in Japan.

The sun was rising over Mount Fuji, and shining down upon the

"palace" of the chief, or emperor—
a fragile, primitive building made
of poles and thatched with rice
straw and rushes.

JIMMU, who was the first emperor, lived, it is now believed,
about this time of Augustus, although the exact date is uncertain
since no early records were kept by
the Japanese who had not yet learned
from the Chinese how to read or
write. Jimmu, Lord of Heaven, had
been the great-great-great-grandson
of the Sun Goddess, Amaterasu-o-
mi-kami. In Japan, the sun was not a
god but a goddess.

The Sun Goddess had been born
when her father, the god IZANAGI,
had wiped his honorable right eye.
Her brother the Moon had been
born when their divine father had
wiped his honorable left eye.

One day father Izanagi and his
wife, Izanami, were standing on the
floating bridge of heaven, the Milky
Way of the stars. With a jeweled
spear they reached down and stirred
up the salty ocean, and then drew
up the spear. The brine that dripped
from the point of the spear piled up
and became the islands of Japan,
which the Sun Goddess then shone
down upon.

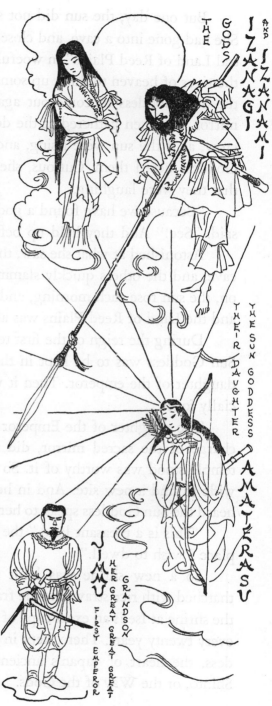

241

But one day, the sun did not shine. The Sun Goddess was angry. She had gone into a cave, and closed the door, leaving the whole "Central Land of Reed Plains" in woeful darkness. Many gods assembled by the river of heaven to think up some plan whereby they might persuade the Sun Goddess to come out again. They wrought a shining metal mirror, and then gathered at the door of the cave. They had the cocks crow, as if the sun were rising, and then they laughed aloud. The Sun Goddess heard them. Curious, she peeped out and asked why it was that they were laughing.

"Because we have found a goddess more beautiful than you," they said. "See!" And they held up before her face the mirror.

Astonished at what she saw, the Sun Goddess stepped out from the cave, and the others quickly slammed the door behind her. From then on, the sun rose each morning, and each day the plain of High Heaven and the Land of Reed Plains was always light.

During the reign of the first ten emperors, the sacred mirror of the Sun Goddess was to be kept in the palace, under the care of a virgin daughter of the emperor. Then it was removed to a temple built especially for it.

The daughter of the Emperor Suinin, who was the twelfth one in charge of the sacred mirror, did not think that the place where the temple stood was worthy of it. So she set forth and wandered far and wide to find a new site. And in her search she came to Ise. There she heard the Sun Goddess speak to her.

"This is a pleasant land," the goddess said. "Here in this pleasant place I wish to dwell."

So a new shrine was built at Ise, a simple building of poles thatched with rice straw like the fragile "palace" of the emperor. Today the shrine at Ise is an exact copy of the first one built. It has been rebuilt every twenty years. There, kept in a box, is the mirror of the Sun Goddess, the heart of Japan's ancient and primitive religion, known as Shinto, or the Way of the Gods.

HEROD IS DEAD

TIBERIUS HAD BEEN LIVING somewhat over two years on the island of Rhodes when, in 4 B.C., shortly after an eclipse of the moon, which occurred in early April, it was learned that Herod was dead. Old Herod, King of Judaea, was no more. Seventy years of age, he had been broken, diseased, half maddened with fear. Thirty-three years had passed since he had made that bloody, never to be forgotten entrance into Jerusalem, to become King of the Jews. There had been no welcome for him then, there was no mourning for him now that he was gone.

It was a long trail of blood that he had left behind him.

The last of the many Maccabeans to meet death at his command were his own two handsome sons—sons of his beautiful Miriamne. Always, Herod had intended that they should be his successors. But of late, in his crazy, fear-maddened mind, he had become convinced that they were criminals, slyly plotting to take his, their own father's, life. Three years later, just before his death, Herod had suddenly grown suspicious of another son, by another one of his wives, and had had him done away with also.

"I would rather be Herod's pig than his son," remarked Augustus, when he heard of it. Pork being a forbidden meat to the Jews, the pig, at least, he assumed, would have a chance to live.

243

Death by poison had been Herod's all consuming fear. Not poison, however, but a lingering, loathsome disease, eventually brought his life slowly to a close. Too slowly for some.

There were those among the people who could not wait for him to die before beginning to undo the evils he had done. While he was still breathing, a crowd of wild-eyed young Pharisees, armed with axes, and carrying a ladder of rope, climbed up the gate of the Temple to where the Roman eagle had been hung. They tore down the hated bird, symbol of Rome's power, and hacked it to pieces.

Ill as he was, Herod roused himself, had the guilty ones, forty of them, summoned before him as he lay on his couch, and later had them sentenced to death.

First he recalled, however, and rather pathetically, all that he had done for the kingdom—the improvements he had made—the help he had given in time of famine—the great Temple he had built for the glory of the Lord. Did all that count for nothing?

Upon his death, Herod's kingdom was divided among three of his remaining sons, according to his will.

Herod ANTIPAS was made ruler of Galilee and Perea.

Herod PHILIP was to be ruler of the northeastern district.

ARCHELAUS was to be king in Jerusalem.

Before Archelaus could leave for Rome to have the will approved, revolt against Rome broke out in Jerusalem. Varus, the Roman governor of Syria, was obliged to rush a legion of soldiers down to Jerusalem in order to quell the uprising. But no sooner had he left than riots broke out afresh. There was bitter fighting in the Temple courts between the Jewish people and the soldiers.

Up in Galilee, also, Herod's death was followed immediately by rebellion against Rome. Judah, son of that old rebel leader Herod had executed unlawfully long ago when he was the young governor of Galilee, was now leader of the rebels. Gathering a band of followers, he broke into the arsenal in the city of Sepphoris, where Herod's royal arms were stored, armed his men, and started out to make trouble.

Varus, the Roman governor, now rushed his soldiers to Galilee to put down that rebellion. As a lesson to the rebels, he set the city of Sepphoris on fire, sold the entire population as slaves, and had 2,000 of the rebels crucified—nailed to the cross. People in the nearby villages, such as the little town of Nazareth, only three miles away, would not soon forget the horror of those days.

Meanwhile in Rome, Augustus was considering Herod's last will. He had to settle a dispute between Archelaus and his brother Herod Antipas who claimed that instead of being made merely ruler of Galilee, he should have been made king of Judaea. Augustus upheld Archelaus—except that he took from him the title of KING, calling him only ethnarch, or ruler.

There was now NO King of the Jews. And there would never be another. But that the Jewish people did not nor could not believe. Had they not long been promised a King, a ruler anointed by God, a descendant of David?

Hope for the Messiah, that promised king, flared up again, stronger now than ever before. Fantastic were the stories of how he would drive out the Romans, "tread down his enemies and trample upon them in fury." Incredible were the predictions of his coming, circulated among the fanatic people. Frenzied was their faith.

Now, at last, surely, the day of the Messiah had come!

News of Herod's death and of the rebellion which followed must have reached Tiberius by letters from Varus, the governor, from Augustus, and from his mother, Livia. By such means he must also have learned how well Herod had remembered the imperial family in his will. Augustus had been left 20,000,000 dollars. And to the empress Livia, Herod had bequeathed two shiploads of gold and silver and, what was more rare and most highly prized by all Roman ladies, a large quantity of that shimmering fabric which came from some remote place in far eastern Asia and was called SERES, or silk.

THE OLD SILK ROAD

OF THE GREAT EMPIRE OF CHINA, which had been for centuries the center of civilization in Asia, the Romans knew nothing. Though China's history had begun almost 2,000 years before Rome was founded, the Romans had heard nothing of it. They had only a vague idea that somewhere in far eastern Asia lived a people who made silk. Therefore far east in Asia, on Strabo's map of the world, appears merely the word Seres.

And of this new Roman empire, which had so recently sprung up, the Chinese knew nothing, except that somewhere out in the west were barbarians who wished to purchase silk.

These were the two great empires of the world, China and Rome. Yet they knew nothing of each other. Their only connection was a slender thread of silk.

Stretching its length across the wide expanse of central Asia, ran a narrow caravan trail, later to be known as the Old Silk Road. Over that trail on camel back bales of precious Chinese silk were carried westward for six thousand miles. Over the silent, burning desert, went the caravans, across barren steppes, through deep mountain passes, in sand storm and blizzard, heat and winter fog.

From Shensi and Huang Ho, the Yellow River, the camels with their tinkling bells and loaded backs, padded out through the Jade gate, the last in the Great Wall, and months later knelt to be unloaded in the capital of the Parthians on the Euphrates River or in the market of Damascus. From there the bales of silk might be taken around the Sea of Galilee, down to Tyre and Sidon, to be embroidered with gold thread, or dyed with the famous Tyrian purple, before being loaded on galleys and shipped on to Rome.

This caravan trail had been opened about one hundred and thirty years before this by a famous Chinese traveler, in the reign of the Emperor Wu. That was the first time that the Chinese had gone outside their own empire.

They had believed and called it "All that is under Heaven."

It was not to sell silk, but because of the Huns, that the "Great Traveller" had been sent out by the Chinese emperor. China was in constant danger of being attacked by the semi-savage tribes of wild horsemen who inhabited central Asia. These savage tribes raided and plundered the civilized nations east and west of them from China to Parthia. The Parthians called them the Scyths. The Chinese name for them was Hsiung-nu or Huns.

As a protection against these barbarians, the Chinese had built a Great Wall which ran over hills and valleys along the northern border for 1,500 miles. Wu Ti extended the wall and added more watch towers. But the wall only helped to keep out the Huns; it did not defeat them. Against these wild hordes the Chinese were obliged to wage almost continual war.

Wu Ti decided that instead of waiting for the Huns to attack, as had been done in the past, he would send an army outside of the Great Wall and drive back the Huns beyond the Gobi Desert.

This still would not be final. The Huns might return, and there were no people outside the western wall to break their advance.

Formerly, just outside the western end of the Great Wall, there had lived a people called the Yueh-Chih. But they had been attacked and defeated by the Huns who had killed their king and used his skull for a drinking cup. Not strong enough to take revenge on their enemies, the sad-hearted Yeuh-Chih had packed up their tents and moved with their herds of sheep and oxen far to the west. On the border of Parthia they had found a new home.

Wu Ti wished them to return to their old place between China and the Huns. So it was with an invitation to these people to return and accept the protection of China that Emperor Wu had sent out a brave young officer by the name of Chang-Ch'ien.

Chang Ch'ien was also to bring back horses. The Chinese needed horses to fight the Huns, for the Huns were wild-riding horsemen.

A caravan of a hundred men started with Chang Ch'ien on the dangerous mission out into the then trackless spaces of Asia. Only two reached their destination in the west, and it was twelve years before the brave Chang Ch'ien, himself, returned to China. He had been captured by the Huns and held prisoner for ten years.

When he returned, he brought word that the Yueh-Chih would not come back; they were contented where they were. But he brought the horses and alfalfa seed to plant for their food. And many were the tales he had to tell. He was hailed and honored by his countrymen, and upon him was bestowed the title of "Great Traveller."

So the way to the west had been opened—the slender trail across the plains, deserts and mountain passes of Asia. Over it silk spun in far off Chinese courtyards was now being carried westward to be worn by unknown ladies of Rome. Along that trail caravans were continually traveling, and would continue to travel for another two hundred years.

Then Chinese control over the tribes of Asia would grow too weak to hold it open. The tinkle of camel bells would no longer be heard along the Old Silk Road. The sand would drift in and cover that slender trail and it would sink back again into the desert.

249

LAND OF THE DRAGON

THE HISTORY OF CHINA began about 2,000 years before Rome was founded. But many centuries before that, the Black Haired people, as the Chinese called themselves, must have begun to till the fertile yellow soil along Huang Ho, the Yellow River. Then, like all other early people, they had felt the world about them to be full of unseen spirits.

In the great winding river, whose water gave life to their fields, there seemed to be a friendly dragon with a winding tail, a helpful spirit, except when he was angry. Then he lashed about, the water rose, flooded the fields and swept away the tiny huts. In the shape of clouds gathering in the summer sky, the Chinese farmer, looking up, could see another dragon—the good sky dragon who sent the gentle summer rain. Against the sky, under the jagged outline of the mountains, could easily be seen the shape of still another dragon which slept beneath the earth, guarding its riches.

And so the dragon, which represented to the Chinese the life and fertility of their land, came to be the symbol of China.

To the question of who had made the world, and how it had been

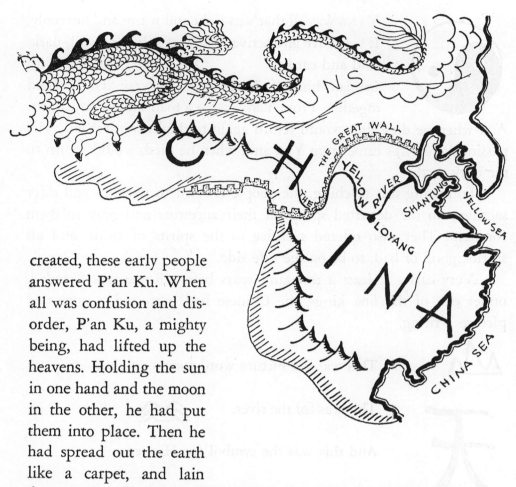

created, these early people answered P'an Ku. When all was confusion and disorder, P'an Ku, a mighty being, had lifted up the heavens. Holding the sun in one hand and the moon in the other, he had put them into place. Then he had spread out the earth like a carpet, and lain down to die. His head had formed the mountains; his bones, the rocks; his flesh, the soil. His blood made rivers and streams; his breath was the wind. And in thunder, could be heard his voice.

Centuries passed. The early myth about P'an Ku no longer satisfied the sages or wise men of ancient China. Looking about them, they saw that everything in the world seemed to have its opposite. There was light and darkness, heat and cold, giving and taking, man and woman, birth and death, good and evil. In that lay the secret of creation, they said. Two forces, acting upon each other, made up the universe. By a circular symbol, half black, half white, they showed how the two forces, YANG and YIN, fitted together and made a perfect whole.

 YANG was all that was light and warm and heavenly. It was alive and active. YIN was solid and still, dark, cold and earthy.

In man, himself, Yang and Yin were also blended together. From Yang, came a man's mind and spirit. And when he died they would return again to the heavenly Yang. His passions and vices came from Yin, and, when he died, would return to the dark earth.

Following this teaching, the people learned to worship and offer sacrifices to the departed spirits of their ancestors and pray to them for help. They also offered sacrifice to the spirits of earth, and all spirits, good or bad, to be on the safe side.

Very early, at least a thousand years before Rome was founded, under one of the first kings, the Chinese had perfected a system of picture writing.

 This was the picture word for mountains.

This was for the river.

 And this was the symbol for Heaven.

There were many spirits in the world, but over and above them all, the Chinese believed, there was one Great Spirit of goodness. They called it Heaven, or T'IEN.

The King was the Son of Heaven, and through him Heaven's will was to be carried out on earth. No ordinary person would presume to make sacrifice directly to Heaven. That was the duty and right of the King alone. He alone could claim Heaven as his ancestor.

This is the Chinese symbol for the sun.

At midnight, on the twenty-first of December, the shortest day of the year, when the sun seemed to stand still, the King, clad in blue, the color of the sky, made his great sacrifice to Heaven.

In the yearly return of the sun, in the regular movement of the planets, in the dignified and orderly return of the seasons, the Chinese felt and recognized the divine order governing the universe. They spoke of it as Tao or the Way of Heaven.

If men would live in harmony with the Great Way of Heaven, said the ancient sages, all would be well upon this earth. To do that man must use the Five Virtues: Kindness, Good Manners, Knowledge, Uprightness, Honor. To properly use the five virtues, a man must know and practice the Five Loyalties, which taught him the right behavior toward every person, and every thing on every occasion. This right behavior the Chinese called the Lı.

Such was the teaching of the ancient wise men of China. Needless to say, it was not always lived up to as the centuries passed.

Tzu is the Chinese word for teacher, or philosopher.

Much later, about the time that Zoroaster taught in Persia, and just before Socrates and Plato lived in Athens, two great teachers or philosophers also lived and taught in China.

Lao Tzu, the old philosopher, and K'ung-fu-tzu whose name people of the western world pronounce CONFUCIUS.

By that time, China had grown into a feudal state, divided into many walled towns and small districts ruled over by feudal lords always at war with one another. The strongest—the ones who ruled over the most of these lesser rulers—were the kings of a dynasty known as Chou. Loyang, in Shensi province, was their capital city.

There, as state historian and keeper of the secret archives, lived the old philosopher LAO-TZU or LAO TZE, as it is also spelled.

Lao-tzu taught of TAO as the way of life.

LAO TZU

老子

"There is a thing," said Lao-tzu, in his quiet voice, "that existed before heaven and earth. It cannot be seen nor heard. Yet it is everywhere. It is the life of all things. It is quiet, yet there is nothing that it does not do. I call it TAO. If princes and kings would keep to it, all things of themselves would be right.

"A man who understands Tao thinks of all people as himself. He gives, and the more he gives to others, the more he has for himself. He treats the good with goodness, and the bad also with goodness, and returns love for great hatred. He does not force his power upon others, nor contend with arms. The strength of his goodness is like that of water. Nothing is so yielding as water. Yet it can wear away the hardest stone. Thus can the gentle overcome the strong. And he who fights with love will win the battle. Let us have sound knowledge to walk on the great way."

Lao-tzu was about fifty years old when, to the eastward, in the

254

province of Shantung, Confucius was born, the youngest of eleven children. Though his father died when he was three, and as a child he had to work hard, he was given, nevertheless, a good education.

Confucius loved to study the ancient Chinese books and wisdom of the sages. When he was about nineteen, he opened a private school himself, which became so popular that his pupils soon numbered 3,000. History, music, sciences, government and rules of good behavior, Confucius taught—but nothing about supernatural or mysterious spirits of any kind. If a man's conduct was right, his relation to the unseen spirits would take care of itself.

In the year 517 B.C., it is said, when Confucius was thirty-four and Lao-tzu was eighty-seven, the younger man journeyed to Loyang to consult the famous "Old Philosopher." He first inquired as to how certain points of etiquette had been taught by the ancient sages, and was dumfounded by the answer he received.

"All that is of no use to you, sir," said Lao-tzu. Goodness was not to be taught by rules and regulations. Pure goodness came from within, not from without. If a man's heart was pure, and in harmony with Tao, his conduct with others would naturally be right.

Confucius then asked Lao-tzu about the Tao, saying that he had read many books, but could not understand nor obtain it.

"And why do you not?" answered Lao-tzu, quietly. "This is the reason. You do not make room for it in your heart."

Confucius left Lao-tzu still bewildered, but with admiration for the beautiful spirit of the older man.

"Today I saw Lao-tzu," he told his pupils. "He is like the dragon. I know that birds fly. I know that fishes swim. But as to the dragon, I cannot know how he can bestride the wind and clouds when he rises heavenward."

Lao-tzu was sad that men would not accept the way of life. The court of the Chou emperor at Loyang he saw filled with corruption and evil. High officials grew rich as they robbed the poor. Lao-tzu was old and discouraged with the evil ways of men. One day he left Loyang, and rode away alone on a water buffalo out through the last gate in the great wall into the desert and was seen no more.

Before he left the city, however, he was met at the gate by the warden who begged him not to depart without leaving some of his wisdom behind. So there, in the gatehouse, the Old Philosopher wrote a book of 5,000 words, containing eighty-one of his sayings.

It is known as the TAO-TE-CHING, Ching meaning text, Tao—the Way of Heaven and Teh—the good life for men.

Confucius had then become Chief Justice of his state, which he promptly put into such good order that the envious ruler of a neighboring state plotted to discredit him, and succeeded so well that Confucius was obliged to resign. Then, for many years, he traveled from state to state with his pupils, teaching good morals.

The last years of his life he spent gathering together all the wisdom of the ancient sages into five texts, or Ching. In centuries following, his pupils wrote four more books, called Shu, about the sayings of their master himself. These nine books became the canon of China.

The heart of his teaching, the best known saying of Confucius, is one upon which all great teachers of every land agree. When he was about nineteen, he was called upon to settle a dispute between some herdsmen who could not understand the fine points of the law. Confucius gave them this simple rule to go by:

DO NOT DO TO OTHERS WHAT YOU WOULD NOT HAVE THEM DO TO YOU.

More than five hundred years had now passed, in these days of Caesar Augustus, since Lao-tzu and K'ung-fu-tzu had lived and taught in China. And since then, what had happened?

The teaching of Lao-tzu, so pure and simple that it seemed a mystery, difficult to understand, had been seized upon and degraded into the religion of TAOISM, which was exactly the opposite of what Lao-tzu had taught. It was a mixture of cheap magic tricks, ignorant superstitions, spirit worship and alchemy.

A Taoist leader had been established whose chief duty seemed to be to take money from the ignorant in exchange for charms against evil spirits. And in the next century, a Taoist "professor" would be trying to manufacture pills that would make people immortal.

The teaching of Confucius, being exact rules of behavior, easily understood, and not so easily changed, had become the rule of life in China. That was good, for they taught self control, order and honest living. But, at the same time, those hard and fast rules, the worship of ancestors and the past, discouraged change and growth. Thus China, which had been for thousands of years a leader in civilization, was eventually to fall behind.

But that was far in the future. In this year 1 B.C. China was one of the two great Empires in the world.

And now, by way of the Old Silk Road, connecting those two Empires, another religion, one from a foreign land, was finding its way into China. It was coming from India.

तै घव देश

Śiva

Brahma

Vishṇu

Pārvatī

Ganesha

Krishṇa

OF INDIA AND THE HINDUS

O F INDIA, that other old and mysterious land to the east, the Romans knew much more than they did of China, and yet very little. Most ridiculous and fantastic tales were told and believed. Some reported that there were tiny wild men

258

living in India, only twenty-two inches tall, who had no noses and carried on war with cranes and partridges. People without mouths, who lived on the smell of meat, and others with ears so long, they went to sleep in them.

"Don't believe all the accounts you hear about India," said Strabo, the geographer. "Most of those who repeat them have not been to India, and what they tell you is from hearsay. Many merchants from Egypt sail to India every year, but only a very small number of them have ever gone as far as the Ganges River."

From the report of an important citizen in Damascus, who also had been a friend of Herod's, Strabo had learned of the unusual delegation once sent by a powerful rajah of India to Augustus Caesar, and received by him on the island of Samos.

Tiberius was no doubt reminded of these strange visitors as he now sailed from Rhodes to Samos to visit his stepson, Gaius. The two grandsons, Gaius and Lucius, had been sent out by their grandfather Augustus, to learn the business of the Empire, before they should be called upon to rule it. Lucius had been sent west to Gaul and Spain; Gaius had now come east, to manage affairs in Armenia and the border of Parthia, just as Tiberius had done himself, twenty years ago. It was that winter, of twenty years ago, which Augustus had spent on the island of Samos, that the extraordinary delegation from India had arrived with rare gifts and messages of friendship.

Strabo, in telling the story, said that the letter which the three Indian ambassadors had carried to Augustus Caesar plainly showed that more than three envoys had started out from India, but only three had survived. The rest, by reason of the long journey, had died. One of the men in the party also later burned himself alive on a funeral pyre at Athens. Not because he was unhappy, he explained, but because he wished "to depart this life, lest something untoward happen to him, if he tarried longer."

Certain other facts about India seemed reliable enough to Strabo, who had never been there, to be repeated in his geography.

He said, "The people in the north of India are like the Egyptians. Those in the south are more like the Ethiopians in color (although their hair does not curl).

"They are divided into seven castes.

"One kind are called Brahmans. They are philosophers, who enjoy high repute. They attend the kings as counsellors, as the Magi attend the Persian kings. They tarry in a grove in front of the city, lying on mattresses of straw and skins, abstaining from animal food, and hearkening only to earnest words, and talking also with anyone who wishes to hear them. The hearer is forbidden to cough or even spit, and if he does, he is banished for that day as a man who has no control over himself. They converse more about death than anything else, for they believe that the life here is as if it were that of an unborn babe, and that death to those who have devoted themselves to philosophy is birth into the true life, that is, the happy life; and they therefore discipline themselves most of all to be ready for death."

It would have been surprising to the Romans, no doubt, had they known that these brown skinned people of India, whose customs seemed so foreign to them, and they themselves had come from the same early ancestors. Both were descended from a race of white people, known as Aryans, who had once lived somewhere on those wide windy plains of Central Asia, across which the Silk Road now made its way.

Long ago, about 2,000 B.C., when the Jews were pushing up out of the Arabian desert, these Aryans, for some unknown reason, had wandered away from their old home in Central Asia. Dividing, they had spread out like branches of a vine. The first group of branch turned south, crossed over the Hindu Kush mountains and settled in the pleasant valley of the Indus River. Another group wandered west as far as Persia; another went on into Greece; another trailed down into Italy; another to Spain, to France, and even across the water to England.

Conquering the more primitive natives, these Aryan people became

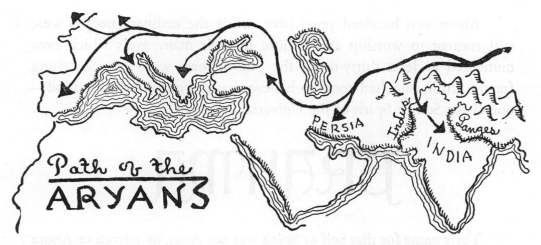

Path of the ARYANS

the ancestors of almost all Europeans, as well as of the Persians and of the Hindus, or people of India.

Wherever these Aryans went, they carried with them all the gods, or spirits of nature, which they had worshipped in their homeland. Greatest of these was the sky or HEAVEN FATHER, called DYAUSH PITAR in their language. In Greece, they pronounced it ZEUS PATER. The Romans called it JU-PITER, Also, wherever they went, these white men out of Central Asia found that the native inhabitants had gods of their own, which they often adopted.

In the valley of the Indus, the newcomers soon began to wonder about these many gods. Which had come first? And how? And the world itself, the thinkers asked, when and how had it been created?

"Who truly knows and who can declare it? The gods are later than this world's creation. Who knows, then, when it first came into being? He . . . whose eye controls this world from highest heaven— does he truly know it? Or does he know it not?"

RIG VEDA

These questions come from the RIG VEDA, a sacred book written in Sanscrit by those people in the Indus Valley about 1,000 B.C. It is the first and oldest sacred book or Bible used in the world today.

261

About two hundred years later, while the ordinary people were still content to worship and believe in their many gods which now numbered at least thirty-three, the philosophers were not. Searching for the truth, they had come to believe that there was but One God — one Great Self or Spirit of the Universe.

BRAHMA

Their name for that Self or Spirit was not Aton, or Jahveh or Ahura Mazda, but BRAHMA. In sacred books, called Brahmana, they described Brahma in this way:

"When people say, sacrifice to this or to that god, each god is but a way in which Brahma is made known, for he is all gods in One. He is the one ruler (of the universe), the Self within all things. His form is not to be seen; no one beholds him with the eye, he is imagined in the heart. Greater than the greatest; smaller than small, the Great Self is always settled in the heart of men. The wise who find him within themselves, to them belongs eternal happiness, eternal peace."

So spoke the philosophers, but the ordinary people did not understand them.

After centuries in the valley of the Indus it became too crowded, and the Aryans, or HINDUS, as they were to be called, were obliged to move south into the hotter, moister valley of the Ganges.

There they found themselves among natives who were black and who worshipped strange animal-headed gods and hideous demons of the jungle.

Fearful that they might become lost among these dark skinned natives, and their religion contaminated, the Brahmans, or priests, drew a color line, or barrier of caste, to keep the two races apart.

It failed, for they intermarried.

And the ordinary people, who had never understood the idea of One God, kept adding new gods to their list, until they numbered more nearly three hundred and three than thirty-three.

Also, sadly enough, the ugly caste system, which had failed to accomplish its first purpose, was then used to divide the Hindus themselves. Unscrupulous priests invented a myth about how people had been created, to prove that the caste system, of which they were the top, was a sacred division.

"From the mouth of Brahma," they said, "had sprung the highest caste, the Brahmans, or priests, who spoke with understanding. From the chest of Brahma had come the strong and brave, the caste of rajahs and soldiers. From his thighs had come the third caste, the active farmers and tradesmen. And from his feet, the lowly serf."

To hold their power, they also loaded down their religion with endless laws and petty rites and regulations, till there was no spirit left.

Such a heartless formal religion failed to satisfy the philosophers. But by that time the hot steamy climate of the Ganges valley had also sapped their energy.

How could one live in this world and be happy, they asked. There was no way to do it. Life itself was a burden from which there was only one escape. Death alone would not set them free. They must be born again and again, until they had purified their souls. Only then, after death, might they be united with Brahma. Lost in the Great Self of the Universe, as a drop of water is lost in the sea, they would at last find peace.

To achieve this, to set the soul free from the body, they believed that they must control all evil feelings that came from the senses—anger, greed, ambition, pride, hate—even hunger and thirst. This led to most extreme practices. Many withdrew from normal life, just to sit and meditate and practice self-control. They tried to feel nothing—not even joy or pleasure. Some starved and tortured their bodies.

But the masses of people went on doing about as they had always done, worshipping one god or many, erecting idols and shrines, obeying the priests, offering sacrifices, and bathing in the sacred Ganges.

There were, however, others who felt that things were not as they should be. About 500 B.C. many reformers arose who tried to free India from customs and beliefs which they looked upon as both useless and false.

One of these was a prince named Gautama, who had been born near Benares, the sacred city of India, on the Ganges River. He gave up his wealth and position to seek a cure for the evils of the world. He led such a holy life that he was called BUDDHA, meaning "the Enlightened One." And after he was dead, his followers declared that he was the son of Brahma, and told stories of his miraculous birth.

Gautama, the Buddha, believed that bloody animal sacrifices were cruel and useless, that extreme torturing of the body was of no avail, and that the caste system was evil and false. He preached a way of life that seemed true to him. Though he gained followers for his teaching, and in time it was to become one of the greatest religions of the world, it was never generally accepted in India.

India continued to be, and still is today, a land of many and widely varying beliefs and practices. All kinds of religion exist, side by side, for all kinds of people, from the most primitive and ignorant to the most intellectual and pure in heart. All these various beliefs and forms, taken together, make up the religion known as HINDUISM. In one of the later sacred books are to be found these words:

"As one can ascend to the top of a house by means of a ladder or a bamboo or a staircase or a rope, so varied are the ways and means to approach God.

"Every religion in the world shows one of these ways."

PATER PATRIAE

TWENTY-SEVEN YEARS AGO the gates of Janus had been closed, signifying peace. Peace, prosperity and order. That is what Augustus Caesar had most desired, and now, to his great satisfaction, had seen established in the Roman Empire. The Roman citizens, too, gloried in the change that had taken place. A whole generation had grown up without knowing the horrors of civil war. Wars of conquest, too, had ceased. Mothers and wives no longer had to send their sons and husbands off to die in foreign lands. Occasional uprisings occurred in the border countries, but they were far away. Food was plentiful. Games and entertainments had never been more lavish. What more could a grateful people ask?

Upon a sudden impulse, one night in the theatre in the winter of 2 B.C. the people rose to their feet in a body, turned to the emperor's box, and hailed him as "Pater Patriae"—Father of his Country!

Soon after that, the Senate, also at a loss to know what further honor to bestow upon Augustus, followed the lead of the people. By unanimous vote they passed a decree, and conferred the title upon the emperor, in these words:

With hearty wishes for the happiness and prosperity of yourself and your family, Caesar Augustus, the Senate, in agreement with the common people, salute you by the title of

PATER PATRIAE—FATHER OF YOUR COUNTRY.

Augustus was deeply moved, and there were tears in his eyes as he replied, "I have now arrived at the summit of my desire, O Senators. What more have I to ask of the Immortal Gods but that this, your affection for me, continue to the end of my life?"

265

His eyes were filled with tears, but only in part with tears of happiness. Mingled with them must have been tears of grief. They had wished for the happiness of himself and his family! As father of his country, he had been honored and successful. But as father of his family—what disgrace had been brought upon him! In that same year—and by his only child—his daughter Julia!

"Ah! would that I had never entered wedlock, and had died childless," he moaned whenever thought of Julia entered his mind. That bright, high-spirited, saucy little girl, whom he had so adored and petted—the ugly truth about her dissolute life had reached her father at last, and it had almost broken his heart. A shocking scandal had been brought to light in which Julia was involved. It was of a nature too dreadful ever to be fully disclosed, quite possibly a political plot against her father himself.

At first, Augustus had been so humiliated by the disgrace that he would see no one. Then, regaining his composure, he called upon the Senate to witness how a Roman father could punish a wayward child. He banished Julia to an island, deprived her of all comforts, allowing her only the bare necessities of life. He took out a bill of divorce against her in the name of Tiberius. Then he sent word to Tiberius in Rhodes that he was freed from his marriage to Julia, and that to the day of his death, he, or her father, never intended to lay eyes on her again.

Tiberius protested in a reply to his step-father against being overly harsh. He also expressed his desire that Julia should keep all the gifts that he himself had given her.

Tiberius also requested permission now to return to Rome. He did not wish to re-enter public life, but would help advance the careers of Gaius and Lucius, the younger members of the family.

Augustus flatly refused. "Since you were so ready to desert your family, you may dismiss all anxiety concerning them."

Tiberius re-read those words, then lifting his near-sighted eyes, squinted off in the direction of the harbor.

When, if ever, he wondered, would he see Rome again?

BUDDHA AND THE KINGDOM OF TRUTH

ONE DAY, in this year 2 B.C. in his imperial palace at Chang-An, the emperor of China, Son of Heaven, robed in yellow, and seated upon his red dragon throne, received an ambassador, a Tartar, who kowtowed before him. Then, having most humbly touched his forehead to the floor, nine times, the ambassador rose and presented his Celestial Highness with "Three Baskets of Wisdom."

267

These so-called "baskets" of wisdom, the emperor need not be told, were the sacred books of Buddhism, the religion which had grown out of the teaching of one Gautama, the Buddha, who had lived in India, when Lao-tzu and Confucius had lived in China.

Five hundred years had gone by since then. Two hundred fifty years ago, Asoka, an Indian ruler, who was a follower of Buddha, had sent missionaries out to all the known world, and some of them must have reached China.

But it was not until about 67 A.D. when Nero, the great-great-grandson of Augustus, was emperor in Rome, that Buddhism, which was to become the third great religion of China, would be accepted officially by the Chinese emperor.

Then, according to a legend, Ming Ti, or the emperor Ming, was to have a dream in which he saw the image of a foreign god being carried into his palace. An embassy would then be sent by him to secure images, books, teachers, and a Buddhist priest from India, to translate the Buddhist gospels into Chinese.

Fu or Fo is the Chinese word for Buddha.

BUDDHA
IN CHINESE

BUDDHA
IN SANSCRIT.

This is the story of Buddha and some words from his pure and beautiful teaching, taken from these "Baskets of Wisdom" now being presented for the first time to the emperor of China:

"There was once a rajah in India, strong of purpose and reverenced by all men, a descendant of those called Gautama. His wife was beautiful as the water lily and pure in mind as the lotus. And immaculate. And the spirit of Truth, glorious and strong as a white elephant, descended upon her.

When she knew that the hour of motherhood was near, her attendants hung a curtain about her and retired. Four pure minded angels of the great Brahma held out a golden net to receive the babe, who came forth from her right side like the rising sun, bright and perfect. All the world was flooded with light, whilst heavenly music rang through the air and the angels rejoiced.

Now there was at that time in a grove nearby, a Brahman, leading the life of a hermit. And the king invited him to see the royal babe. And the seer, beholding the prince Gautama, said:

'Like the moon when full, thou shouldst feel great joy, O King. For this son of thine will rule the world. He will either be a king of every land or he will become a Buddha (an Enlightened One).'

And as the light of the moon increases little by little, so the royal child grew from day to day in mind and in body, and truthfulness and love resided in his heart.

When the prince had grown to youth, his father desired to see him married. Then Gautama chose his cousin, a gentle princess as his wife.

The prince attended to his religious duties, bathing his body in the holy Ganges and cleansing his heart in the waters of the law.

The palace which the king had given the prince was resplendent with all the luxuries of India. All sorrowful sights and knowledge of misery were kept away from him, for the king desired that his son be happy and not know that there was evil in the world.

But as a chained elephant longs for the wilds of the jungles, the prince was eager to see the world. So the king, his father ordered a jewel-fronted chariot with four stately horses to be held ready. And the prince rode with his charioteer through the city and into the country.

By the wayside they met an old man with bent frame, wrinkled face and sorrowful brow, and the prince asked, 'Who is this?'

The charioteer said: 'This is a man in old age.'

And lo! while they were passing on, a sick man appeared on the wayside, gasping for breath, and groaning with pain, and the prince asked, 'What kind of man is this?'

The charioteer told him, and then sped the horses, to escape the sight, when suddenly they were stopped. Four persons passed by carrying a corpse. The prince shuddered. 'What is this they carry?'

The charioteer answered, 'A dead man.' Observing the deep impression the sad sights had made on the prince, he turned his horses and drove back to the city. Having returned home, the prince looked with disdain upon the treasures of his palace.

'Alas,' he cried. 'My heart is heavy. All the world is full of darkness and no one knows how to cure the ills of life.'

It was night. The prince found no rest on his soft pillow; he arose and went out into the garden. He sat down beneath the great jambu tree. Pondering on life and death, his mind became clear, and perfect peace came over him. He said to himself:

'I will sever all ties that bind me to the world, and I will seek the way of truth. Verily I shall become a Buddha.'

The prince returned to the bedroom of his wife to take a last farewell of those whom he dearly loved, his beautiful wife and his beloved son. Then he rode out into the silent night.

Gautama gave up his kingdom, severed all ties, and went into homelessness. He cut his waving hair, exchanged his royal robe for a mean dress the color of the ground, and walked along the highroad with a beggar's bowl in his hand. Now he was a Bodhisatta, one who is seeking to become a Buddha.

Now there were among the Brahmans two who were especially renowned as teachers of philosophy. The Bodhisatta went to them and sat at their feet. He listened to their doctrines of the Brahma Self, as being the 'I' of the mind and the doer of all things. He learned of the law of karma; how souls of bad men had to suffer by being reborn in men of low caste or animals, while those who purified themselves would become brahmans or kings and rise higher and higher. But he was **not** satisfied. There was too much of selfishness in their teaching.

The Bodhisatta then went to priests officiating in the temple. But his gentle mind was offended at the unnecessary cruelty performed on the altars of the gods. And he thought:

'How can the slaughter of an innocent victim blot out the evil deeds of mankind? Purify your hearts and cease to kill; that is true religion. To abandon enviousness; to give up hatred and ill will, that is the right sacrifice and the true worship.'

So the Bodhisatta went in search of a better system and came to a settlement of five bhikkus, or monks, and joined their company. With holy zeal and a strong heart, he continued for six years torturing himself, till at last he ate each day one hemp seed only, saying, 'Let the flesh waste away, if only the mind becomes more clear.' However, seeking true wisdom he did not find it so. He left the monks and wandered away alone.

The Bodhisatta then directed his steps to that blessed banyan tree, beneath whose shade he was to end his search. There he gave himself up to meditation. Pondering on the origin of birth and death, he saw the truth—that Perfect Peace can dwell only where all vanity and thought of self has disappeared. Gifts are great, meditation and understanding, but greater than all is loving kindness.

An Image from India

271

Blessed is he who has conquered all selfishness and pride. He has reached Nirvana. He has become the Buddha, the Perfect One.

And now he thought: 'I have obtained Nirvana. Now I desire to give light to those who are in darkness, and to found the kingdom of truth upon earth.'

So the Blessed One set the wheel of truth rolling, saying: 'the spokes of the wheel are the rules of pure conduct; justice is the equalness of their length; wisdom is the tire; modesty and loving kindness are the hub, in which the axle of Truth is fixed.' To the Brahmans, the Buddha spoke of caste:

'Who is an outcast? Who is a Brahman? An outcast is one who is angry and bears hatred, who does not fear to commit a wrong. He in whom there is truth and righteousness, he is a Brahman. Not by his family or by birth does one become an outcast, or a Brahman, but by deeds. Our good and evil deeds follow us continually like shadows. It is impossible to escape the result of our deeds. Let us then guard our thoughts that we do no evil, for as we sow, so shall we reap. That which is most needed is a loving heart.'

To the monks he said:

'Neither abstinence from fish nor shaving the head will cleanse a man whose heart is not pure. To keep the body in good health is a duty, for otherwise we shall not be able to trim the lamp of wisdom and keep our mind strong and clear.

And to all men, whatever they do, whether they be artisans, merchants, priests or officers of the king, let them put their whole heart into their task, and if they can struggle in life without cherishing any envy or hatred, if they can live in the world, not a life of self but a life of truth, then, surely, joy, peace and bliss will dwell in their hearts.'

And those who heard him gladly said: 'Truly, the Buddha, Our Lord, has set the wheel of Truth rolling, which by no one in the universe can ever be turned back. The kingdom of Truth will spread; righteousness, good-will and peace will reign among mankind.' "

V·IMPERATO
PONTIFEX
MAXIMVS
DIVI
PRIN
AV
PATER PATRIAE

PEOPLE WHO WERE LIVING

GERMANS
ROSE AGAINST THE ROMANS
UNDER HERMANN, THEIR FIRST
HERO
9 A.D.

TIBERIUS
AFTER RETURNING FROM RHODES,
WENT TO THE GERMAN BORDER TO
RESTORE ORDER GERMANICUS, HIS
NEPHEW, (SON OF DRUSUS) WAS WITH HIM

JUDAS OF GALILEE
TRIED BUT FAILED TO START
ANOTHER UPRISING OF THE JEWS
AGAINST THE ROMANS IN 6 A.D

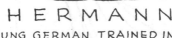

HERMANN
YOUNG GERMAN TRAINED IN THE
ROMAN ARMY AND SERVING UNDER
VARUS, TURNED AGAINST HIM AND
DESTROYED THREE ROMAN LEGIONS,

he was a student

CLAUDIUS
THE SECOND SON OF DRUSUS
AND ANTONIA, WHO WAS TO
BE ROME'S FOURTH EMPEROR
WAS 10 YEARS OLD IN. 1 A.D.

VARUS
WHOSE HEAD, AND NEWS
OF THE DISASTER WERE
SENT TO AUGUSTUS,

HERODS SON
WHO FOLLOWED HIS FATHER
AS KING, WAS BANISHED BY
AUGUSTUS, AND JUDAEA PUT
UNDER A ROMAN GOVERNOR,

AND SOME EVENTS THAT TOOK

WHEN AUGUSTUS WAS OLD

JESUS
WENT FOR THE FIRST TIME
FROM NAZARETH TO JERUSALEM
TO CELEBRATE THE PASSOVER

SAUL
A LITTLE JEWISH BOY
LIVING IN TARSUS, WAS
TO BE KNOWN AS PAUL

GRANDSON OF DRUSUS

"CALIGULA"
THIRD EMPEROR- BORN
12 A.D BROUGHT UP IN AN ARMY
CAMP IN GAUL, THE SOLDIERS
CALLED HIM CALIGULA- OR
"LITTLE BOOTS"

A COIN OF
AUGUSTUS

HIS WILL
LEFT IN THE
CARE OF THE
VESTAL VIRGINS
MADE TIBERIUS
HIS HEIR,

AUGUSTUS
AFTER BIDDING FAREWELL TO LIVIA, HIS
WIFE, DIED AT HIS COUNTRY HOME NEAR
NAPLES, ON AUGUST 19, 14 A.D (76 YEARS OLD,

TIBERIUS
SUCCEEDED AUGUSTUS,
AND BECAME THE SECOND
EMPEROR OF ROME

PLACE BETWEEN 1 AND 14 A.D.

DECEMBER 25, YEAR 1

And now in this world of Augustus Caesar, we have come at last to the year 754, which was to be changed by future Romans into the Year 1. It was again midwinter. The earth had completed another annual journey. That most joyful season had returned, when, all over the world, as through untold ages of the past, fires and lights were being kindled and celebrations held to welcome the return of the sun.

On the Roman calendar it was the month of December. Houses

were gay again with candles and holly berries. Crowded streets were echoing to the merry cry of Io Saturnalia!

In Egypt, under waving branches of palm, the people were rejoicing in the birth of the sun god Horus, picturing him as a new-born infant in the arms of his sacred mother Isis.

In Persia, or Parthia, it was the birthday of Mithra. The Magi, or wise men of the East, gathered about their altars of fire, were singing praise to the mighty Sun who had conquered again the darkness of winter.

Far to the north, in the frozen forests of Europe, the wild boar had been killed and the Yule log was burning.

And under the midnight stars of the far east, sacrifice and thanks were being offered to Heaven by the emperor of China. And it was a small emperor on this winter night of the Year 1 who was climbing the high steps to the altar, there to carry out as perfectly as he could the customs of his ancient ancestors. He was but nine years old, that little boy, who had now become emperor of China. His name was Ping Ti, meaning "Prince of Peace."

Midnight in China was sunset in Palestine, the beginning of a new day in the Festival of Lights. From Jerusalem to the Sea of Galilee, little oil flames had been set burning in the Hanukkah lampstands. In the village of Nazareth, those little lights might have been seen reflected in the shining dark eyes of a small boy who, in years to come, was also to be spoken of as the "Prince of Peace."

In those future years, his birth would be celebrated at this ever joyful season of midwinter, although it may truly have been at another time of year. Perhaps it was on a day when the fertile fields of Galilee were bright with summer flowers. Or, perhaps, when the leaves were falling, and the grapes were being crushed to liquid crimson in the limestone hollows. It may be that he was born when the first white blossoms of the almond trees were budding in the hills.

We do not know, for this small boy was Jesus of Nazareth. Joshua was the name his parents called him—his mother Mary, and her husband

278

Joseph, who was a carpenter. That ancient Hebrew name seemed good to them, for it meant "helper of God." In the Greek language, Joshua is Jesus, and so it has come down to us, for Greek is the language in which his life story was first written for the Roman world.

In this Year 1, which was later supposed to mark his birth, Jesus was perhaps eight, possibly only four or six years old. No one knows exactly, for the two stories telling of his birth do not agree. But that is not to be wondered at, for they were not written until after eighty or ninety years had passed. Seen through the distance of so many years, facts lose their sharp outlines and often appear strange and mysterious like objects seen in starlight.

Matthew and Luke are the two men who wrote the story. Luke was a Greek doctor, writing to a friend in Rome, and so he connected the time of Jesus's birth with a decree issued by the emperor Augustus. Matthew was a Jew. He connected the birth of Jesus with old King Herod, who in the Year 1, had been dead four years. Matthew also was eager to prove to his people that Jesus was the long promised Messiah, so he quoted from the prophets.

This is from the story by Matthew:

"Now, when Jesus was born in Bethlehem of Judaea, in the days of Herod the King, behold there came wise men from the east to Jerusalem, saying 'Where is he that is born King of the Jews? For we have seen his star in the east and are come to worship him.'

And when Herod the King heard it, he was troubled, and gathering together the chief priests and scribes of the people, he inquired of

279

them where the messiah should be born. And they said, in Bethlehem of Judaea, for this it is written through the prophet.

And thou, Bethlehem, in the land of Judah—out of thee shall come a governor who shall rule my people Israel.

Then Herod, when he had privily called the wise men, inquired of them diligently what time the star appeared. And he sent them to Bethlehem, and said, 'Go and search diligently for the young child, and when ye have found him, bring me word again, that I may come and worship him also.'

They departed; and lo, the star which they saw in the east, went before them till it came and stood over where the young child was. And when they were come into the house, they saw the young child with Mary his mother and fell down and worshipped him. And when they had opened their treasures, they presented unto him gifts, gold and frankincense and myrrh. And being warned of God in a dream that they should not return to Herod, they departed into their own country another way.

And behold, the angel of the Lord appeareth to Joseph in a dream, saying, Arise and take the young child and his mother and flee into Egypt and be thou there until I bring thee word: for Herod will seek the young child to destroy him. And he arose and took the young child and his mother by night and departed into Egypt, and was there until the death of Herod: that it might be fulfilled which was spoken of the Lord by the prophet saying: *Out of Egypt have I called my son.*

Then Herod, when he saw that he was mocked by the wise men, was exceedingly wroth, and sent forth and slew all the children that were in Bethlehem, and in all the coasts thereof, from two years old and under, according to the time, which he had diligently inquired of the wise men.

But when Herod was dead, behold the angel of the Lord appeareth in a dream to Joseph in Egypt, saying 'Arise and take the young child and his mother and go into the land of Israel; for they are dead which sought the young child's life.' And he arose and took the young child and his mother and came into the land of Israel. But when he heard that Archelaus did reign in Judaea in the room of his father Herod, he was afraid to go thither; he turned aside into the parts of Galilee. And he came and dwelt in a city called Nazareth that it might be fulfilled which was spoken by the prophets, *He shall be called a Nazarene.*"

This is from the later story written by Luke, a Greek doctor who was born in Antioch, the capital of Syria:

"And it came to pass in those days that there went out a decree from Caesar Augustus, that all the world should be taxed.

And all went to be taxed, every one to his own city. And Joseph also went up from Galilee, out of the city of Nazareth, into Judaea, unto the city of David, which is called Bethlehem (because he was of the lineage of David) to be taxed with Mary, his wife.

And so it was that, while they were there, she brought forth her first born son and wrapped him in swaddling clothes and laid him in a manger, because there was no room for him in the inn.

And there were in the same country shepherds abiding in the field, keeping watch over their flock by night. And lo, the angel of the Lord came upon them, and the glory of the Lord shone round about them and they were sore afraid. And the angel said unto them: Fear not for behold I bring you tidings of great joy, which shall be to all people. For unto you is born this day in the city of David, a Saviour, which is Christ, the Lord. And this shall be a sign unto you; Ye shall find the babe wrapped in swaddling clothes, lying in a manger. And suddenly there was with the angel a multitude of the heavenly host praising God and saying, Glory to God in the highest, peace on earth, good will toward men.

And his name was called Jesus. And, according to the law of Moses, Joseph and his mother brought him to Jerusalem to present him to the Lord and to offer sacrifice—a pair of turtle doves or two young pigeons. And when they had performed all things according to the law of the Lord, they returned to Galilee—to their own city, Nazareth. . . ."

ON A DAY IN THE YEAR 2 A.D. a Roman galley at anchor in the harbor of Rhodes was making ready to depart. Boarding it, followed by slaves carrying his traveling toga, some rolls of books and a few last bags and boxes, was a tall distinguished Roman gentleman, about forty-five years old. He carried his head bent slightly forward, and squinted, as though the sun on the water hurt his eyes.

The traveler was Tiberius. Augustus had finally relented, possibly because Livia would give her husband no peace until he had forgiven her son. Whatever the reason, Tiberius had received the welcome word that he might return to Rome!

Contrary to his mother's ambition, however, he still had no desire to hold public office. But he soon found that his own desire and that of the gods apparently did not agree.

By some strange fate, young Lucius, who was in Spain, was stricken with fever that year, and died on his way home. And within eighteen months, Gaius, who had gone to Armenia, was treacherously wounded and also died.

It was a tragic blow to Augustus—the death of those two young grandsons upon whom he had pinned his hopes. Having now no descendants of his own flesh and blood to follow him, as head of the Roman Empire, Augustus turned at last to Tiberius. And, after all these years of waiting, Livia's hope was realized.

Tiberius was adopted by Augustus as his son and heir.

Tiberius Caesar would become the second Emperor of Rome!

A BOY OF NAZARETH

IN THE GRAY DAWN of a summer morning, while the village of Nazareth was still asleep, a slim boy in a striped tunic might have been seen striding softly along on his sandaled feet toward the edge of the village and the open hillside beyond.

"I will lift up mine eyes unto the hills!" The words of the old psalm were in his heart, as he went swinging along through the cool wet grass of early morning. He climbed to the top of the hill and to a ledge of smooth white rock that caught the first rays of the rising sun.

From that high hill behind the village, one could look far away in all directions. On the western skyline as soon as it grew light could be seen a strip of deepest blue, the waters of the Mediterranean. Soon would come glimpses of bright colored caravans, like miniatures, moving slowly along the distant highway, almost hidden by the hills. Some of these camel trains were going down to Egypt, others coming north along the highway leading to Damascus. From there they might be going on to Parthia or to India, or to some other far-off and mysterious land.

Now, in the dawn, the faint sound of trumpets could be heard, waking a camp of Roman soldiers somewhere in that upland valley.

Rolling hills, covered with green treetops, stretched away to the east, but were cut off abruptly. A jagged line of hills that were barren and gray marked a sharp outline against the eastern sky now growing faintly pink. Between those bare lifeless hills and the green trees, though hidden from sight, lay the gleaming blue sea of Galilee and the Jordan River.

Coming toward Nazareth along the road from that direction, could often be seen the small jogging cart of the publican, who, being a tax collector for the Romans, was thought of as a sinful man. Now in this early morning, there was only a shepherd driving a flock of sheep along the road, and a lone farmer with his two-wheeled wagon bringing an early harvest of grain to the village threshing floor.

Everywhere about lay fields of flax and barley, orchards, and gardens. And directly below were the flat roofs of the small stone houses, the public well and the nearby synagogue.

All this could be seen if a boy looked down to earth from that high hill behind the village. And the earth was very beautiful.

But if one looked up! There was nothing between one and the wide blue sky! Standing there it seemed possible to reach up and touch finger tips to heaven—and to enter into the "secret place of the Most High." And there, in the silence of that most high place, one could feel a rhythmic beating, stronger and more steady than the beating of his heart. And listening—seem to hear within him the whisper of a still small voice—like the small voice that Elijah, the prophet, had heard on Mount Carmel! Within him—within his own heart, then, must also be a secret place of the Most High!

Looking west toward Mount Carmel, he saw the eastern slope of the mountain, now edged with gold. Soon the whole earth was flooded with light—for the sun had risen!

284

It was glorious to see it from that hilltop—joyful just to be walking down the hill again, into so beautiful a world. He could imagine the prophet Isaiah walking beside him and almost hear the words he would be saying,

> With joy shall you go out
> And in peace shall you be led
> And the mountains and hills shall break into singing before you
> And all the trees of the field shall clap their hands.

The psalms and the prophets. There was never a day in his life when a boy of Nazareth did not hear the verses of the psalms or the words of the old prophets. The psalms were the first songs his mother sang to him. The deeds and words of the great Hebrew prophets were taught him each week-day in the school and read aloud each Sabbath in the synagogue.

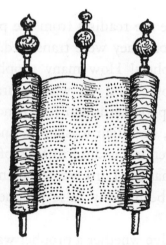

Reading of the law and the prophets was the high point in the service. One sat patiently on a bench waiting for the time when the sacred rolls of parchment would be taken from the Ark. Below the platform, facing the congregation, were the benches of the elders. When they were seated with their long gray beards falling on their chests and their hands folded on their knees, the service began.

"Hear, O Israel, the Lord thy God is One. And thou shalt love the Lord thy God with all thine heart and with all thy soul and with all thy might."

Those well-known words of the first commandment with which the service began were also written on a tiny scroll within a small box fastened to the door post of every house, there to be touched reverently by all who passed.

They were also in the little leather box or phylactery worn on his forehead by a Pharisee. A traveling Pharisee sometimes read from the sacred word on the Sabbath instead of the usual scribe or teacher.

At the appointed time in the service, the doors of the Ark were opened, and the sacred rolls carried from that niche in the back of the platform to the reader's desk. Reading from the law came first. One verse at a time was read in ancient Hebrew, which no one except scholars understood, and then repeated in Aramaic, which was the common language.

After the law came the reading from the prophets, three verses at a time, in Hebrew, before they were translated.

"Those great prophets! How many prophets there had been in Israel!" thought the boy. "And yet what courage it must take to be a prophet! How did a poor herdsman like Amos dare to condemn the wicked lords of Bethel, or Elijah to stand alone against four hundred and fifty priests, or Jeremiah endure to be scoffed at and persecuted? How did they know what the Lord wanted them to say?"

There must have been many false prophets, too, who had been stoned and punished.

But who was to judge whether a prophet was true or false?

How could anyone who did not have the clear-seeing eyes of a prophet understand what a prophet might know or see?

Could those who never left the narrow streets of a village know what there was to be seen from the top of a hill?

שְׁמַע יִשְׂרָאֵל

HEAR O ISRAEL

THE HEBREW PROPHETS

FROM THE DAYS OF MOSES, the first great prophet of Israel who had led his people out of Egypt to the land of Canaan, there had always been prophets among the Hebrews. But most of the great prophets had lived in those few hundred years just before the Golden Age of Greece. Of the three questions which held the interest of the Greek philosophers, the early Hebrew prophets had been interested only in the second.

"How can we live in this world with other people and be happy?" And to that question, this was their one and only answer:

287

"Thou shalt hearken to the voice of thy God and do that which is RIGHT, in the eyes of the Lord."

The Hebrews had been living almost four hundred years in that land of the Phoenicians or Canaanites, to which Moses had led them, when there arose another great prophet, the prophet Elijah.

Like a whirlwind out of the desert came Elijah, out of the wilderness beyond the Jordan River. Dressed only in a hairy skin, held about him with a leather girdle, he came stalking into the city of Bethel. There he bespoke the judgment of the Lord upon the wicked king. For the king and people of Israel had now deserted the God of their fathers for the gods of the Canaanites.

It was not to Jerusalem, but to the city of Bethel, that Elijah went, because the twelve tribes, which David had formed into a nation, were no longer united. After the death of David's son, King Solomon, the ten northern tribes had broken away to form the kingdom of ISRAEL, leaving only two tribes in the kingdom of JUDAH, centered in Jerusalem.

In the days of Elijah, the King of Israel had married a Phoenician princess, and to please his queen, in the city of Bethel, he had built a temple to Baal, the god of the Canaanites.

"For this," cried Elijah, "as the Lord liveth, before whom I stand, there shall not be dew nor rain for years upon this land."

Three years of drought and famine followed, during which Elijah lived beside a brook fed only by the ravens. And then he returned.

"Art thou he who is making trouble in Israel?" grumbled the king.

"I have not troubled Israel," answered Elijah, "but thou and thy father's house. Ye have forsaken the Lord and followed after Baal.

Now, therefore, send and gather all the people of Israel unto Mount Carmel, and the prophets of Baal, four hundred and fifty."

There on Mount Carmel Elijah proposed a test to prove which was the true God, Jehovah or Baal.

First the prophets of Baal laid a bullock on their altar and tried, by crying, and jumping, and slashing their arms with knives, to bring down fire upon it, but in vain.

Then Elijah laid a bullock on the altar to Jehovah, and it was said the people saw fire sent down from heaven to consume the offering. And they fell on their faces, crying:

"He is the true God. The Lord—Jehovah, he is God!"

And Elijah said unto them: "Take the prophets of Baal; let none of them escape." And Elijah slew them, every one. And soon the heaven was black with clouds and wind and there was a great rain. The drought was over.

To escape the vengeance of the angry queen, Elijah fled for his life. In time, he and his disciple Elisha were walking by the Jordan River, near Jericho. . . . "And it came to pass, as they still went on, and talked, that behold, there appeared a chariot of fire, and horses of fire—and Elijah went up by a whirlwind into heaven!"

One hundred years after Elijah came the prophet Amos.

Amos was the first Hebrew prophet to put his words into writing. So the book of Amos, although now placed far from the beginning among the books in the Bible, is believed to be the first one to be written—written about the time that Rome was supposed to have been founded.

Amos was a herdsman. Though he lived in Judah, not far from Jerusalem, he often took his wool north to be sold in Bethel, the rich city of Israel. A plain, honest man, each time he went Amos was shocked by what he saw. Princes, priests, all the rich and powerful of the city were robbing the poor, and yet, before the altar making great show of their religion.

The injustice of it, the falseness of it, burned within him, until one day Amos was given the courage to speak. And his voice was hard and harsh as he prophesied the awful Day of Judgment to come.

"Hear this word ye cattle who oppress the poor and crush the needy. . . . Hear this word that the Lord hath spoken against you, O children of Israel.

Because you tread upon the poor and take from him his share of wheat, though you have built houses of hewn stone, you shall not live in them. I hate, I despise your feast days saith the Lord. Though ye offer me burnt offerings and your meat offerings, I will not accept them. For I know thy many trangressions and thy mighty sins. Behold the eyes of the Lord are on this sinful nation and I will destroy it!"

The high priest of Bethel, unable to bear the true words of Amos, denounced this courageous prophet as a traitor, and had him driven away. But Amos wrote down his words of righteous indignation that they might never be forgotten.

Hosea : Micah

HOSEA and MICAH, who followed Amos very shortly, also feared and believed that God would punish the people of Israel for their sins. Yet they saw him as more gentle and loving than Amos had imagined him. He would turn away his anger and "love them freely" said Hosea, if they would simply do what he required of them.

"And what doth the Lord require of thee," said Micah, "but to do justly, and to love mercy and to walk humbly with thy God?"

Yet if the people of Israel would not listen they must suffer; and the people of Jerusalem, too. Not even the great Temple would save them from the disaster that the Lord would send upon them for their wickedness.

"Because of you, Jerusalem shall become a ruin," said Micah, "and the hill of the Temple as a place in the forest."

And, as they had feared, the blow fell first upon Israel. In the year 722 B.C. the northern kingdom was destroyed and the ten tribes carried off to exile in Babylon, never to return, but to be lost forever. Foreigners were moved into Samaria. That was during the lifetime of the great prophet Isaiah.

Isaiah

Isaiah was a native of Jerusalem and had been counsellor to the kings of Judah for over twenty years when the kingdom of Israel was destroyed. And he could see that just as surely as Israel had fallen, Jerusalem would fall, for the kings of Judah were also wicked.

"Woe unto ye that make unrighteous decrees," he said unto them. "Hear ye the word of the Lord, ye rulers: To what purpose are your many sacrifices? saith the Lord. I will hide my eyes from you. Your hands are full of blood. Wash you; make you clean; seek justice; relieve the poor; watch over the fatherless; plead for the widow.

Come now, let us reason together, saith the Lord. If ye be willing and obedient, ye shall eat the good of the land. But if ye refuse and rebel, ye shall be devoured with the sword, for the mouth of the Lord hath spoken it."

But Isaiah saw further than that to the time when, purged of its sin, Jerusalem would be reestablished as a city of righteousness. And even further he seemed to see to a time when a great and wise king should come forth from the family tree of David.

"And the spirit of the Lord shall rest upon him, the spirit of wisdom and understanding. And his name shall be called Wonderful, Counsellor—the Prince of Peace. Of the increase of his government and peace there shall be no end, upon the throne of David. And he shall judge among nations. And they shall beat their swords into plowshares and their spears into pruning hooks; neither shall they learn war any more."

Such was the vision of Isaiah, while he still continued to warn the kings of their coming destruction. In the end, it is said, one king more wicked than the others did away with the old prophet by having him sawed in two.

This king had now set up an image of the Babylonian goddess Ishtar in the sacred Temple, and altars to the sun, the moon, and all the other planet gods of Babylon, for the people to worship.

And then about fifty years later came the great prophet Jeremiah.

Jeremiah is often called the weeping prophet," for though he worked, pleaded, and prophesied unceasingly, he also wept, as well he might, for he could not turn the minds and hearts of the people from their wickedness. He was mocked at, thrown into a slimy dungeon, and when he predicted that Jerusalem would surely fall, he was seized as a traitor and barely escaped death. And then came the dark days when Jerusalem did fall, the Temple was destroyed, and all but a handful of the people carried off to Babylon.

As a young man, Jeremiah had had hope that the people would be brought back to the God of their fathers. A good king had come to the throne. And, in repairing the Temple, there was found in the wall a book called Deuteronomy, or the laws of Moses, which had been written and hidden there during the evil days of the wicked king who had killed the prophet Isaiah.

But Jeremiah soon realized that enforcing the law could not change the hearts of the people, and that true religion did not come from without, but from within.

And so he predicted that in days to come the Lord would make a new covenant with his people.

"And in those days, saith the Lord
I will put my law in their inward parts
And write it in their hearts.
And no more shall every man teach his neighbor saying
Know the Lord
For they shall all know me.
From the least of them unto the greatest."

Daniel

In time the Persians had conquered Babylonia. And it was a Persian king who set free the Judaeans or "JEWS" as they were from then on to be called. He allowed them to return to Jerusalem.

Like the Roman captives returning from Parthia, the Jews, who had lived there in ancient Babylon, had also learned of the great religion founded by the prophet Zoroaster.

They learned of the Persian idea of Paradise, of angels of light and the devil of darkness.

And the Hebrew prophets began to be interested as they had not been before in the question of what might happen to a man after he was dead, and to believe in life after death. One of these prophets was DANIEL, who lived at the court of the Persian king.

"Many of them that sleep in the dust of the earth," said Daniel, "shall awake, some to everlasting life, some to shame and everlasting contempt."

But this reward or punishment was not to be meted out as soon as each man died, as the Persians believed, but on some awful day of wholesale judgment of which Daniel beheld a vision in the night.

"And I beheld, until the thrones [of the earth] were cast down and the Ancient of Days did sit, whose garment was white as snow and the hair of his head like pure wool. Ten thousand times ten thousand stood before him, the judgment was set and the books were opened.

And behold, one like the Son of Man came with clouds of heaven, and came to the Ancient of Days and they brought him near before him. And there was given him dominion and glory—an everlasting dominion and a kingdom that shall not be destroyed."

It was to be a heavenly kingdom, according to Daniel, ruled over by some celestial being—a Kingdom of Heaven!

Malachi

But this day of judgment, predicted by the prophets, was not to come upon the people without warning. They would be warned of it, said MALACHI, who was the last of the old prophets.

"For behold, the day cometh that shall burn as an oven, and all the proud, yea and all that do wickedly—the day cometh that shall burn them up, saith the Lord. But unto you that fear my name, shall the Sun of righteousness arise, with healing in his wings.

"Behold, I will send you ELIJAH the prophet before the coming of the great and dreadful day."

So Elijah was coming to warn them when the day of judgment was upon them and the Kingdom of Heaven was at hand.

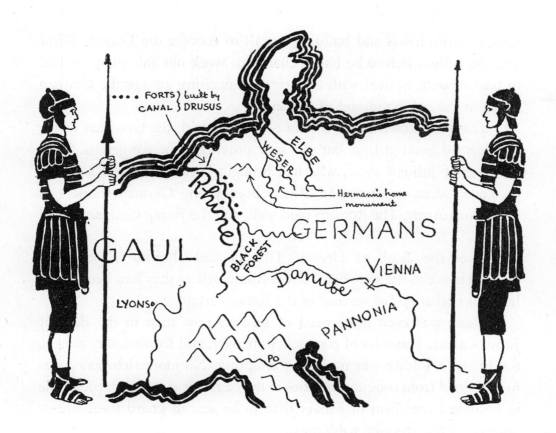

ON THE GERMAN BORDER

A LTHOUGH SO RECENTLY RETURNED, and now raised to a position second only to that of Augustus himself, Tiberius was not able to remain in Rome. The problem of protecting the frontier against the German tribes demanding his attention, and very shortly he left for the German border.

Tiberius went north first, to explore the territory between the Weser River and the Elbe, and was convinced that there was nothing to be gained by going farther into that swampy wilderness.

He considered instead the region of the Black Forest, where fourteen years ago his brother Drusus, exploring that region, had suffered an accidental injury and died. There Tiberius now proposed making

295

strong fortifications and building a wall to connect the Danube River and the Rhine. Before he had a chance to work out this plan, he had to hasten south to deal with a threatened uprising among the German tribes in the neighborhood of Vienna.

This had grown out of a plan of dealing with the Germans which had seemed good at first, but was now proving to be dangerous. Since the days of Julius Caesar, who had brought back from Gaul a legion of 6,000 Germans, there had always been young German soldiers in the Roman Army. The Romans paid well, and the young Germans loved to fight.

After the death of Drusus, Tiberius had allowed 40,000 Germans to move to the west bank of the Rhine, where they had been given land, in exchange for serving in the Roman army.

There was even more need of soldiers now than in the days of Julius Caesar. The wars of conquest were over, and for that very reason, the life of a soldier was no longer tempting. No more rich booty was to be gained from conquering cities in the east. It was far more profitable to become a merchant or banker than to be sent to guard some dreary outpost in the frontier wilderness.

For the Germans, it was quite a different story. It gave the young German chiefs a chance to be drilled in the Roman way of fighting. And right there lay the danger.

After learning all the tactics, it was quite natural that ambitious young Germans should be tempted to practice what they had learned against their former teachers.

That was exactly what had now happened in Vienna.

One of those promising young Germans who had been brought up and educated by Augustus himself had conceived the idea that, by uniting several tribes, he might form a German empire patterned after that of the Romans!

He had gathered his followers near Vienna, on the Danube River, and was drilling them, making preparations.

It was a report of this which had reached Tiberius. Leaving Varus, the same Varus who had been the former governor of Syria, in charge in the north, Tiberius hastened south at once.

In Rome, Augustus also was very much disturbed by the news. Vienna was much too near for safety to Pannonia, which was one of the most explosive and weakly protected spots in the empire.

And his worries never seemed to come singly. From the east, too, as well as the west, came annoying reports. From that ever troublesome little country of Judaea.

Those Jews! thought Augustus. More stubborn and difficult to manage they were than any other civilized people under the rule of Rome.

And with less cause for complaint, so far as he could see. Every effort was made not to interfere with their temple services or religion. In order not to offend their sensitive feelings, the Roman legions did not even carry their standards into Jerusalem. And little or no notice was paid to the fact that they refused to offer the customary sacrifice to him, the emperor.

The utmost consideration was shown them, and yet they were always on edge.

Now they were complaining bitterly against the rule of Archelaus. Complaints came from Samaria as well as Jerusalem. It would be necessary, it seemed, to get rid of Archelaus, and have no more independent rulers in Judaea.

Let Judaea be reduced to a second rate province, and from now on be ruled by governors sent out directly from Rome.

It was now the year 6 A.D.

The time had also come for another census to be taken in Palestine, and that, too, seemed always to be a cause of irritation to the Jews. Especially in Galilee, that breeding place of rebels. Augustus sincerely hoped that Varus and his burning of Sepphoris would discourage another uprising, but one never knew. One never could tell what to expect from Galilee.

THE PASSOVER

EARLY APRIL OF THE YEAR 6, Nazareth and all the villages of Galilee were abustle with excitement—but only in preparation for the annual journey to Jerusalem to celebrate the Passover. There was no rebellion. Although the decree of Caesar Augustus had been received that a census was to be taken for collecting taxes, there was no uprising against the Romans in that year 6, either in Jerusalem or in Galilee.

The high priests in Jerusalem had persuaded the resentful people that it would be of no use to resist. In Galilee, the hot-blooded Judas, who had stirred up the last rebellion, after the death of Herod, ten years before, tried, but failed, to start another. Around the Sea of Galilee he found some ready followers again, but none near that great city which had been ruined by Varus. The men of Nazareth shook their heads. The memory was still too vivid of those rows of crosses upon which thousands of their neighbors had died. They would not run the risk of another wholesale crucifixion.

PASSOVER

The Roman census was taken every fourteen years. So if, according to Luke, Jesus had been born at the time of the last census, he was now fourteen. But, according to Matthew, he may have been only twelve, and this would be his first journey to Jerusalem. To be considered a man, a "son of the Law," and to be going to the great feast of the Passover, that was a thrilling time in a boy's life. He could almost feel how his ancient ancestors must have felt at the time of the first Passover, when they learned they were to follow Moses out of Egypt to the promised land!

The previous weeks and days in the village were filled with preparation. Each traveler must be dressed in his best homespun, and each have a fresh, newly bleached headcovering to wear.

The journey would take three days, so tents had to be provided, sleeping rugs rolled up, baskets of food packed, and bottles of wine filled. Small groups of men arranged to pool their money and purchase a lamb together for the sacrifice. They elected one man to take charge and represent them when they got there.

Then, one early morning, all was ready and the procession started, men and boys on foot, the women riding donkeys. As they left the village, someone burst into song, and they all joined in:

> "I was glad when they said unto me
> Let us go into the house of the Lord."

The House of the Lord, thought the boy. "How wonderful it would be—silent and beautiful, with all the people kneeling!"

"Our feet shall stand within thy gates, O Jerusalem!" they sang.

The shortest route to Jerusalem from Galilee ran directly south through Samaria, but the people from Nazareth were soon turning east instead, toward the Jordan River. There, on the outskirts of a manufacturing city, they were joined by a larger company of pilgrims coming down from Capernaum and other places along the Sea of Galilee.

Here the company divided. Some crossed the Jordan to avoid even the edge of Samaria. Others, less fearful that the dust of the wicked nation would pollute their feet, continued along the west bank of the winding river. The valley sank lower and lower and grew hotter and hotter as they went south. At Jericho, they were joined again by those who had crossed the river.

JERICHO! This city, then, was Jericho, thought the boys who were seeing it for the first time. This was the place where the people from Egypt had entered the promised land. This was the spot to which Joshua had led them after Moses had died. This was Jericho, the city that Joshua had captured. Around the campfires that night, the old legend was told again, of how the walls of Jericho had come tumbling down—how "Seven priests, bearing seven trumpets of ram's horns before the Ark of the Lord, blew with their trumpets, and the armed men before them and the people following, went round the city for six days. And on the seventh day they went round seven times. And at the seventh time, when the priests blew with the trumpets, the people shouted with a great shout, and the wall fell down flat and they took the city."

That had happened 1,200 years ago. Jericho, which then must have been a crude little town, was now a most beautiful city of palaces and theatres, of rose gardens and groves of palms. There to be seen was the palace which Herod had built, and also the new palace and gardens of Archelaus, in which he would never live again. For Herod's son had now been banished by the Romans.

The first new governor sent out from Rome would be in Jerusalem for this Passover.

Jerusalem was now only fifteen miles away! In the morning, leaving the Jordan River, which would soon lose itself in the Dead Sea, the pilgrims began the long climb to Jerusalem. Up and up they went, over steep, barren hills, through a treeless, stony wilderness, wild and uninhabited, bleak and awful compared to the fertile fields of Galilee. But who should complain? Was not the Temple of the Lord at the end of that long, thirsty climb?

It was late afternoon when they rounded the top of the last hill, the Mount of Olives, and there, across the valley, was the Temple! There Jesus saw it for the first time—the beautiful golden roof of the Temple shining in the sun!

That night the country people of Nazareth pitched their little tents among the thousands of others on the hillside. The next evening, at sundown, the first day of the Passover would begin.

Early in the morning they were on the viaduct leading over the valley to the Temple. Crowds of people from everywhere were moving in the same direction. There were crowds, as they entered the Porch of Solomon. They were gathering about the teachers of the Law— some of whom had phylacteries on their wrists as well as on their foreheads. Roman soldiers in their helmets were marching along the roof and crossing the great outer court, into which they now passed. That, too, was filled with a seething crowd of all kinds of people. Country folks like themselves, haughty townsmen dressed in long silk robes banded with fur and glittering with jewels, and with gold chains swinging from their necks. Paupers, beggars in rags, handsome Greeks in short tunics, rich Jews from Egypt and Asia, visitors from Rome in fashionable togas. Old men in tightly curled beards, young men in high striped turbans. White skins—brown skins—black. Slaves following their masters, carrying bags of gold. Tailors with bright yarns threaded through their ear lobes, money-changers with earrings of gold coins, tradesmen of all kinds going to or coming from the southern porch where each trade had its booth. Scribes with goose-quill pens sat at tables writing prayers on parchment for the crowds of onlookers to buy. Porters passed carrying crates of pigeons. Back and forth went the people, gathering in knots to talk, arguing, laughing, squabbling, chatting, in every kind of voice and language.

Confusion and babel was everywhere. The sound of bugles came from the fortress. From the inner court came the sound of trumpets, the chanting of psalms, singing, the muffled bleating of sheep, the nearby rattle of money being dropped into the funnels along the wall. For now they had climbed the steps and were inside in the Inner Court, the court of the women. There was a balcony over the next gate where the mothers could sit.

But a twelve-year-old boy could go into the Court of Israel with the men. Some pushed in front of them, to get nearer to the railing, for a better view. Priests in their white robes were moving back and forth. The altar was smoking.

A chorus of Levites were singing, but the words were soon drowned by the sound of hoofs.

The man elected from Nazareth had gone around to the north gate to bring in the lamb when his turn came. The priests now raised their silver trumpets and blew three blasts. Twenty or more men came in leading as many lambs. Each placed his hand on the head of the lamb to lay upon it the sins of those for whom it was being sacrificed. Then, twisting its head to face the Temple, each one threw his lamb on the pavement, and slit its throat. The blood gushed out. Priests caught it in golden bowls and poured it on the base of the altar. The dead lamb was then hung on a hook, the hide removed by the butchers, the fat cut off and burned with a piece of meat on the altar. That was all. The part of Nazareth in the service was over. They went out while the priests blew three blasts on the trumpets and more lambs came in. . . .

The evening air was cool and sweet on the hillside as they ate the Passover meal just after sunset. Over an open fire, turning on a spit, the lamb, brought back from the Temple, was roasting whole. A pale moon came up.

Seated in a circle, they sang the psalm which the Levites had sung at the altar, each word full of meaning.

"Oh praise ye the Lord. Praise, O ye servants, the name of the Lord . . . our God, who dwelleth on High. . . . When Israel went out of Egypt . . . from a people of strange language . . . the sea saw it and fled; Jordan was driven back. . . . The mountains skipped like rams and the little hills like lambs."

The wine was blessed and each one drank a cup. Bitter herbs were eaten, dipped in vinegar, sweetened only with dates and raisins.

"What mean ye by this service?" a boy's voice asked. And in each circle, a father's voice replied:

"It is the sacrifice of the Lord's Passover, who passed over the houses of the children of Egypt while he smote the Egyptians and delivered our houses."

Unleavened cakes were then eaten with another cup of wine. And then came the Passover lamb, which must all be finished by midnight. In closing came the singing of three more psalms of praise.

"O praise the Lord all ye nations: praise him all ye people.
For his merciful kindness is great toward us
And the truth of the Lord endureth forever.
Praise ye the Lord.
O give thanks unto the Lord, for he is good
For his mercy endureth forever."

Jesus did not sleep at once. He lay awake watching the stars above the roof of the Temple, now shining softly in the moonlight. Was the Lord there now, he wondered? Confused and puzzled over many things he had seen and heard, he found many questions he wished to ask the teachers in the Temple. They could tell him, he felt sure—not the ones who made great show of praying, with their arms upraised, but those others, with the wise quiet eyes.

In the morning he was there in the Porch of Solomon, talking with the wise men. One of the teachers he may have heard that morning was the great rabbi Hillel, for he was still living. So absorbed was the boy that he was not aware of it when the company from Nazareth left for home.

Nor did Joseph and his mother know that he had tarried behind. But, according to the story told by Luke:

"Supposing him to have been in the company they went on a day's journey; and they sought him among their kinsfolk and acquaintance. And when they found him not, they turned back again to Jerusalem, seeking him.

And it came to pass, that after three days they found him in the Temple, sitting in the midst of the teachers, both hearing them and asking them questions. And all that heard him were astonished at his understanding and answers.

And when his parents saw him, they were amazed.

And his mother said unto him, Son, why hast thou thus dealt with us? Behold, thy father and I have sought thee sorrowing.

And he said unto them, How is it that ye sought me? Knew ye not that I must be about my Father's business?

And they understood not the saying which he spoke to them. And he went down with them, and came to Nazareth, and was subject unto them; but his mother kept all these sayings in her heart.

And Jesus increased in wisdom and stature, and in favor with God and man."

And that is all we know of Jesus of Nazareth until twenty-three years later when he was over thirty.

AUGUSTUS CAESAR was growing no younger. In August of the year 7 he would celebrate his seventieth birthday. This past year, however, had brought him much more cause for anxiety than for celebration. Feeling weak and miserable from a recent illness, he sat one day with a shawl about his shoulders at his desk in the tablinum, writing a letter to Tiberius, who was still in camp on the frontier.

"I swear to you, my dear Tiberius," he began. Then stopping to adjust his pen, he held it poised for some time, lost in his anxiety over the safety of Tiberius and the empire.

As he had long feared, rebellion had now broken out in the empire's most weakly defended spot—in Pannonia. Fortunately there had been no uprising in Palestine, and from the ambitious young German chieftain in Vienna there was nothing more to be feared. He had been quickly cowed and frightened into seeing the folly of his ways by the mere approach of the Roman legions. But scarcely had Tiberius come to peaceful terms with him, when this more serious rebellion had broken out in Pannonia.

There on the Adriatic Sea—not ten days' marching time from Rome—the natives had suddenly attacked and slaughtered not only merchants, salesmen and tax-collectors traveling from town to town, but Roman citizens, who had lived there peacefully for many years!

Tiberius had gone at once to the scene of the rebellion. He was still there, and his young nephew, Germanicus, the son of Drusus, was with him, getting his first taste of active service.

Augustus had faith in Tiberius. He felt sure that he would restore the province to order—if the gods were willing. But what if they were unwilling? What if Tiberius, also, should be taken from him? His fears, magnified by his weakness, made Augustus' hand shake, as he continued writing:

"I swear to you, my dear Tiberius, when I hear that you are getting thin under the continuance of your labors, may I be confounded if my body is not all one shudder and I implore you to spare yourself, lest, if we hear that you are in bad health, your mother and I may expire and the Roman people be in danger of losing its imperial position. It does not matter a bit whether I, myself, am ill or well, if you are not well. I implore the gods to preserve you to us, and give you your health now and always, if they do not utterly hate the Roman people."

Having finished his letter, Augustus rose and walked slowly down the few steps into the peristylium, putting on a broad-brimmed hat to shield his head from the bright light of the open courtyard.

There he sat down to exchange a few words with the three favorite women of his family. They were women to be proud of, these three, Augustus thought, looking from one to another. There was Livia, his wife, as handsome and attractive in his eyes as the day he married her. And Antonia, his niece, who was the mother of young Germanicus. She must be all of forty-five, and yet she still had the gentleness and sweetness she had as a young girl. And Agrippina, his slim pretty granddaughter, who was the young wife of Germanicus. There was one of Julia's children who was truly a joy and comfort to her grandfather.

These three, all mothers of future Emperors, were sewing, trying to keep up a cheerful conversation although they too were filled with anxiety.

Augustus, only half listening to what they were saying, soon became absorbed again in his own thoughts.

If the rebellion continued over many months, he was thinking, Tiberius's need for soldiers would become very critical. It might be necessary to require every man and woman in Rome to free a certain number of their slaves to be enrolled in the army and sent to the front. . . . Ten days' marching time from Rome! That was bringing rebellion dangerously close to the heart of his empire!

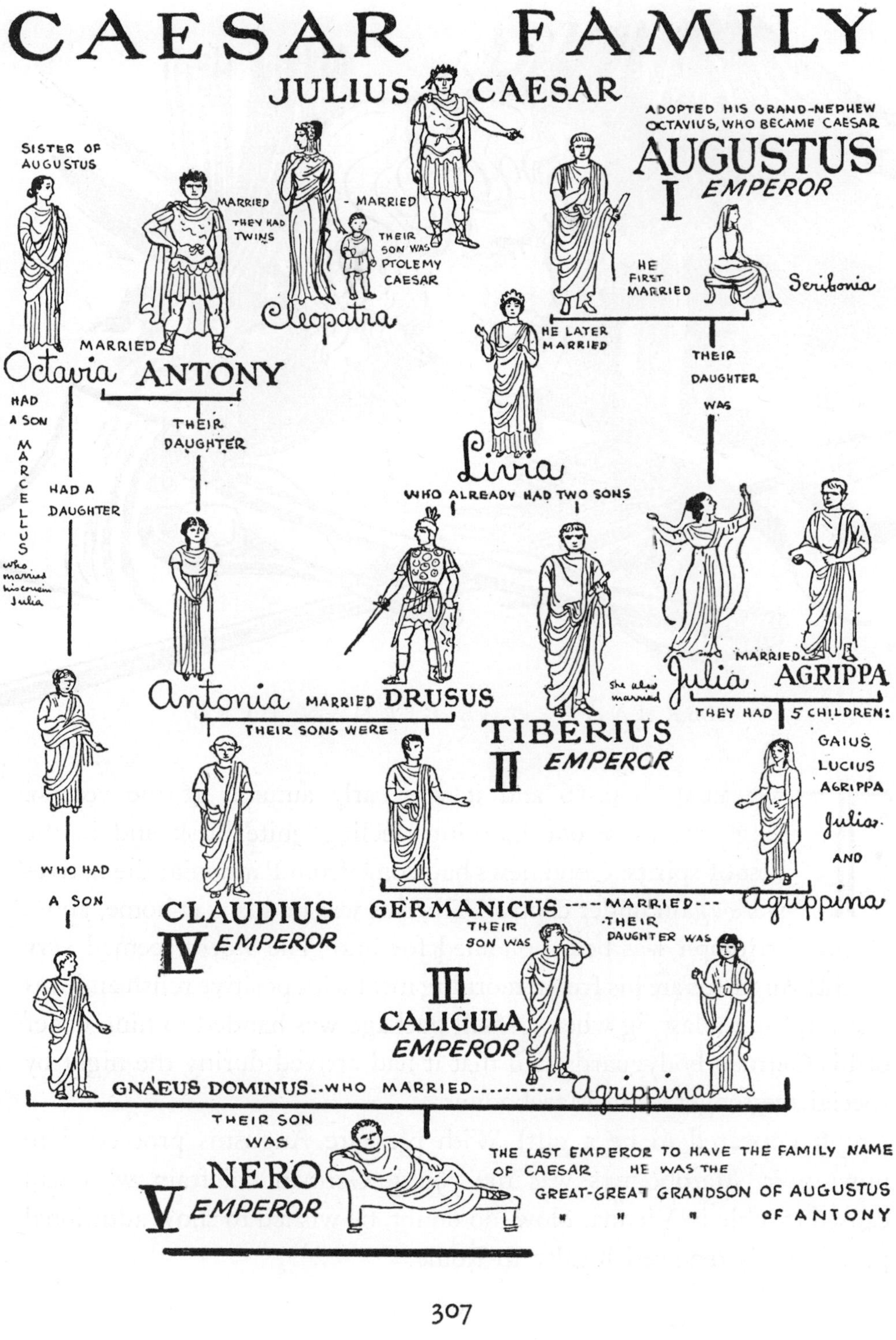

CAESAR FAMILY

JULIUS CAESAR

ADOPTED HIS GRAND-NEPHEW
OCTAVIUS, WHO BECAME CAESAR

AUGUSTUS
I EMPEROR

SISTER OF
AUGUSTUS

MARRIED
THEY HAD
TWINS

THEIR
SON WAS
PTOLEMY
CAESAR

Cleopatra

HE
FIRST
MARRIED

Scribonia

MARRIED

Octavia **ANTONY**

HE LATER
MARRIED

THEIR
DAUGHTER
WAS

HAD
A SON
MARCELLUS
who married
his cousin
Julia

HAD A
DAUGHTER

THEIR
DAUGHTER

Livia

WHO ALREADY HAD TWO SONS

She also
married

MARRIED

Julia **AGRIPPA**

THEY HAD 5 CHILDREN:
GAIUS
LUCIUS
AGRIPPA
Julia.
AND

Antonia MARRIED **DRUSUS**

THEIR SONS WERE

TIBERIUS
II EMPEROR

WHO HAD
A SON

CLAUDIUS
IV EMPEROR

GERMANICUS ---- MARRIED --- *Agrippina*
THEIR
SON WAS

THEIR
DAUGHTER WAS

III
CALIGULA
EMPEROR

GNAEUS DOMINUS..WHO MARRIED............ *Agrippina*

THEIR SON
WAS

NERO
V EMPEROR

THE LAST EMPEROR TO HAVE THE FAMILY NAME
OF CAESAR   HE WAS THE
GREAT-GREAT GRANDSON OF AUGUSTUS
"   "   "   OF ANTONY

HERMANN, THE GERMAN HERO

TWO YEARS PASSED and it was early autumn of the year 9. Augustus woke one morning, feeling quite brisk and in the best of spirits. Good news had come from Pannonia; the natives were again under control. Tiberius was on his way home, and a splendid triumph was being planned for him. The world seemed very bright! Augustus ate his frugal morning meal with positive relish and was just finishing a last fig when a small package was handed to him. Chief of his German bodyguards said that it had arrived during the night by special messenger from Maroboduus.

It appeared to be a gift! With pleasure Augustus proceeded to unwrap it. Maroboduus was the young German chieftain who had caused trouble in Vienna. Now, no doubt, he wished to show additional proof of his renewed loyalty to Rome.

308

Then, as the contents lay revealed, the Emperor's face turned gray. He stared as if he could not believe his eyes. What he saw was the head of a man, cut off at the neck!

"Varus!" he gasped hoarsely, as he recognized the face of the former governor of Syria, whom Tiberius had left to govern the Germans near the mouth of the Rhine.

"O Varus! O my legions!" moaned Augustus as he learned of the full tragedy. Not only had Varus been murdered, but thousands of soldiers, almost three Roman legions, had been slaughtered by the Germans. "O Varus, Varus!" he moaned, "give me back my legions!"

This is the story of what had happened. To the Romans, it was a tale of treachery. To Germans of later years it would be a story of patriotism. Either way, it is one of the deciding events in the history of Europe.

The chief character in the story is Hermann, a young German prince or chieftain whose Roman name was Arminius.

It was from Hermann that Maroboduus had received the bloody head of Varus. Hermann had sent it to him hoping, with this proof of prowess, to enlist his rival's help against the Romans. But Maroboduus, now preferring safety to freedom, had sent the gruesome trophy on to Augustus, with sympathetic report of the disaster.

Hermann, who was about twenty-five years old, was another one of those young Germans who had been sent to receive training as a Roman soldier and was an officer commanding one of the legions under Varus. When Varus had been sent to guard or govern the German territory near the Weser River, young Hermann was back in his own native homeland. His father was king of one of the tribes inhabiting that half-conquered Roman province.

Hermann found many of his tribesmen boiling with hatred for the Romans. Not all of them, to be sure. They were divided. Some thought it best to accept the Roman rule, and adopt the Romans' more civilized way of living as well as their way of fighting. But there were just as many who resented being forced to give up their old law and

309

customs, and abide by Roman law. That encouraged young Hermann in his dream of fighting for independence. As a beginning, he formed a daring plot against his commander.

As governor, Varus had spent the summer going about, holding court here and there, handing out judgments, settling disputes, in a harsh, unfeeling manner that was characteristic of him.

September came, and, considering that his work was done for that season, Varus was about to move from his summer quarters near the Weser River back to winter quarters on the Rhine.

Just the night before leaving, however, Hermann told him at dinner that trouble had arisen between two tribes that ought to be settled before he left. It meant going northwest again into difficult country. And winter storms were on the way.

Other Germans, friendly to the Romans, saw and warned Varus that it was a trap.

Varus laughed loudly, being a man who could be told nothing, and said that he could rely on his own judgment—that he trusted Hermann implicitly. Indeed, he so trusted that young officer, that the next morning, when they set out for the northwest, he put Hermann in charge of the soldiers guarding the supply wagons.

It was a stormy day, wet leaves were blowing. Hermann went along until they were well on into the thick forest; then he slipped away to gather his own troops, recruited among the Germans.

Varus and the Romans went on hacking their way through the wet tangled thicket while the rain increased. Soon huge trees began to topple down on every side of them—trees which had been sawed half through by the Germans during the night.

The second day, the attack came suddenly. As they were struggling through a swamp, whizzing out from all directions came spears and arrows, hurled by an unseen enemy hidden in the underbrush.

On the third day came the end. The Romans, retreating, had struggled to the top of a ridge on the very peak of which stood a ring of huge stones, as an altar to the German gods.

They were descending toward an open plain ahead, when, down upon them like wild men, with their blond hair and beards flying in the wind, came the Germans, in their iron helmets, shouting and singing songs of battle.

Varus fell upon his sword, so that he was dead when they cut his head off. Only a few of the soldiers escaped to tell the tale. All the rest were dragged up to the ring of stones on top of the mountain and there sacrificed on the altar to the gods. Their heads were found later fastened to trees in the sacred grove.

By this victory, Hermann had gained control of all the Roman forts and outposts on the German side of the Rhine. It was feared that he might cross the river and go sweeping down through Gaul.

But Tiberius, rushing to meet him, held the Rhine line secure. And that was enough to do, it was decided by both Augustus and Tiberius. Never again were the Romans to establish their authority beyond the Rhine. The Germans would remain independent—slowly, and their own way, develop and become civilized.

And so, by blocking the spread of the Roman civilization into Germany, this victory of Hermann changed the future of Europe. How it might have differed, what future wars might have been avoided, had this not been so, no one can say.

Hermann's ambition was to unite the German tribes, but this was never to be accomplished. They continued to disagree and fight with one another. Only part of Hermann's own tribe ever stood behind him, and even members of his own family were against him. He was to die, ten years later, stabbed in the back by one of his own kinsmen.

But future fellow countrymen were to look back upon this young Hermann as the liberator of Germany. Poems, songs and plays would be written about him. And today a monument, a tremendous bronze statue of this first German hero, stands on top of the mountain where the victory is said to have taken place. It is encircled by that ring of altar stones upon which the Roman soldiers were sacrificed to the old gods of Valhalla.

AUGUST, THE MONTH in which the greatest good fortune had always come to him, and which bears his name, also brought the life of Augustus Caesar to a close. He died on the 19th day of August in the Roman year 767, which we call 14 A.D. He was at his small country house near Naples. A few days before, though in miserable health, he had sat through and tried to show pleasure in an exhibition of gymnastic games given in his honor. Following the games, Tiberius, who had been his stepfather's almost constant companion for the past two years, left on an important mission. He was recalled almost immediately, as Augustus felt himself growing weaker.

The nineteenth of August was a breathlessly hot day. The dying emperor talked with such difficulty that it was not long before he relaxed and gave no more attention to affairs of state.

Calling for a mirror, he ordered his hair to be combed. His cheeks were badly shrunken, and he wanted them pulled out. Then he looked at the circle of friends standing about the room, and asked:

"Do you think I have acted my part on the stage of life well? If so," he added, quoting a Greek poet, " 'with joy your voices raise in loud applauses to the actor's praise.' "

Other people entered, who had just arrived from Rome. Augustus inquired about one of the younger members of the family who was ill. Then he dismissed them all—except Livia. He turned to the wife with whom he had lived happily for over forty years.

"Live mindful of our union, Livia; and now—farewell," he said and passed away quickly and quietly, as he had always wished he might.

Because of the extreme heat, the soldiers carrying his body traveled only by night, so they were several days in covering the distance between Naples and Rome.

Meanwhile the emperor's will, written on parchment in his own distinctive handwriting, was brought to the Senate by the Vestal Virgins.

312

Tiberius called the meeting. The Senators were extravagant in their proposals to do honor to the man who had been first on their roll call for almost forty-five years. Outside on the forum and in the streets, the people, too, were extreme in their sorrow and desire to honor the first citizen of Rome. Tiberius urged the Senators to be moderate, and warned the people not to go to excess, as they had at the time of Julius Caesar's death.

The ceremony was therefore dignified and orderly, as Augustus would have wished it to be. On the day of the funeral, the coffin, which was in the shape of a golden couch, was carried from his home on the Palatine to the Forum. It was draped in purple, and on it lay an image of the emperor, dressed as he had been on the day of his triple Triumph. Another image of the great statesman, cast in gold, was carried from the Senate House, followed by images of his famous and mythical ancestors, back to Aeneas and the goddess Venus.

Two funeral orations were spoken in his praise: one by Tiberius, in front of the Temple to the god, Julius Caesar; the other in front of the rostrum.

Then, following the coffin, borne on the shoulders of the Senators, a long line of mourners, headed by Tiberius, walked slowly through the narrow streets, to the sound of trumpets and muffled drums—out past the Capitoline, past the theatre Marcellus, and the Pantheon—and out along the Tiber to the Campus Martius, where the pyre had been erected.

Wine, oil and spices were then ceremoniously poured upon it.

The name of the dead Caesar was called, three times. And when no answer broke the silence, the torch was laid to the funeral pyre and soon it was ablaze. Flames and smoke rose high.

And as they watched, many believed that they saw in the smoke the shape of an eagle, rising toward heaven, carrying the spirit of the dead to his eternal place of glory among the stars.

"Farewell," they cried. "Farewell!"

And when the fire had died down at last, and the ashes were cool— barefooted, and with loosened tunics, the most distinguished of those

Romans bearing the rank of Knight gathered up the ashes and, in company with Livia, deposited them in the Imperial Mausoleum.

Thus ended the life of the man who had reorganized the Roman empire so soundly, and so established it in the way of peace and order, that the time in which he ruled was to be known to future generations as the great Augustan Age—the "Golden Age" of Rome.

THE KINGDOM OF HEAVEN

THE AGE OF AUGUSTUS is now behind us. His day is past but in order to know the end of the story, which began in Judaea in those peaceful days of Augustus when the gates of Janus were closed, we must look with that old god into the future.

Had this truly been a "Golden" Age?

Not for the Jews. They were still waiting for the Kingdom of Heaven to be established, which would be their Golden Age.

The Sadducees were satisfied with the rule of Rome. And the princes and high priests appointed by Rome had prospered as always. But the majority of the nation chafed under the Roman rule.

Most of the Pharisees believed that the evil would end in God's own time; they had only to be patient and wait.

The rebels or Zealots refused to be patient. They wanted to hurry along the day of judgment. They wanted armed rebellion against Rome. Then the Lord would be obliged to send his Messiah, and the evil kingdom of the world would be destroyed!

Years passed on. Fifteen years went by with little change under the rule of Tiberius, until the year 29. Then a Roman by the name of Pontius Pilate became governor of Judaea. He allowed the legions to carry their golden eagles into Jerusalem—a thing they had never done before. He also tried to use the money in the Temple treasury to build an aqueduct. In short, he so antagonized the people that they felt that now, certainly, the day of judgment must be near, that day when Rome would be destroyed.

And suddenly it seemed to many as though the warning had come! In the fall of the year, on the bank of the Jordan River, suddenly near Jericho—where Elijah had last been seen—there appeared a strange man, clothed like the old prophet himself in a hairy skin and a leather girdle.

Calling the people to repentance, he cried out that the awful day of judgment was upon them—the Kingdom of Heaven was at hand! All the wicked would perish—those in their own nation, as well as the Roman. All who did evil in the sight of the Lord would burn in the fires of that judgment day!

Many went to hear this preacher. Among those standing on the river bank one day was Jesus of Nazareth.

This is from the story of the days that followed, taken partly from Mark, who wrote it forty years later, and partly from the books of Matthew and Luke:

"Now in the fifteen years of the reign of Tiberius Caesar, Pontius Pilate being Governor of Judaea and Herod Antipas being tetrarch of Galilee . . . there came John the Baptist preaching in the wilderness of Judaea, saying:

Repent ye, for the Kingdom of Heaven is at hand!

And John was clothed in camel's hair, and a leathern girdle about his loins, and his meat was locusts and wild honey.

And they went out from Jerusalem and all the region round about and were baptized by him in the river Jordan, confessing their sins.

And Jesus came from Nazareth of Galilee and was baptized by John in the Jordan. And when he went up out of the water, lo! it seemed as if the heavens were opened and he saw the spirit of God descending like a dove upon him, and heard a voice from heaven saying, This is my beloved son, in whom I am well pleased. And immediately Jesus was led by the Spirit into the wilderness and was there forty days and forty nights [tempted by the devil, and ministered unto by the angels].

Now Herod, the tetrarch of Galilee, reproved by John [the Baptist] for having married his brother Philip's wife, shut up John in prison. Now when Jesus heard that, he went into Galilee and began to preach the good news of the Kingdom of God.

And as he walked one day by the sea of Galilee, he saw Simon [called Peter] and Andrew, his brother, casting a net into the sea, for they were fishermen.

Follow me, he said, and I will make you fishers of men.

And they forsook their nets and followed him. And a little farther hence, he saw James and John, his brother, the sons of Zebedee, and they immediately left their ships and followed him.

And on the Sabbath day, Jesus entered into the synagogue in Capernaum and taught the people. And they were astonished, for he taught as one having authority and not as the scribes. And immediately his fame spread abroad through all the region about Galilee.

And when Jesus left the synagogue and was come into Peter's house he saw Peter's wife's mother lay sick of a fever. And he touched her hand and the fever left her. And at even when the sun was setting, they brought him many that were sick and possessed with devils, and he cast out the evil spirits with his words.

And they went out and blazed it abroad, so that Jesus could not enter into the city, such multitudes came together to be healed, but stayed out in desert places, and they came to him from every quarter.

And after some days he returned to Capernaum. And Pharisees and teachers of the Law were sitting by, who had come out of every town in Galilee and Judaea and Jerusalem.

And as Jesus passed hence, he saw a man named Matthew, a tax collector, and he said unto him, follow me and he followed him. And Matthew made a great feast in his house, and sat at meat with Jesus and his disciples. And when the Pharisees saw it, they said to his disciples, Why does your master eat with sinners and tax collectors?

And Jesus went through the cornfield on the Sabbath day, and his disciples who were hungry began to pluck the ears of corn and to eat. And when the Pharisees saw it, they said unto him, Behold, thy disciples do that which is not lawful on the Sabbath day. Why?

And the Pharisees and scribes complained and asked him, Why walk not thy disciples according to the tradition of the elders but eat bread with unwashed hands?

Jesus answered and said unto them. There is nothing from without a man that entering in can defile him. For from within, out of the heart of men come evil thoughts, and all evil things. A good man out of the treasure of his heart brings forth that which is good.

Every tree is known by his own fruit.

And when he was demanded by the Pharisees when the Kingdom of God should come, he answered them and said, The Kingdom of God cometh not with observation. Neither shall they say, Lo here, or lo there, for, behold, the KINGDOM OF GOD IS WITHIN YOU!

And Jesus went into a ship and sat, and great multitudes stood on the shore and he taught them in parables, saying, To what shall we liken the Kingdom of Heaven? The Kingdom of Heaven is like leaven [or yeast], which a woman took and hid in three measures of meal, till the whole was leavened!

And a certain ruler asked him, saying What shall I do to inherit eternal life, Good Master?

And Jesus said unto him, Why callest thou me good? None is good, save One, that is God. . . . Thou knowest the commandments, Do not kill, do not steal, do not bear false witness, do not defraud, honor thy father and mother?

He answered, Master, all these have I observed from my youth.

And Jesus loving him, said unto him, One thing thou lackest. Go, sell what thou hast and give to the poor, and thou shalt have treasure in heaven.

And the man went away grieved, for he had great possessions.

And Jesus said to his disciples, How hard it is for them that trust in riches to enter the Kingdom of God!

Have faith in God. Seek ye first the Kingdom of God and His righteousness and all things shall be added unto you. Give and it shall be given unto you. Forgive and ye shall be forgiven. Judge not that ye be not judged.

ALL THINGS WHATSOEVER YE WOULD THAT MEN SHOULD DO UNTO YOU? DO YE EVEN SO TO THEM.

For this is the Law and the prophets.

And one of the scribes came and asked him, 'Which is the first commandment of all?'

And Jesus answered him, The first of all commandments is, Hear, O Israel, the Lord our God is one. And thou shalt love the Lord thy God with all thy heart and with all thy soul and with all thy mind and with all thy strength. And the second is: Thou shalt love thy neighbor as thyself. There is no other commandment greater than these.

And the scribe said unto him, Well, master, thou hast said the truth: for there is one God, and to love him with all the heart and with all the understanding and with all the soul, and with all the strength, and to love his neighbor as himself, is more than all whole burnt offerings and sacrifices. And Jesus said unto him,

Thou art not far from the Kingdom of God."

Each human being then holds the key to the Kingdom of Heaven, for it lies within.

A NEW RELIGION FOR ROME

IT WAS IN JERUSALEM, in the spring of 30 A.D., that Jesus of Nazareth was crucified, by order of the Roman governor. The city was crowded with those who had come for the celebration of the Passover. Jesus and his twelve disciples were among them. Though the disciples had been fearful, their master had been steadfast and unwavering in his purpose.

"Behold, we go up to Jerusalem," he had said to them, "and all things written by the prophets concerning the Son of Man shall be accomplished."

They did not understand him. As they journeyed along, they fell to quarreling as to which one should have the best seat next to him in the Kingdom of Heaven! When they drew near Jerusalem, and came to the Mount of Olives, two of the disciples brought a small donkey to Jesus, and he entered the city riding upon it. And many, seeing in him the long promised Messiah, went before him and after, crying, "Hosanna

to the Son of David! Blessed is he that cometh in the name of the Lord!"

The next day, Jesus went into the Temple. Overthrowing the tables of the money-changers and of those who sold doves, he cried, "It is written my house shall be called a house of prayer, but ye have made it a den of thieves!"

And many, hearing him, declared that one of the old prophets had risen again—Elijah—or Jeremiah!

The chief priests and captain of the Temple, who heard and saw him attacking their management of the Temple, were alarmed, but hesitated to lay hands upon him, for fear of causing trouble for themselves among the people.

The Roman officers were also on the alert, lest another rebel from Galilee should excite the crowd to rebellion.

But the hotheads in the crowd were watching for rebellion.

If this leader failed to call for a revolt, they would lose faith in him, as they had in many others who had also been hailed as their long promised king.

The Pharisees watched him anxiously, for they had long feared that he intended to undermine the Law, which they studied so diligently and in which no peasant from Galilee could possibly be versed. So all eyes were upon him during the next two days, as he went quietly about the Temple.

And after two days came the Passover. In the evening, Jesus sat with his twelve disciples in a large upper room in Jerusalem, eating the meal of unleavened bread, bitter herbs and wine.

And as they sat and did eat, Jesus said, One of you which eateth with me shall betray me. And when they had sung a psalm, they went out into the Mount of Olives. And they came to a [garden] which was named **Gethsemane.** He took with him Peter and James and John and said unto them, Tarry ye here and watch while I pray. And when he returned he found them sleeping. And as he spoke, came Judas one of the twelve, and with him a great multitude with swords and staves. And they led Jesus away to the high priest."

And in the morning the chief priests held a consultation with the elders and scribes and the whole Council, and, judging him guilty of blasphemy against the Lord, they brought him to Pontius Pilate. And Pilate delivered Jesus to be crucified.

That was Friday, April 14, 30 A.D.

In no book or document written at that time, however, was there any mention of Jesus of Nazareth, and he left no written record of his teaching. One might well expect that his memory would be erased and his name forgotten. Instead, from the day he died, his name was to be constantly repeated, at first by only his little band of heart-broken followers whose grief and fear soon turned to joy and courage.

Mary Magdalene, "out of whom Jesus had cast seven devils" and Mary, the mother of James, told of how they had gone to the tomb early on the morning after the Sabbath and had found it open and empty except for a young man clothed in white, who had told them that Jesus had risen from the dead. Later, Mary Magdalene said that she had seen Jesus himself. Two others soon reported that they had also seen him, and walked with him along a country road. Later, in Galilee, the eleven disciples believed that they had felt his presence with them as they sat at meat. They had seen him, they declared, and heard him speak! And he had said to them:

"Go ye and preach the gospel to every creature, teaching them to observe all things whatsoever I have commanded you, and lo! I am with you always even unto the end of the world."

So they returned to Jerusalem and were continually in the Temple, teaching and preaching. Crowds gathered about them and many joined their company, convinced that what they said was true.

The high priest and captain of the Temple and the Sadducees were annoyed, alarmed, and wondered what "this would grow into." They seized Peter and the other apostles and brought them before the council of elders in the Hall of Hewn Stone, to consider "whether they should be killed or what should be done about them."

Then there stood up one in the council, a Pharisee, named Gamaliel, a doctor of the law, held in high honor among the people for his own understanding, as well as for the fact that he was the grandson of the great rabbi, Hillel, who now was dead.

And Gamaliel said unto them, "Ye men of Israel, take heed to yourselves, what ye intend to do about these men. Before these days, Judas of Galilee rose up, in the days of taxing. He also perished and all who obeyed him were scattered abroad. And now I say unto you, Refrain from these men and let them alone, for if this work be of men, it will come to naught. But if it be of God, ye cannot overthrow it."

And the council agreed and called the apostles, commanded that they should speak no more in the name of Jesus and let them go. But the apostles continued to preach daily in the Temple. And many who heard them were alarmed and shocked and angered, thinking that they heard blasphemous words against the Temple and the Law.

And when an apostle named Stephen cried out and accused them of having killed the Just One, as their fathers had slain and persecuted the prophets that came before him, they reached down and raised their arms and stoned him to death. They persecuted and drove out many of the others, who scattered through Judaea and Samaria.

Then a strange thing happened. Among those who had seen Stephen stoned that day was a young man whose name was Saul. He was a pupil of Gamaliel. Now, in spite of his teacher's disapproval, Saul became most active in persecuting the followers of the new faith. He was on his way to Damascus, to stamp out a group which had sprung up there, when, suddenly along the highway, he fell. And as he lay there in the dust and heat, he had a vision. Jesus seemed to speak to him, saying, "Saul, Saul, why persecutest thou me?" From then on, instead of persecuting, Saul became a champion of the new order.

Using the Greek name for Saul, he became Paul the Apostle.

And using the Greek word Christos or CHRIST for the Hebrew word Messiah, Paul traveled through the cities of the Roman empire, preaching that Jesus of Nazareth, whom they had crucified, was the Christ, the Anointed One, the Savior, the Son of God!

From Jerusalem, Paul went back to his native city of Tarsus, the city where Cleopatra and Antony had met aboard her ship. He went to Antioch, the capital of Syria, where Agrippa had taken Julia to live when he was governor. He went to Philippi, where the battle had been fought against Brutus and Cassius; to Athens, where he was questioned by the Stoics and Epicureans on Mars Hill; to the islands of Rhodes and Samos, and finally over a rough winter sea, the tireless missionary sailed for Italy. His ship was wrecked and washed ashore on the island of Malta, but another ship, from Alexandria, took him on to Puteoli, the summer resort near Naples. From there, over the Appian Way, Paul traveled to Rome.

It was then about the year 63. Nero, the fifth and last ruler to bear the family name of Caesar, was now emperor of Rome. He was the great-great-grandson of both Augustus and Antony. The two other emperors who had come between him and Tiberius were Caligula, the son of Julia's daughter, Agrippina, and Claudius, who was the son of Antonia and Drusus.

Paul lived two years in his own rented house in Rome, receiving all that came to him and teaching them. And so, because of Paul's teaching, the belief that Jesus was the Messiah or Christ, though it died out among his own people, spread in ever-widening circles through the Roman world.

Slaves, freedmen—all the poor and oppressed—eagerly accepted the new religion, for they had need for it. Finding in it hope and courage, they clung to it through torture and persecution. Nero ordered the Christians (who like the Jews would not worship the emperor) to be thrown to the lions in the arena. Still the numbers continued to grow— on through the next two centuries—until finally they included the emperor himself.

In the year 312, the Emperor Constantine had a vision in which he seemed to see a cross in the sky, and the words "in hoc signo vinces" (in this sign you conquer). Therefore he made Christianity the official religion of the Roman Empire, the last religion to be adopted by Rome.

Seventy-four years later, 386 A.D., the Bishop of Rome decreed that the birth of Jesus should be celebrated on December 25th, the birthday of the sun.

And in 532, a priest, by the name of Dionysius, who was a Scyth by birth and an astronomer, brought into use the custom of counting from the Roman year 754, supposed to mark the birth of Jesus, calling that year the Year 1.

And so out of this world of the Caesars came another story of the triumph of life and courage over fear and death, a triumph seen anew in every spring that follows winter and with the rising of the sun each day.

INDEX OF CHARACTERS

Eve, wife of Adam: 188
Elijah, Hebrew prophet: on Mt. Carmel, 284, 288; prophecy about, 294
Epicurus, Greek philosopher: 223
Eratosthenes, Greek geographer: 231
Esau, son of Isaac: 189

Frey, Norse and German god: 176
Freya, Norse and German goddess: 176
Fulvia, wife of Antony: 30; makes trouble, 90, 92

Gaius, son of Agrippa: born, 169; two years, 177; adopted by Augustus, his grandfather, 192
Gamaliel, grandson of Hillel: 183; a rabbi, 323
Gautama, Prince of India, who became the Buddha: 264, 269
Germanicus, Roman general: son of Drusus, 305

Ham, son of Noah: 188
Hercules, Greek god: and Antony, 30; son of Jupiter, 164
Hermann, German hero: 309
Herod, King of the Jews: governor of Galilee, 66; and Cleopatra, 91; in Rome, 100; besieges Jerusalem, 108; and Cleopatra, 112; and Mariamne, 122; builds Temple, 177; and star, 227; death, 243
Herod Antipas, son of Herod: 244; tetrarch of Galilee, 316
Herodotus, Greek geographer: 231
Herod Philip, son of Herod: 244
Hillel, the rabbi: 182, 304
Horace, Roman poet: 80; with Virgil, 106
Horus, Egyptian god: 200, 278
Hoseah, Hebrew prophet, 290
Hyrcanus, High Priest of the Jews: 63, 67; prisoner, 91; killed, 125

Isaac, son of Abraham: 189
Isaiah, Hebrew prophet: 95, 285, 291
Ishtar, Babylonian goddess: 292
Isis, Egyptian goddess: and Cleopatra, 17; and Osiris, 200, 278
Israel, or Jacob: 189; in Egypt, 203
Itzamna, Mayan god, 237
Izanagi, Japanese god: 241
Izanami, Japanese goddess: 241

Jacob, son of Isaac: 189
James, disciple of Jesus: 317
Janus, Roman god: 40; gates closed, 128; in early days, 161
Japeth, son of Noah: 188
Javeh, Hebrew name for God: 64, 187
Jeremiah, Hebrew prophet: 292, 320
Jesus of Nazareth: boy, 278; stories of his birth, 279; in Nazareth, 283; at Passover, 298; life and teaching, 315–322
Jimmu, first Japanese emperor: 241
John, disciple of Jesus: 317, 322
John the Baptist: 316, 317
Joseph, son of Jacob: 189; his wife, 203

Joseph, husband of Mary: 278; search for Jesus, 304
Joshua, Hebrew leader: conquered Jericho, 300
Jove, Roman god: 160
Judas, disciple of Jesus: 322
Judas Maccabeus, Hebrew hero: 65
Judas, rebel leader of Galilee: 244; fails to start uprising, 298; mentioned, 323
Julia, daughter of Augustus: born, 100; at twelve years, 143; married Marcellus, 145; widow, 153; married Agrippa, 168; to Syria, 177; married Tiberius, 192, 225; divorced, banished, 266
Julius Caesar: killed, 10–12; and Cleopatra, 15; and month of July, 38; in Gaul, 44, 144; and Germans, 296
Juno, Roman goddess: queen of heaven, 155, 163
Jupiter, Roman god: sacrifice to, 49; triumph, 128; and Aeneas, 155; son of Chronus, 163; planet, 227; and Aryans, 261

Lao Tzu, Chinese philosopher: 253
Lepidus, Roman general: in Triumvirate, 51
Livia, wife of Augustus: 107; and sons, 142; and Julia, 226; inherits silk, 245; and Tiberius, 282; and Augustus, 306, 312
Livy, Roman historian: boy, 41; writes history, 164
Lucius, grandson of Augustus: baby, 177; father dies, 192; heir of Augustus, 224; sent to Gaul, 259; died, 282
Luke, author: 279, 316

Maat, Egyptian goddess: 199, 201
Maecenas, friend of Augustus: 12, 78; with Virgil and Horace, 106; advises Augustus, 134; patron of art, 154; dead, 225
Malachi, Hebrew prophet: 294
Marcellus, nephew of Augustus: infant, 58; in triumph, 127; marries Julia, 145; dead, 153
Mariamne, wife of Herod: child, 63; with Herod, 111; death, 122–125
Mark, author: 316
Maroboduus, German chieftain: 308
Mars, Roman god of war: 40; father of Romulus and Remus, 42; first god, 160; father of twins, 164; planet, 227
Mary, mother of Jesus: 278; at Passover, 304
Mary Magdalene, follower of Jesus: 322
Matthew, author: 279, 316
Matthew, tax collector: 318
Mercury, Roman god: 155; son of Jupiter, 164
Micah, Hebrew prophet: 290
Ming Ti, Chinese emperor: 268
Mithra, Persian sun god: 170, 173, 278
Moses, Hebrew prophet: 187; and Passover, 190, 287

Nero, Roman emperor: 100, 324
Neptune, Roman god of the sea: 155; brother of Jupiter, 163
Noah, Hebrew patriarch: 188

Octavia, sister of Octavius: 19; and her son, Marcellus, 58; marries Antony, 97; daughter

328

GENERAL INDEX